W9-BVV-932

Praise for *Fanatical Prospecting*

"Prospecting is the core, the foundation, the heart of every successful sales effort. *Fanatical Prospecting* leverages the prospecting success of author Jeb Blount, one of the most successful sales leaders of this decade, and provides answers to every aspect of successful prospecting."

"The techniques and concepts contained in *Fanatical Prospecting* are not theories from an ivory tower occupant or the ideological wishes of a university professor. This is a step-by-step field guide to every aspect of prospecting in the Internet era."

"Blount explains core principles of prospecting in a storytelling style that begs you to write in the margin and put your own action plan into place. Whether talking about 'the 30 Day Rule' or the difference between 'Golden Hours' and 'Platinum Hours,' he keeps his guidance at a personal level, understandable and easy to relate to. Clear, simple pillars like the Four Objectives of Prospecting ring true for any sales effort, in any industry and for every customer size."

"Straightforward, easy-to-follow visual maps of 'five step guides' for telephone prospecting, voice mail prospecting, and in-person prospecting will prove valuable throughout your entire career in sales and in sales management. I recommend buying two copies—one to read and one to write, draw, highlight, and add sticky notes to. It is that powerful."

—**Miles Austin**, Publisher, FillTheFunnel.com

Fanatical
Prospecting

Law of the Universe: Nothing happens until something moves.
Law of Business: Nothing happens until someone sells something.

—Jeb Blount

Fanatical Prospecting

The Ultimate Guide for Starting Sales Conversations and Filling the Pipeline by Leveraging Social Selling, Telephone, E-Mail, and Cold Calling

Jeb Blount

WILEY

Cover image: Gold © iStock.com/idal

Cover design: Wiley

Copyright © 2015 by Jeb Blount. All rights reserved

Published by John Wiley & Sons, Inc., Hoboken, New Jersey.
Published simultaneously in Canada.

For general information on our other products and services or for technical support, please contact our Customer Care Department within the United States at (800) 762-2974, outside the United States at (317) 572-3993 or fax (317) 572-4002.

Wiley also publishes its books in a variety of electronic formats. Some content that appears in print may not be available in electronic books. For more information about Wiley products, visit our web site at www.wiley.com.

Library of Congress Cataloging-in-Publication Data:

Blount, Jeb, author.
  Fanatical prospecting : the ultimate guide for starting sales conversations and filling the pipeline by leveraging social selling, telephone, e-mail, and cold calling / Jeb Blount.
      1 online resource.
  Includes bibliographical references and index.
  Description based on print version record and CIP data provided by publisher; resource not viewed.
  ISBN-13 978-1-119-14475-5 (cloth); ISBN 978-1-119-14477-9 (ePDF);
ISBN 978-1-119-14476-2 (ePub)
  1. Selling. 2. Business referrals. 3. Customer relations. I. Title.
  HF5438.25
  658.8'72—dc23

                                                                        2015027909

Printed in the United States of America

20 19 18 17 16 15 14 13 12

For Bob Blackwell

Contents

Foreword

For 25 years I've hoped for a book like *Fanatical Prospecting*, and never has this powerful message and valuable advice been needed more than it is today.

Like a prophet, Jeb Blount boldly points out the lies of the loud, popular nouveau sales "experts" whose deadly advice leads sales-people and sales leaders astray. These experts preach to all who will listen that prospecting—*proactively pursuing prospects*—no longer works. What's particularly dangerous about this false teaching is that it is exactly what the struggling, reactive salesperson wants to hear. Why do the hard work to prospect and self-generate new sales opportunities when some "guru" lets you off the hook by telling you that it's "old school" and "doesn't work anymore"? Why block time to pick up the phone if instead you can tweet, write blog posts, or play for hours posting comments in a LinkedIn group?

The truth, as Jeb so eloquently shares, is that there is no Easy Button in sales. There is no magic bullet or secret sauce. No one sales tool, gimmick, or mystical new process guaranteed to fill your pipeline. In spite of what the social selling Kool-Aid pushers and inbound marketing companies tell us, the truth is that top producers and sales superstars are fanatical prospectors who take personal responsibility for identifying and creating their own sales opportunities.

When a company's sales organization is failing to make its number or reach its potential, it is not because its salespeople can't present well, are ineffective closers, or lack the skills for offering insight or challenging prospects. It's rarely because of a deficit of talent. The reason most sales organizations are not making their numbers is that the pipeline is anemic because the sales team is not prospecting.

Prospecting not only still works, but it's the fastest and most effective way to accomplish exactly what this book's subtitle promises: *opening sales conversations and filling the pipeline!*

Jeb Blount knows prospecting. He is an authority on this subject because he was an all-star, record-setting salesperson and executive sales leader before building his own wildly successful sales training and talent management company. Today he transforms sales organizations by helping them accelerate performance and speaks to hundreds of companies across the globe each year that are eager to hear his inspiring message about what it takes to reach peak performance—fast.

In *Fanatical Prospecting*, Jeb leaves no stone unturned and holds nothing back. He shares why we need to prospect, exactly what to do, and how to do it.

New sales are the lifeblood of a business. Nothing is more important than securing discovery meetings, conversations, appointments, and sales calls with potential customers. And that is exactly why this is the most important book ever written on this topic.

If you are a sales leader or salesperson looking for help creating more new sales opportunities, then this book is for you. But be warned, once you read *Fanatical Prospecting*, there will be no more excuses. From understanding why and how we must interrupt prospects, to jealously guarding our precious golden hours for selling, Jeb provides a comprehensive guide to increase sales fast. There is practical, powerful advice on using every means (social selling, e-mail, telephone, text messaging, networking, referrals, in-person prospecting) available to start sales conversations and create new opportunities.

If you picked up this book because you've never prospected for new business or you are struggling to hit your numbers, congratulations. I promise that if you follow the prescription Jeb provides, your results are about to improve dramatically. And if, like me, you're a long-time believer in prospecting, this book will take your game to completely new levels.

—Mike Weinberg, The New Sales Coach and
author of *New Sales. Simplified.*

Special Note: Free Prospecting Resources

This is the longest book of the seven I've written and still, it was impossible to cover everything you need to know about prospecting. Also, with the shifting landscape of technology, prospecting tools, apps, and social media, things are changing so fast that I needed a place to keep you updated on tools, trends, and techniques that will give you an edge while filling your pipe.

So, I built FanaticalProspecting.com. There you will find dozens of free guides, articles, podcasts, videos, virtual training programs, and reports that supplement the book and expand your knowledge base. As a special bonus to thank you for purchasing this book, you get free access (valued at $499) to these resources.

You'll find a special, exclusive code that gives you free Pro-Level access located in Chapter 7.

1 | The Case for Prospecting

There are bad salespeople, mediocre salespeople, good salespeople, consistent salespeople, and then there are Superstars. The elusive talent that companies and sales organizations spend billions of dollars to identify, recruit, retain, and emulate—the coveted top 20 percent that produce 80 percent of sales.

Superstars outearn other salespeople—taking home almost all of the available commissions and bonuses. They win the trips, prizes, spiffs, and the recognition that the also-rans so badly crave.

They are not one-hit wonders. Superstars deliver year in and year out and tend to stay on top over the long haul.

Superstars are good at selling. They've got the talent and the skills. They're competitive and have the drive to perform. They understand how to manage the sales process, ask great questions, deliver winning presentations, and close the deal. They have exceptional people savvy, high emotional intelligence, and a winning mindset.

But, here's the thing: So do lots of salespeople. Lots of sales-people possess the drive and hunger to succeed. Lots of salespeople have the intelligence, talent, skills, and education to be top per-formers. Lots of salespeople are competitive, understand the sales process, and know how to ask for the business. Yet they consistently underperform the superstars.

That's what leaves so many salespeople and executives scratch-ing their heads and wondering how the elite top 20 percent produce such massive results year in and year out. It's why:

- HR managers are frustrated that their complex and expensive hiring assessments aren't as predictive of sales success as promised.
- Legions of academic researchers spin their wheels searching for the holy grail of sales that they believe will magically turn all salespeople into top performers, and why corporate executives eagerly consume their flavor-of-the-day promises.
- CSOs and sales VPs chase one fad after another, desperately clinging to the latest expert who wins the annual "everything-in-sales-has-changed" beauty contest, in hopes of reviving their failing sales organization.
- So many salespeople and entrepreneurs yearn for the secret to gaining income stability through real, lasting success in sales, yet that secret always seems just out of reach.

The Real Secret to Sustained Sales Success

The path to superstar-level success in sales is brutally simple. Simple, mind you, not easy. It's a Paradox of Basics: A truth that is so blatantly obvious it has become impossibly invisible. A truth that remains frustratingly elusive for most salespeople, causing so many promising, intelligent, talented people to fail miserably in sales, and, likewise, businesses to close their doors and entrepreneurs to crash and burn.

What's the secret that separates superstars from everyone else, and why do they consistently outperform other salespeople? *Fanatical prospecting*.

Superstars are relentless, unstoppable prospectors. They are obsessive about keeping their pipeline full of qualified prospects. They prospect anywhere and anytime—constantly turning over rocks looking for their next opportunity. They prospect day and night—unstoppable and always on. Fanatical!

My favorite definition of the word fanatical is "motivated or characterized by an extreme, uncritical enthusiasm."[1]

Superstars view prospecting as a way of life. They prospect with single-minded focus, worrying little about what other people think of them. They enthusiastically dive into telephone prospecting, e-mail prospecting, cold calling, networking, asking for referrals, knocking on doors, following up on leads, attending trade shows, and striking up conversations with strangers.

- They don't make excuses: "Oh, this is not a good time to call because they might be at lunch."
- They don't complain: "Nobody is calling me back."
- They don't whine: "The leads are bad."
- They don't live in fear: "What if she says no?" Or "What if this is a bad time?"
- They don't procrastinate: "I don't have time right now. I'll catch up tomorrow."
- They prospect when times are good because they know that a rainy day is right around the corner.
- They prospect when times are bad because they know that fanatical prospecting is the key to survival.
- They prospect even when they don't feel like prospecting because they are driven to keep their pipeline full.

Fanatical prospectors carry around a pocket full of business cards. They talk up strangers in doctors' offices, at sporting events, in line to get coffee, in elevators, at conferences, on planes, trains, and anywhere else they can get face to face with potential customers.

They get up in the morning and bang the phone. During the day they knock on doors. In between meetings they prospect with e-mail and text. At night they connect with and engage prospects on social media. Before they quit for the day they make even more calls.

The enduring mantra of the fanatical prospector is: *One more call.*

Prospecting is the air they breathe. They don't whine like babies about not having enough leads or cry at the coffee machine with all of the losers about how they don't understand why no one is buying today. They don't blame the sales manager, company, products, services, or economy. They get moving, take responsibility, and own their territory. They generate their own leads and through hard work, determination, and perseverance, their own luck.

Superstars are aware that failure in sales is not caused by a deficit of talent, skills, or training. Not a poor territory or inferior product. Not subpar communication and presentation skills. Not a failure to ask for the business and close. Not terrible sales managers.

The brutal fact is the number one reason for failure in sales is an empty pipe, and, the root cause of an empty pipeline is the failure to prospect.

Yet countless salespeople and sales leaders who marvel at the consistent year-in-and-year-out performance of superstars are blind to the real reason for their success. Unwilling to accept that the foundational root of all success in sales is a fanatical focus on prospecting, they waste time tilting at windmills on their quixotic pursuit of fads, silver bullets, and secret formulas they believe will deliver them into the arms of success with little effort.

In Search of the Easy Button

"Lose weight effortlessly," the announcer says over an image of models admiring their ripped abs. "With this revolutionary, break-through pill you'll never have to worry about your weight again. Eat what you want. Forget about exercise. Just take this pill and you'll have the body of your dreams."

If these commercials didn't work, the companies that run them would quit. But they do work.

In his book, *Spartan Up: A Take No Prisoners Guide to Overcoming Obstacles and Achieving Peak Performance*, Joe De Sena explains that "easy is the greatest marketing hook of all time." So companies promise, again and again, that you can lose weight, flip houses, or get rich with no pain, no sacrifice, and no effort. Their phones ring off the hook, even though intuitively, most people know these promises are over-hyped and not true. It is just human nature to seek the easy way out.

It is disappointing to observe how many salespeople today have this attitude—always looking for an easy way out. They have some-how deluded themselves into believing that they are owed some-thing. They whine and complain endlessly about their company, prospects, leads, coworkers, CRM, product, prices, and on and on.

This is the brutal truth: In sales you are owed nothing! You've got to get your ass up and go out there and make things happen yourself. You have to pick up the phone, knock on doors, make presentations, and ask for business. Sales is not a nine-to-five job. There are no days off. No vacations. No lunch breaks. The great salespeople are skipping meals and doing deals—whatever it takes to win.

This mindset is the difference between driving a Mercedes or a Hyundai. Wearing a Rolex or a Timex. Savoring a juicy, bone-in, prime, cowboy rib eye in a five-star restaurant or surviving on ramen noodles. It's the difference between watching a 60-inch, flat-screen, ultra high-def TV or sock puppets on a 12-inch flea market hand-me-down.

In sales there will always be something to complain about. That is just how it is. There will be obstacles, roadblocks, bad managers, rude prospects, product and service challenges, and changes to the commission plan. There will always be rejection. There will always be hard work. You can sit around and complain and whine, but trust me, you are only hurting yourself.

It is critical that you awaken from the delusion that somehow you are going to be able to make prospecting easier and come to grips with the truth: If you had a choice between prospecting and swimming with sharks, you would choose the sharks.

The first step toward building an endless pipeline of new customers is acknowledging the truth and stepping back from your emotional need to find Easy Street. In sales, easy is the mother of mediocrity, and in your life, mediocrity is like a broke uncle. Once he moves into your house, it is nearly impossible to get him to leave.

The next step is keeping it real. In sales, business, and life, there are only three things you can control:

1. Your Actions
2. Your Reactions
3. Your Mindset

That's it. Nothing more. So instead of whining about the things that are out of your control, focus your energy on what you can control—your attitude, choices, emotions, goals, ambitions, dreams, desires, and discipline (choosing between what you want now and what you want most).

Stop Wishing That Things Were Easier and Start Working to Become Better

Developing a fanatical prospecting mindset starts with coming to grips with the fact that prospecting is hard, grueling, rejection-dense work.

There is no sugarcoating it. Prospecting sucks. This is why so many salespeople don't do it and instead spend their time and energy seeking silver bullets, secret formulas, and shortcuts, or ignore prospecting all together until it is too late.

However, if you dream of having a superstar income and living a superstar lifestyle, you must face the reality that prospecting sucks and get over it. To get what you want, you must prospect consistently.

Jim Rohn once said that you shouldn't wish that things were easier; you should wish that you were better. That's the promise I make to you. When you adopt the techniques in this book, you will get better.

Will the techniques I teach you in this book make you a more efficient prospector? Absolutely. I will teach you how to get more prospecting done in less time so that you can get back to the fun part of selling: meeting customers, discovery, presentations, proposals, negotiation, closing deals, and cashing commission checks.

Will the techniques I teach you in this book make you a more effective prospector? You can count on it. I will teach you how to get the highest return on the time you invest in prospecting. You will learn how to balance prospecting using multiple methodologies and gain insight on how to engage qualified prospects in sales conversations and get them into your pipeline. You'll get better results, open doors you thought would always be closed to you, and ultimately close more sales.

Will the techniques I teach you eliminate rejection, make prospecting more palatable (to use the words of one author who promises that prospecting can be "fun and easy"), make it painless, or remove the emotional and mental roadblocks that lead to prospecting procrastination?

Nope. Not a chance.

I will not lie to you about prospecting. I am not going to promise you that I will make prospecting easier, eliminate rejection, or turn it into something that you will learn to love. Only you can make the decision to do the hard work, pick up the phone, approach strangers, and get past your own mental hang-ups. The choice to act, the choice to adopt a new mindset, is yours and yours alone.

Here's the brutal truth: There is no easy button in sales. Prospecting is hard, emotionally draining work, and it is the price you have to pay to earn a high income.

How do I know this? I've been selling in the trenches my entire life. I've got trophy cases full of awards for my sales achievements. I started a successful multimillion-dollar business from the ground up and survived and thrived because my only option was to pick up the phone and start dialing. I am considered a leading expert on sales because of these accomplishments, and people pay me big bucks just to teach them the things I know. I've made millions of dollars in commissions. Bought big houses, boats, cars, and all of the toys a successful career in sales affords.

All of this was courtesy of fanatical prospecting. All of it! Yet, even though I know what brought me to the dance, even though I am fully aware that prospecting generates my income, the truth is prospecting is still the hardest, most mentally exhausting part of my sales day. There is always something more fun I would rather do, and although I know it will never get easier, the one thing that separates me from most other people is this: I get over it and do it anyway.

2

Seven Mindsets of Fanatical Prospectors

We like to think of our champions and idols as superheroes who were born different from us. We don't like to think of them as relatively ordinary people who made themselves extraordinary.
—Carol S. Dweck, *Mindset: The New Psychology of Success*

Merriam-Webster dictionary defines *mindset* as "a mental attitude or inclination." It can also be defined as "a mood, disposition, inclination, or intention" (reference.com).

Mindset is completely and absolutely within your control and drives both the actions you take and your reactions to the environment and people around you.

Success Leaves Clues

Success leaves clues. Highly successful people, from ancient philosophers like Aristotle to modern-day thought leaders, have always made the point that there is little need to "reinvent the wheel." If you study what successful people do, you find patterns. When you duplicate those patterns, you'll be able to duplicate their success.

Developing and maintaining a fanatical prospecting mindset is the ultimate key to success in sales. This mindset keeps you focused, persistent, and driven to open doors in the face of inevitable setbacks, challenges, and rejection. When you adopt a fanatical prospecting mindset, you'll grow in the face of adversity rather than shrink before it.

I've spent a lifetime studying fanatical prospectors. Along the way I discovered seven core mindsets that define them. These are their success clues. Duplicate these mindsets and you'll guarantee yourself success in filling your pipeline and crushing your number.

1. *Optimistic and enthusiastic:* Fanatical prospectors have a winning, optimistic mindset. They know that negative, bitter people with a victim mindset do not succeed in sales. Fanatical prospectors attack each day with enthusiasm—fired up and ready to rock. They view each day as a fresh new opportunity to achieve. Because of this, they seize the day, brush past naysayers and complainers, and dive into prospecting with unequaled drive. Even on bad days they reach deep inside and find enough stored enthusiasm to push themselves to keep going and make one more call.

2. *Competitive:* Fanatical prospectors view prospecting through the eyes of a fierce competitor. They are hardwired to win and will do whatever it takes to stay on top. They begin each day prepared to win the battle for the attention of the most coveted prospects, and outwit and outhustle their competitors at every turn.

3. *Confident:* Fanatical prospectors approach prospecting with confidence. They expect to win and believe they are going to win. They have developed mental toughness and the ability to manage the disruptive emotions of fear, uncertainty, and doubt. They leverage confidence and self-control to persuade prospects to give up time and resources to engage in sales conversations.

4. *Relentless:* Fanatical prospectors have a high need for achievement. They do whatever it takes to reach their goal. They never, ever give up believing that persistence always wins. They use rejection as motivational fuel to get up and keep going with a determined belief that their next "yes" is right around the corner.

5. *Thirsty for knowledge:* Fanatical prospectors welcome feedback and coaching. They seek out every opportunity to learn and invest in themselves by voraciously consuming books, podcasts, audiobooks, blog posts, online training, live seminars, and anything else they believe will make them better. They have an unshakable belief that everything happens for a reason and through this lens view setbacks as opportunities to learn and grow.

6. *Systematic and efficient:* Fanatical prospectors have the ability to execute with near-robotic and systematical efficiency. They are skilled at their craft like a pro athlete. They protect the golden hours, block their time, and concentrate their power to tune out distractions and avoid disruptions. They systematically develop their prospect database to build more effective and targeted lists, and squeeze every moment from each sales day.

7. *Adaptive and flexible:* Fanatical prospectors have acute situational awareness. Because of this, they are able to respond and adapt quickly to changing situations and circumstances. They leverage the three As in their approach to prospecting: adopt, adapt, adept. They actively search out and adopt new ideas and best practices, then adapt them as their own, and work at it until they become adept at execution. Fanatical prospectors are constantly trying new things and flexing with the world around them—whatever it takes to keep their pipeline full. They tend to be

early adopters of new prospecting techniques, cutting-edge technology, and game-changing tactics.

Look around you. I guarantee that you will find that the highest-earning sales professionals in your town, city, networking groups, and company are fanatical prospectors. From insurance to real estate to industrial products to software to mobile to autos to trucks to medical device and pharmaceutical—in every industry and every company—they share these seven mindsets.

As you move forward through this book, use these seven mindsets as a foundational reference point to assess where you have room to grow and further develop your mindset.

3 | To Cold Call or Not to Cold Call?

To be, or not to be, that is the question.
—William Shakespeare, *Hamlet*

It seems these days that everywhere you look there is some so-called expert pontificating that *cold calling is dead*. This is usually an inbound marketing, Sales 2.0, social-selling-obsessed nitwit with an agenda and a vested interest in telling you that everything you thought you knew about sales prospecting is "old school"—except their narrow version of "new school." By vested interest, I mean they've got something they want to sell you that promises to fill your pipe with no fuss, no muss, no rejection, and little effort.

These folks pander to the sales masses' desire to stop cold calling. You've seen the ads and headlines plastered everywhere: "Never cold call again!" Buy their system and you'll be set free of the burden of reaching out and touching prospective customers.

With their top-secret system, you'll happily and painlessly blog and post on social media sites, and prospects who are already 70 percent (or 57 percent or 68 percent or whatever the latest statistic is these days) through the sales process—all by themselves—will miraculously *call you* at exactly the right time. You'll answer the phone or check your e-mail or social inbox and boom—closed deal. It's easy, they'll tell you. Why work hard when, with their little magic pill, you can just kick back, relax, and wait for the phone to ring.

Welcome to Fantasy Island.

Likewise, there are experts who bill themselves as cold-calling queens and kings. They preach loudly that cold calling is the real key to prospecting success and offer top-secret formulas they say will eliminate rejection, cause your targeted prospects to swoon when you call, and guarantee your success.

It feels like the sales profession's twisted version of a Shakespearian play: *to cold call or not to cold call.*

Give me a break!

The Fine Art of Interrupting

So the gurus and thought leaders rage on over whether to cold call or not to cold call. But their bluster is really just an inane argument focused on semantics of degrees—cold, warm, smoldering, hot, smoking hot—and mostly centered on how to avoid ever having to make an outbound call to a prospect again.

This is why I'm going to let you in on the truth—the *real truth* that all of these so-called experts continue to ignore, and it has nothing to do with cold calling.

Here's the deal.

If you want sustained success in your sales career, if you want to maximize your income, then you've got to interrupt prospects. You'll have to pick up the phone, walk in the door, send an e-mail or text message, or ping a prospect on LinkedIn, Twitter, Google+, or Facebook and interrupt someone who is not expecting you to contact them (i.e., you don't have an appointment or they are not waiting for you to call or write) and with whom you are not currently engaged in a sales discussion.

You can argue the degrees, warm, hot, cold, whatever. It could be a prospect that filled out one of your web forms or downloaded your latest white paper. Maybe they just connected with you online. It could be an old customer you are trying to reactivate, or a prospect in your defined database, or a new business that you've stopped by to qualify, or a prospect you met at a trade show.

No matter the circumstance, the simple fact remains that you are interrupting their day to talk about something you want them to hear, do, or buy, and you do not have a scheduled appointment with them to have that conversation.

This is what gets missed in all of the useless noise about how cold calling is dead. All of the talking heads who promise an easy way out if you'll just join their little cult ignore the real reason that prospecting is so hard, no matter how you choose to do it. It has *never* been about degree of the call; it is has *always* been about the willingness on the part of the salesperson to interrupt.

Which, by the way, is why most sales reps protest so loudly and will do anything to avoid making an outbound call. It is so much easier to speak to someone who is calling you.

The problem is, most companies can't create enough qualified inbound leads to keep the pipeline full. And, by the way, the reps that work for companies that do generate enough inbound leads to keep the phones ringing are making far less than sales pros who are reaching out and interrupting prospects to create opportunities.

Case in point, I have one client that spends $1.2 million a month to generate leads for their inbound sales team. It is still not enough. Those reps are idle more than half of the time. The only way they can achieve their number is to make targeted outbound calls.

Another client has a robust inbound-marketing and social-selling process that generates a consistent stream of leads. However, the biggest and most lucrative prospects in their marketplace, the ones they need to sell to achieve their goals, rarely respond to inbound-marketing or social-selling efforts. They have no reason to engage this way. Their accounts are so lucrative, there's always a long line of salespeople knocking on the door. The only way to start a sales conversation with these high-value prospects is to interrupt them.

Stop Seeking the Easy Way Out and Start Interrupting and Engaging

It is difficult and awkward to interrupt someone's day.

You can't control their response. That unknown leaves us vulnerable and causes fear.

Your prospect's initial reaction to being interrupted—usually a brush-off or reflex response in a not-so-friendly tone of voice—feels like rejection. As a human it is natural to abhor rejection; we are social creatures at heart who desire to be accepted.

These are the core reasons mediocre salespeople spend an inordinate amount of time finding excuses not to prospect rather than just doing it.

This past year one of my clients wanted to set up an outbound prospecting team to call and reactivate dormant customers. They hired a few young, inexperienced reps to make the calls.

While training them, I observed the reps obsess over the unknowns, the "what ifs" of the highly qualified "warm" calls. They wanted to be sure they had all of their ducks in a row before they ever picked up the phone. They hesitated and agonized. Planning to plan to plan to call.

But these were not calls to strangers. We were calling people who had done business with the company in the past. There was history here. In fact, the calls were warm lay-ups. Yet, the two reps demonstrated the exact same anxiety I've observed in reps who were calling complete strangers—in degrees, very cold prospects.

So I demonstrated by grabbing the list, picking up the phone, and dialing numbers. The customers who answered the phone were receptive, and other than being initially irritated at being interrupted, took time to talk to me about their next buying window. Over the course of 25 dials, three of these former customers indicated that they were ready to buy again.

Once the reps learned how to interrupt those inactive customers and initiate sales conversations, they became phenomenally successful, going on to produce, as a team, $100,000 each week in sales. This, by the way, became my client's most successful new sales initiative of the year, and they have expanded the outbound team and are now attacking the entire database.

I observe salespeople demonstrate this same behavior pattern with hot prospects (prospects that have been generated via inbound marketing efforts, referrals, or trade shows and are extremely receptive). I even see the pattern when current customers are being called for cross-sell opportunities. These salespeople agonize, procrastinate, and stare at the phone—afraid to pick it up.

A few months back I was working with a group of insurance agents from one of the most well-known companies in the industry. They were tasked with calling a list of clients that were already doing business with their agency. The objective was simple: Set an appointment with the client to review their coverages and ensure there were no gaps. The goal of the appointment was to find opportunities to cross-sell additional financial products where it made sense.

This was a low-impact call to a current client. The approach was simple:

"Hi, Roger, this is Jeb from XYZ agency. The reason I'm calling is, in reviewing your current coverages, I noticed that you have your cars and home insured with us, but we don't have an umbrella liability policy set up for you. I want to schedule a short meeting with you to review your current situation and identify any coverage gaps that could create a risk for you and your family. How about Thursday morning at 11 AM?"

Yet the agents had come up with every excuse in the book for not making the calls. One even complained to me that "he didn't 'sign up' for cold calling." I politely explained that calling a current client—someone who is already doing business with you, familiar with you, and most likely to take your call—was about as far from cold calling as Perth, Australia, is from New York City.

Just Afraid to Make the Call—Not Cold Call

Today most people, including the experts and the insurance agent I mentioned above, have no idea what a cold call really is. They think that any outbound call or visit is a cold call.

They've turned the fear and anxiety they feel about interrupting prospects into a hobgoblin and relabeled it "cold calling." This has provided the perfect excuse to sit and wait for prospects to interrupt them instead—and, of course, complain about not having enough leads.

It is not the "cold" call that is hard; it is the interrupting. Reps are just afraid to make the call, not the cold call.

Now, for sure, some prospects will be more receptive than others. A prospect who fills out your web form will be easier to speak to than a prospect you are contacting with no pretense. A prospect who is familiar with your name from social media may be more engaged than a prospect you found via a Google alert and contacted through their switch board. A prospect who has a contract expiring with your competitor will be more likely to engage in a conversation than a prospect who just signed a new contract. If you are calling a former customer, you'll likely receive a better reception than from a prospect who has never purchased from you or your company.

Interrupting your prospect's day is a fundamental building block of robust sales pipelines. No matter your prospecting approach, if you don't interrupt relentlessly, your pipeline will be anemic.

So the question is not, to cold call or not to cold call.

Instead, the question is how to strategically balance prospecting across the various prospecting channels to give you a competitive advantage when interrupting prospects in the crowded, competitive marketplace.

4 | Adopt a Balanced Prospecting Methodology

Poor people choose now. Rich people choose balance.
—T. Harv Eker, *Secrets of the Millionaire Mind*

"But Jeb," Janice said emphatically, "I'm so much better in person!"

It was a refrain I'd heard hundreds of times from salespeople who were quick to tell me that they were so much better at one type of prospecting than another.

The "I'm so much better at . . ." excuse is just that: an excuse to avoid other prospecting techniques that salespeople find unpalatable. More often than not, it's an excuse to avoid phone prospecting.

The pipeline always reveals the truth. Salespeople who gravitate to a single prospecting methodology seriously sub-optimize their productivity.

I can guarantee that when the words, "But you don't understand, I'm so much better at . . ." come out of a salesperson's mouth in response to a prospecting technique I've just introduced, that salesperson is underperforming against their number and cheating themselves out of thousands of dollars in commissions.

The Fallacy of Putting All Your Eggs in One Basket

Imagine that a friend comes to you seeking advice on investing for retirement. They explain that they went to a financial seminar where an investment "guru" presented a "sure-thing stock." The guru advised that they immediately move their entire nest egg into this stock. What would you tell them?

If you were a good friend, you would be incredulous. "Putting your money into a single stock is stupid. You'll lose your retirement money!" you'd exclaim.

"But the guy says this investment is a sure thing," your friend responds emphatically. "He says I can make a ton of money!"

You grab him by the collar and shake him. "Are you kidding me? Are you a moron? There are no sure things in investing. That's why sane people do something called diversification—they spread their money out across multiple investments to reduce their risk. This guy is feeding you a line of bull. If you follow this advice, you're courting financial disaster."

In sales, consistently relying on a single prospecting methodology (usually the one you feel generates the least amount of resistance and rejection), at the expense of others, consistently generates mediocre results. However, balancing your prospecting regimen based on your industry, product, company, territory, and tenure in your territory gives you a statistical advantage that almost always leads to higher performance and income over the long term.

Not unlike investing, there is an expert or so-called sales guru on every corner preaching to salespeople that their method is the one way to prospecting salvation. They push phone prospecting, e-mail prospecting, social selling, trade shows, referrals, networking, or inbound marketing as the one true way while disparaging all other forms—usually by labeling the forms they don't like "cold calling" to create the ultimate turnoff. "Do it my way," they'll tell you, "and you'll get unlimited qualified leads. All for only $999!"

These promises and your own justifications that "I'm just so much better at . . ." sound good in a seminar, book, webinar, article, and in your own head. But in the real world, where real salespeople actually have to engage prospects, make a number, feed families, pay mortgages, and buy food, it rarely works out over the long haul.

Avoid the Lunacy of One Size Fits All

Think of me as your friend grabbing you by the collar shaking you into reality. Putting all your prospecting eggs into a single basket is stupid. It's career suicide. Using the "I'm better at . . ." excuse to run from prospecting techniques you don't like is short-sighted.

The foundation of a winning prospecting strategy is balance.

The very best salespeople have mastered balanced prospecting in the same manner that wealthy people have mastered balance in their investment portfolios. Balance simply means that to get the best return from your prospecting time investment, there should be a mixture of telephone, in-person, e-mail, social selling, text messaging, referrals, networking, inbound leads, trade shows, and cold calling. The relative distribution of your time investment in each prospecting methodology should be based on your unique situation.

There isn't a one-size-fits-all formula for balanced prospecting. Every territory, industry, product, service, and prospect base is different. As are the demands of the sales plan, economic drivers, and the strategy and direction of the business—all of which are certain to change over time. It's also important to have a clear understanding of where you are against your goals because that may also determine the appropriate mix of prospecting channels.

For example, in some industries or with certain products or services, if you spend the majority of your time cold calling rather than professional networking, you will fail. In others, if you don't prospect in person, you will die a quick and painful death. In some verticals, referrals are everything, and in others, trade shows deliver the highest-quality prospects.

Social selling might be a primary driver in a consulting business, while inbound marketing might carry a heavier weight with certain software products. If you work for a large company, you may have a ready-made database of prospects, and the telephone and e-mail are the most efficient and effective channels for getting in doors. If you work for a small company or a start-up, you'll need to balance your prospecting to both build your database with long-term opportunities and fill the pipe with deals you can close now.

The key is designing your prospecting regimen based on what works best in your industry and with your product, service, deal complexity, customer base, and tenure. In some cases, this may even be market or geographic specific. For instance, in high-density zip codes like Manhattan or downtown Chicago, you may be more efficient and effective prospecting in person rather than via phone.

Likewise, tenure in your territory matters. If you are new to sales, new to your company, or have just taken over a new territory, your balance of prospecting techniques will likely need to be different than that of a tenured rep who has been in the same territory for years.

In fact, this is how many rookies get themselves into big trouble. They see Joe, the 20-year veteran, generating million-dollar months with what appears to be little effort. Then they emulate this behavior. On their way to failure, they miss the fact that Joe spent years qualifying his database and now he is tuned into his prospects' buying windows and knows exactly when to engage them. The rookies fail to understand that Joe's success was paid for in advance with years of fanatical prospecting.

If you are brand new in your territory, company, or industry, you must be prepared to pick up the phone and do lots of dialing or hit the streets and do lots of knocking. You may have to do a good bit of cold calling to qualify and build your database. On the other hand, if you have been in your territory or industry for years, it is likely that cold calling will become a smaller portion of your prospecting balance while referrals, social selling, lead nurturing, and timely calls to qualified prospects who are moving into the buying window will become your primary focus.

Look around you. Find out what the top salespeople in your organization are doing to generate qualified prospects. Then do what they do. The sale pros who are bringing home the big commission checks know the formula. Beware, though. If you sell to small and mid-market accounts and adopt the same prospecting regimen as the regional account executives or enterprise account managers, you'll likely fail.

Striking a balanced approach with prospecting is the most effective means of filling your sales pipeline no matter your industry product or service. With few exceptions, the combination of multiple techniques and channels is the most effective path to building a winning pipeline.

5

The More You Prospect, the Luckier You Get

Inaction breeds doubt and fear. Action breeds confidence and courage. If you want to conquer fear, do not sit home and think about it. Go out and get busy.

—Dale Carnegie

The unrelenting daily imperative for every salesperson is keeping the pipeline full of qualified prospects.

Top sales professionals spend as much as 80 percent of their time on prospecting and qualifying activities for one important reason: They want to get up to the plate often and put together a consistent string of singles, doubles, triples, and a few home runs.

There are three core laws of prospecting that, when heeded, will ensure that you are moving a steady stream of prospects into the pipe:

1. The Universal Law of Need
2. The 30-Day Rule
3. The Law of Replacement

In this chapter, we discuss the implications of these universal laws for success in sales. You will also learn why ignoring these laws causes sales slumps and how to get out of a slump if you find yourself in one.

The Universal Law of Need

It is when pipelines are empty that salespeople find themselves face to face with the Universal Law of Need. The Universal Law of Need governs desperation. It states that the more you need something, the less likely it is that you will get it. This law comes into play in sales when lack of activity has left your pipeline depleted.

When all of your hope for survival rests on one, two, or even a handful of accounts, the probability of failure increases exponentially.

Consider Jerry. His prospecting is inconsistent at best. Several of the deals he was counting on and put into his forecast pushed off decisions to next quarter or were lost to a competitor. Because of this, he has only a handful of viable opportunities left in his pipeline. Now, with the end of the quarter looming, Jerry is under tremendous pressure. He desperately needs one of these deals to close. As Jerry becomes more desperate to close anything, he comes face to face with a cruel reality: Desperation magnifies and accelerates failure and virtually guarantees that he won't close the deals he must have to survive.

There are several reasons why desperation increases the probability that Jerry will fail when he needs to succeed the most. The first is that desperation taps into the downside of the Law of Attraction, which states that what you focus your thoughts on, you are most likely to get. When you are desperate, you no longer focus your thoughts on what is required for success. Instead, you focus on what will happen to you if you don't get what you need, thereby attracting failure.

The next problem with desperate need is that other people can sense your desperation. Through your actions, tone of voice, words, and body language, you send the message that you are desperate and weak. Prospects and customers naturally repel salespeople who are needy, desperate, and pathetic. Instead, they gravitate toward sales professionals who exude confidence. When you reek of the foul stench of desperation, people don't want to do business with you.

Finally, when you are desperate, you become emotional and act illogically, which causes you to make poor decisions. These poor decisions exacerbate an already bad situation, leaving you stressed, miserable, and digging a deeper hole.

In contrast to Jerry, Sandra is consistently prospecting, networking, gaining referrals, and systematically moving her accounts through her pipeline. Her hard work has resulted in more than 30 opportunities in her funnel.

Will they all close? Not likely. However, Sandra feels little pressure. She is consistently replacing the prospects that fall out of her pipeline and as a result, her sales have been regular, predictable, and on target. She knows exactly what she will close tomorrow, next week, and next month and she has earned her sales manager's trust because she keeps her forecast promises.

Under little pressure, she gets a huge boost when several of the accounts in her pipeline that were long shots suddenly go her way. She blows away her quota and earns a huge bonus. Sandra didn't need this extra sales gravy, yet, because she was disciplined in her activity, it fell right into her lap.

The 30–Day Rule

"Hey, Jeb, got a minute?" The voice on the line was familiar.

"Sure, Greg, what's up?" Greg is a sales pro who lives in my town. We've known each other for years.

"I was wondering if you might have a minute to talk."

I was stuck in traffic on the parking lot called I-285 in Atlanta and had nowhere to go, so Greg started telling me his story. He explained that for some reason nothing he was working on was closing. He was getting frustrated, feeling that he'd lost his edge, and looking for tips that would help him get some deals closed. It was early March and he was worried that he was going to end up having a bad quarter. Slumps can quickly erode confidence and create a feeling of desperation.

"Greg," I asked, "just by chance are you calling the same prospects over and over? And are these prospects the same ones you were trying to close in February?"

"Yes. They keep putting me off. I was wondering if you might have some closing techniques or something I can say to get them to pull the trigger."

"Greg, this is going to sound like a weird question, so bear with me. How much were you working in December?"

"Well, we had a lot going on in December and I didn't get in as much time as I had hoped. We also took a couple of weeks off at the end of the year. You know how it is around the holidays."

"So you weren't doing as much prospecting as usual?"

There was silence on the other end of the line. "Oh, crap, Jeb—the 30-Day Rule! I didn't even see it."

Greg didn't have a closing problem; he had a prospecting problem. He'd stopped prospecting in December and it was biting him in the rear in March. However, because his activity gap happened way back in December, he didn't immediately connect it to his slump in March. To him it felt like a closing issue. Because he treated his slump as a closing technique issue rather than a prospecting issue, he continued to call on stale, dead-end prospects over and over again, unwilling to mentally admit that those deals were never going to close.

That is when he started to dig the hole even deeper. The irony was, as his frustration at not closing sales increased, he stopped prospecting altogether. Instead he just called the same old prospects over and over again, deluding himself that this was prospecting activity.

This death spiral is common and happens to the best salespeople. Let's get real: It's hard to find the energy and motivation to start prospecting when you feel like a loser.

As this cycle continued, Greg failed to replace the stale prospects with new opportunities, became more desperate, hit a slump, and started looking for a silver bullet that would solve his problem. That is when he called me looking for top-secret closing techniques that would save him.

In December Greg stopped prospecting because it was easy to become distracted during the holidays with things that are way more fun than prospecting. Ninety days later his pipeline was stale and stalled. This is what happens when you ignore the 30-Day Rule.

The 30-Day Rule is almost always in play in B2B and high-end B2C sales. In shorter-cycle transactional sales, the 30-Day Rule may become the "One-Week Rule," but the concept remains the same.

The 30-Day Rule states that the prospecting you do in this 30-day period will pay off for the next 90 days. It is a simple, yet powerful universal rule that governs sales and you ignore it at your peril. When you internalize this rule, it will drive you to never put prospecting aside for another day.

The implication of the 30-Day Rule is simple. Miss a day of prospecting and it will tend to bite you sometime in the next 90 days. Miss a week and you will feel it in your commission check. Miss the entire month and you will tank your pipeline, fall into a slump, and wake up 90 days later desperate, feeling like a loser, with no clue how you ended up there.

The Law of Replacement

Rick sat in in front of his VP of sales. He had made big promises at the beginning of the month on his forecast—predicting a record month. Now he was apologizing for a huge miss. He tried to explain how the sales they were counting on failed to materialize for one reason or another. In a desperate Hail Mary, he pointed out that in the two previous months of the quarter his team had delivered ahead of the forecast. His excuses fell on deaf ears.

Rick came to me looking for answers. "My team let me down, and I can't let that happen again. The one thing my VP expects is that we make the forecast. How do I keep my team from quitting on me in the future?"

I asked Rick to walk me through his team's activity over the past few months since he had taken over as sales manager. He explained that when he first started working with the team, the pipe was weak. He'd pushed his team hard to prospect and get it filled with opportunities.

"And it worked!" he said emphatically. "Two months ago we had the best month we've had in two years. The next month was even better. That's why I don't understand what happened this month. It's like everybody just gave up."

"Rick, were your salespeople prospecting at the same intensity during those two big months as they did when you were pushing them to fill the pipeline?" I asked.

"No, once we got the pipe full of opportunities, we got out there and started closing deals."

"Okay, so what does your pipeline look like for next month?"

"Well, that is another thing I had to explain to my VP. We've been so busy working on closing deals that we've let it get weak again."

Problem identified.

I had to break the news to Rick that his salespeople had not given up on him. Instead he had allowed his team to jump on the classic sales roller coaster because he had failed to heed the Law of Replacement.

Here's a math question: Becky has 30 prospects in her pipeline. Her closing percentage is 10 percent. She closes one deal. How many prospects remain in her pipe?

Most people answer 29.

The real answer is 20.

So why 20? Here's the math. Becky has a 1 in 10 probability of closing a deal. That means on average she will close only one deal out of 10 prospects she puts in her pipeline. The net result is when she closes one deal, the other nine are no longer viable prospects. This means her pipeline will be reduced by 10 prospects rather than one. She must now replace those 10 prospects to keep her pipeline full.

The Law of Replacement can be a difficult concept to understand because it is a statistical formula. You may in fact argue how we could possibly know that the other nine prospects are no longer closeable. To do, however, is missing the point. We are talking about statistical probabilities based on Becky's average closing ratio. The stats tell us, over the long run, that she must replace those prospects to keep her pipeline healthy and full.

The Law of Replacement is a critical concept to internalize because failure to heed this law is the reason salespeople get on, *and* stay on, roller coasters. Up and down. Up and down. Until one day they get so far down that they can't get back up again.

The lesson the Law of Replacement teaches is that you must constantly be pushing new opportunities into your pipeline so that you're replacing the opportunities that will naturally fall out. And, you must do so at a rate that matches or exceeds your closing ratio. This is where a fanatical prospecting mindset really begins to pay off.

The Anatomy of a Sales Slump

Ninety-nine percent of sales slumps can be linked directly to a failure to prospect. The anatomy of a sales slump looks something like this:

- At some point you stopped prospecting (see the 30-Day Rule).
- Because you stopped prospecting, your pipeline stalls (see the Law of Replacement).

- Because the prospects in your pipe are dead, you stop closing deals.
- As you experience this failure, there is an erosion of your confidence.
- Your crumbling confidence creates negative self-talk and that further degrades your confidence, wrecks your enthusiasm, and causes you to feel like a loser.
- Feeling like a loser saps your energy and motivation for prospecting activity.
- Because you don't feel like prospecting, you call the same old dead-end prospects over and over and get nowhere.
- The lack of prospecting activity makes your already stale pipe even worse.
- You start hoping for silver bullets. But, because hope is not a strategy, nothing changes.
- You sink deeper into your slump, get desperate, and then *bam!* You get slapped by the Universal Law of Need.
- Your sales days become depressing black holes of misery.

Early in my sales career I hit a bad slump. The previous quarter I'd closed a ton of new business and allowed myself to get caught up in the administrative work required to set up those new customers.

The truth is, I took the easy way out and justified my lack of prospecting with the admin work. Ninety days later I woke up to a new quarter and a sales manager in my face demanding that I get my sales back on track. It was my up-front and close experience with the brutal reality that in sales it is not about what you have sold but rather what you have sold today.

My sales manager pulled me aside and explained the 30-Day Rule to me. He pointed out that I was in a precarious situation. My bone-dry pipeline was testament to this sad state of affairs. He gave me one strong piece of advice: "Go get on the phone and start dialing."

Truthfully, I was depressed, angry, and full of excuses. I felt like a total loser. But I took his advice and started prospecting. Just taking action to save my hide boosted my spirits.

At first, though, it didn't feel like I was making any progress—when you are desperate, you try to will the world to conform to your unreasonable deadlines. I felt that I was just going through the motions and sinking deeper into quicksand because I wasn't actually selling anything. But each day of calling added opportunities to my pipe.

I stuck with it and by the end of the quarter, miraculously, I was the number-one sales rep in my region. The impact of daily prospecting on my performance that quarter—from zero to hero in just three months—made an indelible impression on me. It was a lesson I never had to learn again.

Sooner or later, we all let down our guard and find ourselves in desperate need of a sale. The cumulative impact of our poor decisions, procrastination, fears, lack of focus, and even laziness have added up and suddenly we are desperately scrambling to survive.

You can recover, but first you must acknowledge where the blame for your predicament lies. You see, often, when we find ourselves in desperate situations, we fall back on human nature and blame everything and everyone for our plight except, of course, ourselves. The Universal Law of Need doesn't punish others, though. It punishes you for your failures in executing the daily disciplines required for success. Once you look in the mirror and accept your own culpability and take responsibility, you have a chance to change your future.

The First Rule of Sales Slumps

The first rule of holes is when you are in one, stop digging, and the first rule of sales slumps is when you are in one, start prospecting. The only real way to get out of a sales slump is to get back up to the plate and start swinging.

When you find yourself in a slump, take a breath, acknowledge that your negative emotions are just making things worse, and commit yourself to daily prospecting. Do whatever it takes to get your mind focused on prospecting and committing to daily goals.

Don't spend a moment in thought about what might happen to you if you don't get what you need. Worry won't change the future. Likewise, don't get mired down in regret over what you have failed to do. Your future does not lie in your past.

Instead, put all of your energy, emotion, and effort into actions that you control. Success in sales is a simple equation of daily, weekly, monthly, quarterly, and annual activity. In other words, you are in complete control of your future. Even in a desperate situation, if you go back to the basics and focus on the right activity soon, the results will come. It will usually take about 30 days of dedicated daily activity to get back on track.

One of my absolute favorite quotes is from Arnold Palmer: "The more I practice, the luckier I get."

There is a parallel singularity in sales: The more you prospect, the luckier you get.

Will training, experience, and technique make you a better prospector? Of course. However, it is far more important that you prospect consistently than that you prospect using the best techniques.

When you prospect consistently—and that means every day— amazing things happen. The cumulative impact of daily prospecting is massive. You begin to connect with the right people, in the right accounts, at just the right time. Suddenly, opportunities drop in your lap out of nowhere (my team at Sales Gravy calls this phenomenon "The Sales Gods").

Most salespeople never get lucky because they only do the minimal amount of prospecting required to just squeak by, and when they do start prospecting (usually out of desperation), they expect instant miracles. When those miracles don't happen, they gripe that prospecting doesn't work and crawl back into the warm comfort of mediocrity.

You can't expect to make prospecting calls for a single day and expect miracles any more than you could expect to hit the driving range once and go on to win a golf tournament. It requires consistent commitment and discipline over time—a little bit every day.

So go hit the phones, knock on doors, send e-mails and text messages, pound LinkedIn, ask for referrals, attend networking events, and talk to strangers. Be fanatical. Don't let anything or anyone stop you.

The more you prospect, the luckier you get.

6

Know Your Numbers

Managing Your Ratios

Everything around you is mathematics. Everything around you is numbers.
—Shakuntala Devi

There are people who will tell you that sales is not a numbers game. This statement is often followed with "That's old-school thinking" or something I heard more recently, "Thinking of sales as a numbers game is stupid."

Well, being stupid is stupid.

Sales is and always has been governed by numbers because, in sales, the formula for success is a simple mathematical formula: What (quality) you put into the pipe and how much (quantity) determines what you get out of the pipe.

Numbers, or the "how much," are the science of sales. The "what"—the size of the prospects, the quality of the prospects, the qualification level of the prospects, the depth of your penetration and relationships with decisions makers, influencers, and coaches—that is a little bit of science and art.

Elite Athletes Know Their Numbers

Take a moment and think of your favorite professional athlete. If we were to walk up to that person and ask them to tell us about their latest stats, what do you think the probability is that they'd be able to recite a litany of detailed statistics on their performance?

I'll guarantee it would be 100 percent. I know this because elite athletes know their numbers. They know their numbers because their entire focus as competitors is reaching peak performance. Knowing their numbers gives them the data they need to evaluate how they are doing at any given time and most importantly, to make adjustments.

It is no different in sales. Elite salespeople, like elite athletes, track everything. You will never reach peak performance until you know your numbers and use those numbers to make directional corrections.

At any given moment, you should know how many calls, contacts, e-mails, responses, appointments, and sales you have made. You should track social prospecting activity on sites like LinkedIn, text messages sent, and even smoke signals (if that is relevant). You should measure how many new prospects or new information points you've gathered about existing prospects that you've added to your database.

Once you are tracking your numbers consistently, the door is opened to an honest assessment of both the efficiency and the effectiveness of your sales activities.

- Efficiency is how much activity you are generating in the time block allotted for a particular prospecting activity.
- Effectiveness is the ratio between the activity and the outcome.

Your drive is to optimize the balance between the two and maximize the outcome.

Efficiency + Effectiveness = Performance

$$(E + E = P)$$

For example, you could be highly efficient in making prospecting calls on the phone. You are able to crush it and make 100 dials in an hour. But if those 100 dials result in no new information, no appointments, or appointments with low potential prospects (LPPs), then you were not effective and essentially wasted your time.

Conversely, you could make 10 calls in the same period, setting one appointment with a highly qualified prospect and updating two records in your database. You would be more effective than the previous scenario but extremely inefficient because you wasted a ton of time and suboptimized your phone block.

Without a doubt, there are dozens of variables that drive efficiency and effectiveness for every potential prospecting channel. Those variables include the quality of the list you are working from, industry vertical, time of day, time of year, day of week, decision-maker role of your contact, product or service, complex sale versus transactional, call objective, prospecting channel, quality of your approach, methodology, message, confidence, your mindset, and much more.

Once you know your numbers, you also gain the power to consider these variables objectively. With that information you'll make small adjustments that can increase or even double your sales.

This is why you must gather the courage and self-discipline to track, analyze, and make regular adjustments based on your prospecting performance stats. Keeping count keeps you grounded in reality and focused on your daily goal. It ensures that you remain honest with yourself about where you really stand against your targets and what you need to do or sacrifice to get back on track if you are missing your number.

You Cannot Be Delusional and Successful at the Same Time

Last summer I walked into my office after getting back from an appointment. It was midafternoon as I strolled into the sales bullpen to check the temperature of our sales team. I stopped and asked one of my reps how the day was going.

He shook his head and whined, "It's awful. No one is pulling the trigger today. I don't know what's going on out there, but I'm hitting a brick wall on every call."

"Well, that's not good," I said. "Tell me how many calls you've made today."

He rolled his eyes and shook his head. "A lot! And I'm getting nowhere!"

"Help me understand," I responded. "When you say 'a lot,' what do you mean?"

He grimaced like he was in pain. "Well, I don't know exactly. I'm guessing it's easily 50 calls so far today. You don't understand, Jeb. Something has changed out there. Nobody wants to do anything."

"Okay, let me see your tracking sheet." I looked down at his desk, searching for the sheet we use at our office to visually track daily stats.

He stared blankly at his screen for a moment to gather his thoughts and then responded, "Oh, I forgot to use the tracking sheet today. I've been so busy it just slipped my mind. But I'm tracking my calls in SalesForce."

"All right then, let's go in and take a look at each of your calls and see if we can find a pattern."

I had him walk me through each of the calls he'd made that day, and while we were doing that checked the call log on our phone system. As we walked through calls and I asked questions, he became more and more aware of just how few calls he'd made that day. When we finished our conversation the final tally was 12.

Twelve calls over a seven-hour period. Completely inefficient and a big question mark about what he'd been doing with this time.

At the conclusion of our short coaching session, he said that it felt like he had made far more calls than he actually had. Because he hadn't been visually tracking his activity, he had no idea where he stood.

In retrospect, he was derailed early in the day after two prospects rejected him harshly. That tripped up his confidence and shifted his mindset. It happens to the best of us. Here's where he made his mistake though: Because he failed to track his activity (basically allowing the system to do it for him), he had no visibility into what was actually happening with his prospecting activity. With his emotions reeling, he lost touch with reality and deluded himself into believing that he was being productive.

One of the commonalities that I observe among top salespeople and fanatical prospectors across all market segments—inside and outside—is manual tracking of activity. They each have their own style and means of tracking their numbers, but the one thing they all know is exactly where they stand.

The majority of salespeople don't track their numbers. Why? Because it is so much easier to delude themselves into thinking that they have made far more calls or prospecting touches than they have really made. The false comfort of delusion is warm and fuzzy and far more inviting than the cold edge of reality.

When you choose delusion over reality, you are making a conscious choice to not only lie to yourself but to lower your standards and performance. Reality is the realm of superstars, and joining reality is one of the first steps you'll need to take on the road to developing a fanatical prospecting mindset.

7

The Three Ps That Are Holding You Back

Start by doing what's necessary; then do what's possible; and suddenly you are doing the impossible.

—Francis of Assisi

There are three mindsets that hold salespeople back from prospecting: procrastination, perfectionism, and paralysis from analysis.

Procrastination

You've no doubt heard the children's riddle, "What is the best way to eat an elephant?"

The answer, of course, is, "One bite at a time."

It's a simple concept. But when it comes to the real world and real problems, not that easy.

41

Far too often we try to eat the elephants in our lives all in one bite, which results in stress, frustration, and ultimately failure. You can't do all of your prospecting for the month in one day. It is impossible and it will never get done.

Yet salespeople put prospecting off—always with the promise that they'll "get around to it" tomorrow or later this week or Monday or whatever the prevailing excuse of the day is. They delude themselves into believing that they can prospect once or twice a week and it will be okay. But I know the real truth, and so do you. It never works out like that.

Procrastination is an ugly disease that plagues the human race. No one is immune. You've got it and I've got it. In fact, I have a PhD in procrastination—a bona fide expert. One year I bought a book called *How to Stop Procrastinating* (my New Year's resolution). That book sat unread on my bedside table for three years until I finally sold it at a garage sale.

Every major failure in my life has been a direct result of a collapse in my self-discipline to do the little things every day. Frankly, that is all failure really is. The cumulative impact of many poor decisions, slips in self-disciplines, and things put off until it is too late. To add insult to injury, my failures were often accompanied by an embarrassing crescendo of desperate, hurried, and wasted activity trying to catch up and do it all at once, to save my hide.

It is in our nature as humans to procrastinate. It is normal and easy. It's easy to say, "Oh, I'm tired, I'll exercise tomorrow." It's easy to say, "I'll start my diet tomorrow, I'll quit smoking after this pack, I'll make up today's prospecting on Friday, I'll start reading that book next week!" It's in our nature to fool ourselves with these promises.

But there is no reward for procrastination. The failure to do the little things every day will cripple your efforts to achieve your goals. Lack of discipline will slowly but surely tug at your success and will eventually steal it away.

To be a fanatical prospector, you must develop the self-discipline to do a little bit of prospecting each day. You can't wait until the end of the year or even the end of the month to prospect. You have to prospect every day.

Procrastinating is easy, but the cost is great. Many salespeople don't understand the price they have paid until they wake up one day and realize that they are facing down the Universal Law of Need with an empty pipe and an angry sales manager while sitting on top of a big pile of "shoulda-dones," regret, and failure.

As the saying goes: "Procrastination is the grave in which opportunity is buried."

Perfectionism

I looked on as Jeremy arranged his desk perfectly. Organized his computer. Made sure that he had his script just right. He carefully researched each prospect on his list. Google search, LinkedIn search, company website search, and reviewed in detail the history and call notes in the CRM.

An hour went by. Then two. Finally he made the first call—a call to a prospect on which he had done meticulous research. His call went to voice mail, as did the next call, and the next one. He sighed, "No one answers the phone these days."

After three calls he stopped to arrange things on his desk just so. Twenty minutes later he packed up his things and headed out into the field to visit customers he was already doing business with. In Jeremy's quest for perfectionism, he managed to make seven prospecting calls in about three hours, getting nothing in return for his effort.

Valarie has an office right next door to Jeremy. As soon as she sat down at her desk that same morning, she ran a list on her CRM and started dialing. An hour later she'd made 53 calls, spoken to 14 decision makers, and set two appointments with qualified prospects.

Then she sent 39 prospecting e-mails. It wasn't perfect. She ran into a few snags and had a couple of calls that would have gone better had she researched in advance. However, she accomplished far more than Jeremy. Valarie was also earning more than Jeremy—almost $100,000 more in commissions—and was the number one–ranked sales rep in her division.

In her *Huffington Post* article, "14 Signs Your Perfectionism Has Gotten Out of Control," Carolyn Gregoire writes, "The great irony of perfectionism is that while it's characterized by an intense drive to succeed, it can be the very thing that prevents success. Perfectionism is highly correlated with fear of failure (which is generally not the best motivator) and self-defeating behavior, such as excessive procrastination."[1]

This statement describes perfectly why perfectionism is the arch enemy of fanatical prospecting. It generates both procrastination and the fear of rejection (failure).

The late, great Zig Ziglar said, "Anything worth doing is worth doing poorly." I've always believed that messy success is far better than perfect mediocrity. I'll beat the rep that spends a call block meticulously researching each prospect on any day by just picking up a targeted list and calling. Sure, I'll miss a few things here and there if I don't read every note in the CRM, but there won't be enough of a delta to compensate for the activity gap between me and the rep who gets everything perfect before making a single prospecting call.

To be clear, I am not saying that researching or organizing your prospecting block is a bad idea. If you are calling C-level prospects, or you sell a complex and expensive product, it is a good idea to research your prospect in advance so that your message is relevant to their unique situation. *Advance* is the optimal word, though. Do research before and after the Golden Hours so that it does not encroach on your prospecting block.

However, when perfect research, perfect organization, or finding the perfect time to call becomes an obsession that you use to shield yourself from potential rejection, or if you delude yourself into believing that you are working when you are accomplishing nothing, you've got to get control of it.

Most of the problem with perfectionism is self-talk. The voice inside your head telling you that when you get all of your little ducks in a perfect row, prospects will be putty in your hands. This self-talk manifests itself in behaviors that tend to have you working hard getting everything ready and perfect, but not actually doing anything.

Paralysis from Analysis

Call reluctance is a common label that gets slapped on salespeople who fail to prospect. The term conjures up the image of a salesperson staring at the phone or at their prospect's front door—knees shaking, palms sweating, drenched in anxiety, unwilling to take the next step.

Call reluctance is an easy label to apply because it seems to cover all sales sins. But some people aren't reluctant—they are just in the wrong job. If you are that person, so afraid to call that you can't will your fingers to dial the phone or your feet to move, so afraid of calling on strangers that you find it hard to go to work or even get out of bed—quit. Go do something else. This book won't help you. You don't have call reluctance, you are doing something you hate, and trust me on this: Life is too short to spend doing something you hate.

Another, more common reason for what appears to be call reluctance is paralysis from analysis. This problem is driven in part by perfectionism and is totally fixable. Here is what analysis paralysis sounds like emanating from the mouth of a salesperson:

"Well, what if they say no?"

"What if they say this or that?"

"How will I know if . . . ?"

"What should I do if . . . ?"

Rather than just dialing the phone, sending the e-mail, or walking in the door and dealing with what comes next, the rep goes on a "what if" binge, often followed by an attempt to get every duck in a perfect row.

Disrupting the 3Ps

When I'm working with salespeople who are being held back by all or one of the 3Ps, I get them focused on making just one call. Then the next. Then the next. One call at a time. Sometimes I get a list and sit next to them and dial too. When they see that I'm not getting blown out of the water by prospects, it gets easier for them to let go and take action.

Sometimes I have to be a bit more direct to get them to jump into prospecting. The solution is to push them hard to "just do it." Just pick up the phone and make the call. Let the "what ifs" take care of themselves. I know that might sound a bit harsh, but a push is sometimes what is required to break this destructive cycle. It's not much different from how I learned to swim.

I was six and shivering. My toes hung precariously off the edge of the diving board that jutted out over the lake at Athens Y Camp in north Georgia. The hulking, six-foot-five frame of Coach Poss, the waterfront director, towered over me.

We'd spent that last five days learning strokes, how to kick, and how to breathe, all in the safety of the shallow end. Now it was the moment of truth. Each student had to jump from the diving board into the dark, cold, deep lake and swim the 10 feet or so to shore. It seemed like a mile to me.

I looked back at Coach Poss. "What if I can't swim? What if I don't come back up?" I pleaded. I stood on the end of that diving board staring at the water, running all of the worst-case scenarios over in my head.

Coach Poss began walking toward me. He was neither amused nor swayed by my pleading. There was only one thing I feared more than jumping into the lake, and he was getting closer by the second. He'd already unceremoniously hurled a couple of reluctant beginner swimmers from the diving board. I did not want that embarrassment, so I jumped.

I hit the cold water and went under. For a moment I panicked. Then I stroked my arms and kicked my feet and burst through the surface. I remembered my lessons and paddled my way to the shore. The strokes were not perfect—more dog paddle than breast stroke—but I made it. I made it!

After that, you couldn't keep me off of that diving board. Coach Poss taught me to swim because he forced me to do it. He wasn't worried. He knew I wouldn't drown.

We've all found ourselves in the crushing grip of the 3Ps. I observe salespeople endlessly obsessing and overthinking the potential outcomes of prospecting calls almost every day of my professional life. They convince themselves that they need to gather more facts, just need a little bit more training, or that the timing is not right. They squander time worrying about what ifs and look at me with puppy dog eyes pleading for more time to get it right before diving in.

The human mind abhors the unknown. In its natural state, it wants to be safe and secure. It doesn't like jumping off of a diving board into a cold lake or picking up a phone and calling a stranger. It panics in the face of change and clings to the status quo. Then it begins to convince us that all kinds of awful, dire consequences are imminent. But at some point, you've got to do something. Sometimes you just need a Coach Poss or a Coach Jeb to push you to take action.

Regardless of your situation, the one thing you can be sure of is that allowing the 3Ps to stand in the way of prospecting extracts a high emotional and financial cost.

Free Membership to FanaticalProspecting.com

As a BONUS for purchasing this book you've earned FREE Professional Level Membership Access to Fanatical Prospecting—a $599 value. Use the following special code to claim your bonus.

2BZR37AG

8

Time

The Great Equalizer of Sales

To succeed in sales, simply talk to lots of people every day. And here's what's exciting—there are lots of people!

—Jim Rohn

At the beginning of every Fanatical Prospecting workshop, seminar, and boot camp, we ask participants to tell us their greatest sales challenge. We've asked the question more than 10,000 times. Eighty percent of the sales professionals and sales leaders who attend our sessions say that they struggle most with time management.

"I just never seem to have enough time for prospecting with everything else I have to get done" is a constant refrain.

Yes, salespeople and sales leaders are busy. Yes, sales organizations are asking more of their salespeople than ever before. Yes, there are proposals to create, contracts to get approved, orders to enter into the system, calls to record in the CRM, meetings to attend, and asses to kiss. For salespeople, though, most time management problems are self-inflicted.

The difference between top performers and all of the other salespeople who are picking crumbs up off of the floor is top sales pros are masters at maximizing prime selling time for . . . selling.

Top performers organize their day into distinct time blocks dedicated to specific activities, concentrating their focus and eliminating distractions within those blocks. They develop outside sales territory plans that minimize drive time and inside sales plans that organize their database and resources to get the most out of each sales day. They delegate nonessential and nonselling tasks to their support teams. They are flexible, adaptive, and creative in their quest to maximize time for selling and minimize distractions that steal their commission checks.

24

The one constant for every salesperson is time. Time for prospecting, time for discovery, time for meetings, time for demonstrations, time for presentations, time for closing, and, unfortunately, time for administrative tasks, CRM data entry, and paperwork.

Every salesperson has exactly 24 hours each day, and only a handful of these hours are available for selling. It's how you efficiently and effectively use these "Golden Hours" that is the ultimate difference between failure, average, and superstardom. When you master time, territory, and resource management, you'll lower your stress level and make more money.

This chapter is not an ad nauseam treatise on time-management tools. Time-management tools abound. From Google apps to the Outlook calendar to your CRM to the thousands of cutting-edge apps for mobile devices, there is no shortage of tools available to help you manage time, tasks, and resources. My recommendation is to find the ones that work best for you and then use them in the way that works best for you. You'll find an updated list of time and territory management tools at FanaticalProspecting.com.

My primary objective is to generate awareness for how critical time management is to your success and income and, help you shift your mindset about how you schedule and manage time for prospecting and other sales activities. I want you to take an honest look at the consequences of the choices you are making about where and how to spend your time and how those choices may be holding you back.

Adopt a CEO Mindset

The CEO mindset is the most critical component of time, territory, and resource management. Unless and until you are willing to accept complete responsibility for owning your time, nothing else matters. When you adopt a CEO mindset, you choose to see yourself as the CEO of You, Inc.

For dramatic effect, I ask the salespeople in our Fanatical Prospecting Boot Camps to take out their business card, scratch out whatever title is on it, and write in CEO. It's a little corny, but it drives home the point that in sales you control your own destiny. This is the very reason that I love sales so much.

CEOs are ultimately responsible for the results of their organization. They can't push blame off on anyone else. They are expected to deliver and the buck stops with them. However, CEOs have constraints because resources are scarce. The CEO is tasked with generating the highest return on investment possible with the scarce resources available to them.

Likewise, in sales, you are constrained by scare resources. Your job is to generate the highest ROI possible for your company and the largest possible commission outcome for yourself with those scarce resources. And your scarcest resource is time.

Fanatical prospectors adopt a CEO mindset. They believe that they and they alone are accountable for their own success or failure.

They take complete responsibility and accountability for managing their time, territory, prospect database (CRM), and resources.

As the CEO of their own selling company, they do not allow anything to intrude on the Golden Hours and they are diligent and disciplined with how and where they spend their time. They are also aware that they don't live in a perfect world.

No matter how much you plan and how disciplined you are with your time, prospects, customers, the boss, and sometimes life will throw you curve balls. The true test of CEOs in the business world is their ability to find creative solutions to inevitable road-blocks. Likewise, fanatical prospectors do not allow unexpected obstacles to slow them down. They do not blame others. They do not make excuses. Instead, when faced with roadblocks, distractions, and surprises, they adapt and find creative solutions that allow them to work around problems while they continue to fill the pipe.

Protect the Golden Hours

The single biggest challenge for salespeople is keeping nonrevenue-generating activities from interfering with the Golden Hours. It's a challenge for many reasons:

- There will always be clients, managers, and peers who will make requests of you that are nonsales activities but require your attention.
- When your prospecting activity levels are high, you will naturally generate more follow-up tasks like demos, presentations, proposals, CRM data entry, contacts, approval requests, implementations, follow-up calls, inbound calls, and so on.
- Doing nonsales activity feels important—like you are getting things done.
- Nonsales activity is the perfect excuse to avoid the hard work of prospecting. This is the core reason salespeople dig holes for themselves. Busy work becomes an excuse for not prospecting.

Let me make this crystal clear. Salespeople get paid to sell. Period. End of story. Whine and complain about all the stuff you've got to do if you like, but it will not change the fact that your job is to be interacting with qualified prospects during the Golden Hours and moving them into and through the pipeline.

Therefore, if you are a salesperson and you are not doing things that are directly related to selling during the Golden Hours, then you are not doing your job.

I've heard the same BS excuses a million times:

- "Wait a minute, Jeb, what about all of those things my manager or customers need me to do? When am I supposed to get it all done?"
- "If the company didn't put so much on me, I might have time to actually sell something [eyes rolling—sarcastic tone]."
- "What about my work-life balance? I don't get paid to do this stuff after work. I've got a family, dog, golf game, friends, stuff I've got to do!"

Here are your choices:

Delude yourself. You can continue along the same track, deluding yourself that doing busy work during the Golden Hours is actual sales work, but you cannot be delusional and successful at the same time.

Just say no. One of the most effective ways to unload nonsales activity is to just say no. You don't have to take on or do everything that others bring to you. Whenever someone brings a task to you that has the potential to derail your Golden Hours and it is not mission critical—say no. This won't be easy. However, if you consistently create reasonable boundaries, it won't take long for others to get the message.

Prioritize. Get your priorities straight. I have never known of a salesperson who was consistently hitting her numbers and got fired for not getting nonsales administrative tasks done. Harassed, maybe, but fired—never. On the other hand tens of thousands of salespeople get canned for not making their number. Not everything is a priority, and in some cases, this means that there are tasks that may not get done. That's okay. Keep the pipe full and get the deals closed and no one will ever remember.

Do important nonsales activities before or after the Golden Hours. There will always be nonselling activities that you must do to be successful in your job. Proposals, pre-call preparation, contracts, orders, reports, and CRM data entry are all important, but they are not sales activity. Do these things before and after prime selling time—in the Platinum Hours.

Yes, I already know the excuses: "But Jeb, I've got a family, a life . . . things to do." Here's the deal. In sales time is money and the money is in the Golden Hours. If you want to make more money, you will have to make some sacrifices. If you want to maximize your income, you will need to get up early, go to bed late, and do some work on weekends to ensure that you don't waste your Golden Hours on nonsales activities.

Delegate. One of the most effective things you can do with nonsales-related tasks is to delegate them. Leverage your support staff to the fullest. In every organization, there are people assigned to solve specific problems and get stuff done. If you don't know who these people are, ask questions and keep asking until you find out. Sometimes these people are assigned to help you on a formal basis and sometimes there is an informal system.

If you don't have sales support available, consider hiring someone to help you. You can hire someone locally or easily find virtual assistants who will work for you, on demand, by the hour. If you are an independent sales rep like a real estate broker, financial advisor, or insurance agent, getting an assistant is a smart move.

Top sales pros fiercely protect the Golden Hours. They say no a lot. When a fellow rep stops by to chat them up about the weekend or bellyache about a recent policy change, they do not engage. When managers and corporate staff attempt to dump busy work on them, they push back. The best reps put "Do not disturb" signs on their doors when they are on prospecting blocks to keep distractors at bay.

Your daily mission is simple: Squeeze as much out of the Golden Hours as possible by managing that time wisely. If you are not prospecting, qualifying, information gathering, presenting, or closing during Golden Hours, you are hurting your career and your income and you are not doing your job.

The Fine Art of Delegation

Delegating is how you scale yourself. It is how you get more done with the same 24 hours. However, delegating also requires you to have to let go of control and trust other people.

The desire to control everything that is happening with their customers and accounts is how many salespeople get themselves into trouble and cause themselves immeasurable stress. They made promises to their customers and they want to control the outcomes. I get that. The problem is they cannot scale themselves and eventually stop prospecting because they are bogged down with nonsales activity that others could do. You can only scale when you tap into the talents of others to accomplish more.

Effective delegation begins with effective communication. Salespeople create havoc and communication breakdowns when they fail to give clear instructions to their support team. Then, when mistakes are made, these same salespeople throw their hands in the air and proclaim, "If you want it done right, you've got to do it yourself."

Your support staff cannot read your mind. When you take time, in advance, to develop a plan, articulate clear instructions, make sure everyone knows where they are going and have a map to get there, you'll find that you add hours back to your sales week. It may seem tedious in the moment but the discipline to slow down and do things right up front will actually allow you to speed up.

Follow up, follow up, follow up. Once you have delegated a task to your support team, you must provide consistent and ongoing communication and follow up. One of my favorite sayings is "In God we trust; everyone else, we follow up on." If you fail to systematically follow up on tasks you have delegated, you'll find yourself scrambling at the last moment because critical tasks were left undone or incomplete.

Invest in building relationships with your support staff. I've always been appalled at salespeople who treat their support teams with indifference and disrespect. In a recent *Harvard Business Review* article, "3 Behaviors that Drive Successful Salespeople," Ryan Fuller cites a compelling VoloMetrix study that indicated a direct correlation between success in sales and the salesperson's investment in building a strong internal support system and network.[1] Never forget that the people on your support staff are human—just like you. Show them you care, listen, give them the same respect that you expect in return, and, above all, say thank you.

Blocking Your Time Will Transform Your Career

The sales VP was desperate for a solution. His sales team was behind on their number and things were not getting better. I spent a day on-site observing his sales team, going through the pipeline, and analyzing the activity numbers. It was shocking. The standard for each rep was 50 teleprospecting dials each day, with the goal to set three discovery appointments.

I analyzed the call data for the previous 90 days. On average, each rep was making less than half of the required dials and setting only two appointments a week. Think about this for a moment. This is an inside sales team. Their entire day is dedicated to setting appointments with prospects over the phone and they were barely averaging two prospecting calls an hour.

The lack of prospecting activity was putting the entire company at risk. When I pulled the sales team together and confronted them with the numbers, there were excuses—lots of excuses. "You don't understand, Jeb! We've got so many other things to do—meetings, following up on deals in the pipe, admin work. The CRM is clunky, the coffee is decaffeinated, it takes so long to send voice mail, people don't answer their phones in the morning, afternoon, Wednesdays, or during full moons . . ." and on and on.

Been there, done that, got the T-shirt. I'd heard it all before. So, I pointed out the fact that the pipeline was empty and asked how they could be spending so much time on follow up calls and admin when, essentially, there was nothing to follow up on. They stared back at me. The room got cold.

Before they could launch into more excuses, I gave them 10 minutes to go to their offices and pull together a list of 50 prospects and meet me back in the training room when they were done.

Ten minutes later, with lists in hand, I gave them 30 minutes to call 25 prospects with a goal of setting two discovery appointments. The stunned look on their faces told the whole story. They fidgeted in their seats and stared at their phones. Two people said they felt better calling in their office. I wasn't budging. No more excuses. So with a little more prodding, they got down to work.

Thirty minutes later, on average, each rep had made 22 dials and set at least one appointment. More dials and appointments than they'd been making in an entire eight-hour day. After some additional training and coaching, they were averaging 29 dials in 30 minutes and setting two appointments.

I had their attention. The salespeople were shaking their heads, saying that they had no idea it was possible to get that much done in such a short period of time. The VP of sales and his CEO were blown away. They couldn't believe what we accomplished in such a short period of time. All I had done though was leverage the Horstman's Corollary to Parkinson's Law.

Horstman's Corollary

Parkinson's Law states that work tends to expand to fill the time allotted for it. Horstman's Corollary is the converse. It describes how work contracts to fit into the time allowed. I simply changed the paradigm the reps were working under—instead of giving them an entire day to make their prospecting calls, I gave them 30 minutes.

I repeat this exercise with salespeople within organizations across the globe, and the results are always the same. Salespeople and leaders are absolutely stunned at how much they get done when they block their time, focus on a single activity, and set an outcome goal for that activity.

Time blocking is transformational for salespeople. It changes everything. When you get disciplined at blocking your time and concentrating your power, you see a massive and profound impact on your productivity. You become incredibly efficient when you block your day into short chunks of time for specific activities. You get more accomplished in a shorter time with far better results.

For example, the average Sales Gravy inside sales rep makes around 120 outbound prospecting calls a day selling employment advertising to companies that are hiring salespeople. To most people, that seems like a huge number of calls, and it is. But what really causes a double take is when they learn that we do this in just three hours. Which leaves plenty of time for updating the CRM, building presentations, making follow-up calls, creating proposals, closing deals, and cross-selling existing customers.

We schedule our prospecting blocks into three "Power Hours" that are spread across the day—morning, midday, and afternoon. During Power Hours we do nothing but make teleprospecting calls. We stay off of e-mail and remove all other distractions. We don't do research, allow ourselves to get sucked into CRM management, drift off into social media sites, or accept any excuses. We don't take breaks to get coffee or go to the restroom.

We minimize the downtime between calls by having our targeted call lists prepared and researched in advance (Platinum Hour work). We take notes during the block and wait until after the block concludes to log our calls and update the CRM—time that is blocked specifically for CRM activity. We also schedule blocks for e-mail and social prospecting.

Don't get me wrong. It is intense, draining, rejection-dense work. We make calls as fast as we possibly can. However, Power Hours work brilliantly for two reasons:

1. Our work contracts to fit the time allotted, so we get more done in less time.
2. Anybody can stay focused for an hour.

The good news is most salespeople can set all of the appointments they need to keep their pipeline packed with new opportunities in an hour or two each day when that activity is concentrated into set prospecting blocks. If you invest just an hour a day to make 25 to 50 teleprospecting calls and another hour for e-mail and social prospecting, I can absolutely and unequivocally guarantee that in less than 60 days, your pipeline will be packed.

Stick to Your Guns

Let's suppose that you had an appointment with a hot prospect to do an online demo and presentation. You'd been calling this customer for almost two months to get the appointment. It is on your customer's calendar and she is expecting you to be on the conference line at 9:00 AM. At 8:50 AM one of your fellow reps comes by your desk and says he's going out to get coffee and wants to know if you want to go.

Would you? Would you just walk out the door and blow off that meeting? Of course not! That would be completely irresponsible and stupid. You would tell your peer that you have an important appointment and that you can't go.

Prospecting blocks should be scheduled or "blocked" on your calendar like any other commitment. They are appointments with yourself. The key to making prospecting blocks work is to treat them as sacred—in the same manner you view a set meeting with a customer, prospect, your boss, or an important event with your family.

When it comes to time blocking, you've got to stick to your guns. Let nothing or no one—not even yourself—interfere with or steal that time. Many of the sales professionals who go through our courses hang signs on their doors to warn others to leave them alone while they are on their phone blocks. (Get your own "Do Not Disturb" door hanger at FanaticalProspecting.com.)

It is discipline, pure and simple. You, above all others, must hold yourself accountable to schedule your prospecting blocks and keep them sacred. No one else but you can do that.

Concentrate Your Power

What makes prospecting blocks so productive is the concentration of all of your power on a single focus. Of course this flies right in the face of a culture that has elevated the multitasker to mythical status.

Perhaps you're the kind of person who believes you can multitask. You can field text messages from your mom, scan your Facebook feed, take calls from existing customers, answer e-mails, and dig through your CRM to research each prospect, all while you are making prospecting calls. You pride yourself on being a multitasker and even brag about your ability to do so many things at the same time.

Here's the truth: *You suck at it!*

Basic neuroscience refutes the delusional human belief that we are good at multitasking. Our brains don't actually multitask. Instead, when we are working on more than one thing at a time, our brain cycles back and forth between those things. It does this so fast that we have the illusion of multitasking. Which is why we suck at it.

Your brain was not made to multitask. Sure, it was designed to operate in complex environments and process multiple streams of data at once. You can cook dinner and watch TV at the same time, drive and talk. But your brain was not made to talk, walk, rub your belly, and chew gum. You simply cannot do multiple tasks all at one time and do them well.

When you have too many things going on at once (especially complex tasks), your brain begins to bog down and you start slowing down. It is no different from what happens when you have too many complex programs running at the same time on your computer. At some point the processor can't handle it and it begins running slower and slower.

Be honest. You know you've banged into another person or almost been mowed down by a bus while you were staring at your phone screen texting. You know you've escaped death more than once while applying lipstick, talking on the phone, or checking e-mail while you were driving your car.

Most salespeople I work with believe that multitasking is what they are supposed to be doing. They make a call, log it into their CRM, research the next prospect through a web or social query, answer an e-mail from the boss, take calls from customers, monitor social media streams, send LinkedIn InMail, send a prospecting e-mail, send text messages, instant message their peers . . .

When I point out that with all of this going on, it took them an hour to make four prospecting calls, they stare back in disbelief. "No," they'll explain, "I made way more than that." Delusion brought on by multitasking.

You secretly know you suck at multitasking, so why not just admit it? That makes it so much easier to see the truth about your prospecting blocks: You are making maybe one prospecting touch every three to five minutes because you've got so many things going on at once. Prospecting efficiency decreases in direct proportion to the number of things you are attempting to do at one time.

Recently I was working with a group of commercial insurance sales reps who were averaging seven telephone prospecting dials during a one-hour phone block. That's eight and a half minutes per dial. It wasn't like they were sitting around doing nothing. They were busy, busy, busy multitasking. Yet they were barely making enough calls to keep the lights on and feed their families. The next day they averaged 47 dials an hour. What changed?

It was a simple concentration of power.

- Rather than focusing on multiple tasks at one time, they focused on one: Dial the phone.
- Instead of logging the result of each call into their CRM at the time of the call, they created a list in advance and made their notes on the list. They blocked 30 minutes after the call block to log everything in.
- Mobile devices were turned off and placed into drawers.
- E-mail was turned off.
- Signs were placed on doors alerting others that they were in a phone block.
- Research was done and call objectives set prior to the phone block.

The result was both efficiency and effectiveness. Performance improved exponentially—more prospects were qualified, more appointments were booked, and more new opportunities were dropped into the pipe. With all their prospecting calls for the day knocked out in just an hour, they were able to concentrate their power on other activity blocks like lead generation, social selling, outbound e-mail prospecting, discovery meetings, proposals, and closing.

Beware of the Ding

Laura abandoned the prospecting call she was about to make, looked down, and reached for her phone. The sound it had just made compelled her to check it. Two text messages, a Facebook post, and a YouTube video later, she finally shifted her attention back to her prospecting list but couldn't remember where she'd left off. Seven minutes had gone by since she'd looked down at her phone. She was oblivious.

During the two hours I observed her, she'd lost her focus more than 11 times. When e-mails came in, her computer would ding and she'd stop and look at each one—sometimes for a moment, and twice she stopped completely to fret and respond.

When her two-hour prospecting block ended, she'd achieved just a fraction of her activity target. Then (I can't make this stuff up) she turned to me and said, "See, these call targets they give us are ridiculously unreasonable. There is no way anybody can possibly make that many calls."

The two biggest prospecting derailers for sales professionals are e-mail and mobile devices (text, social media, e-mail, web surfing, apps). When something new hits your inbox or social stream—*ding, buzz, lights, action*! Like clockwork, your concentration shifts to e-mail or a smartphone. Twenty minutes later, you find yourself watching a video of a chimpanzee riding a giraffe around a circus tent and can't remember how you got there.

Making things worse is the addictive nature of our mobile devices. The average person looks at their phone screen every seven minutes. Look down—*ding*—and just like that, you get sucked in. Even as I write this paragraph my iPhone is calling to me. I put it in another room so I'd stay focused on my writing block, but I miss it!

You cannot be efficient when you are constantly being distracted. Besides the distraction itself, it takes time to remember where you left off before you were distracted. This is why time blocking and concentrating your power inside those prospecting blocks will make you so much more productive. Placing your attention on one thing at a time is the key.

This means that during prospecting blocks or building proposal blocks or follow-up call blocks or whatever block you are in, you need to turn everything else off. Schedule alternate time blocks for dealing with e-mail, watching cat videos, or hanging out on Facebook.

What Lurks in Your Inbox Can and Will Derail Your Sales Day

Anthony Iannarino, author of *The Sales Blog*, advises salespeople not to check e-mail first thing in the morning. Maybe "advises" is a little weak. He's passionate about it and calls it prospecting rule number one.[2]

Most salespeople have a really hard time getting started with prospecting each morning. There are dozens of convenient distractions. Iannarino says that one of the best ways to "avoid these distractions is to never check your e-mail first thing in the morning."

E-mail is the great time-sucker of the twenty-first century. It is an always-on stream of consciousness. It follows you everywhere (on your phone, tablet, laptop, and now trains, planes, and automobiles) and demands your attention.

E-mail is the derailer of all derailers. The time-sucker of all time-suckers. If you are itching for a few unproductive hours that you will never get back, just open up e-mail and dive in.

In our always-on society, e-mail has become an addiction. We feel compelled to check it, file it, manage it, rate it, flag it, spam it, and respond to it immediately. We delude ourselves into believing that if we don't jump right on it we'll be judged as nonresponsive or worse.

Consider this: When you are with a customer, do you interrupt them with a "Hey, could you hold a second? Mary over in billing just sent me an e-mail. It's nonsense but I need to answer her." Do you leave your phone or laptop sitting on their desk dinging and beeping while you are in the middle of a sales conversation? Sound ridiculous? Of course it does. Yet we'll interrupt a prospecting block (an appointment with ourselves) to answer trivial e-mails that can easily wait for an hour—or never—to be answered.

If you were to get up early with me, grab a cup of coffee, and sit in sales offices observing salespeople in the wild (sort of like one of those Discovery channel nature films with the Australian narrator), you'd see salespeople walk through the door in the morning, sit down at their desk, take a sip of coffee, and dive headlong into e-mail.

"Look closer, at the sales rep's intense concentration on her inbox," says the narrator with the Australian accent. "Just a click here and a response there. Respond to the boss. Fire off a nasty e-mail to accounting. Oh boy, we've got a customer service issue. Well, you know how it is: 'If you want it done right, you've got to do it yourself.' Check on an order status, read a newsletter, read a personnel announcement from HR—oh, that looks like an interesting link. Three hours later our well-intentioned sales rep is mired down and getting nowhere."

When you open e-mail first thing in the morning, there is almost never good news. That big client you've been trying to close didn't suddenly come to her senses at 2:00 AM and send over a note telling you that you have the deal.

Nope. You've got four messages from your boss giving you nonsales busy work to do; an e-mail from HR telling you that you have not completed the compulsory compliance training on the company intranet; a handful of clients asking questions about when they will get their orders; one livid customer who wants you to stop your world and call them because they called customer service at 4:00 AM and no one was there; and 72 CYA, FYI, BTW, and OMG e-mails that require no action. But you feel compelled to respond immediately to all of them just so people will know that you are still breathing.

Blocking out the first one to two hours of each day for a focused telephone prospecting block is the mark of fanatical prospectors. This is why Anthony is so passionate about moving e-mail to a later time in your day. He explains that "once you open yourself to the demands of the outside world, it is very difficult to bring your full attention and focus to the most important tasks you need to complete each day and the most important task you need to complete each day is prospecting."

"But Jeb, what if one of the e-mails is important? What should I do then? You know it is bad to ignore a client." This is one of my favorite whines from salespeople who are unwilling to face the truth about e-mail. Of course, some e-mails are going to be important. But important does not mean urgent. You will rarely get an urgent e-mail first thing in the morning, and if you do, Anthony says it best: "If something is really important, they will call or text you on your mobile phone—not just send an e-mail."

Take care of your prospecting block first, then manage e-mail.

Leverage the Platinum Hours

During the Golden Hours, time is money. Literally. To maximize sales productivity and your income, your total focus must be on prospecting and customer engagement activities. That, of course, means that there will be a number of tasks that will have to wait until before or after the Golden Hours. We call these periods the Platinum Hours.

Top-earning sales pros set aside time early each morning or late each afternoon to attack important nonselling activities before the demands of the sales day kick in or after they've been addressed. They use the Platinum Hours for:

- Building prospecting lists
- Research
- Precall planning
- Developing proposals and presentations
- Creating contracts and getting approval
- Social selling activities
- E-mail prospecting
- Prospect research and call objective planning
- Planning and organization
- Administration and reports
- Responding to e-mail
- Calendar management
- CRM management

The objective of the Platinum Hours is to set up your sales day so that all of your focus can be spent on high-value selling activities.

Measure Your Worth

When I was in my twenties, I worked for an entrepreneur. The man was worth millions and ran several successful companies. He was also a hands-on leader who for some reason took an interest in me. Because of this, I had the chance to spend time with him whenever he traveled in to visit my location.

One day over lunch, he asked me what I did on the two days I'd taken off the week before. I was blown away that he would even know that. He had several thousand people working in his company. But that was Phil. He knew everything.

I explained that I'd done some home repairs. I proudly told him (and I was proud of my accomplishment) how I had learned new plumbing and electric skills and made the repairs on my own.

He leaned forward and asked, "How many hours did it take you to do that work, including going back and forth to the hardware store to get and exchange parts?"

I replied that it had taken up most of the two days. "But it didn't beat me," I exclaimed. "I got the job done!"

"So about how many hours do you think it actually took you?" he asked.

I thought about it and said, "I'd guess about 12 in all."

"Let me ask you a question," he said. "How long do you think it would have taken a skilled plumber or electrician to do that same work?"

"I don't know—probably a couple of hours. It was pretty simple stuff. I'm just not good at things like that, so it took me longer. Nothing's ever easy." I said sarcastically.

"Well, why didn't you just hire a specialist to do the work?" he asked.

"Plumbers are so expensive," I said. "Why pay them when I can do it myself?"

"How expensive?"

"The ones I called quoted $150 for the repair. That's way too much for something that simple!"

He pulled out a pen and paper and said, "All right, why don't we do some math. You're one of our top people. How much do you think you'll earn this year with your base and commissions?"

I thought about it for a moment, doing the math in my head. "Probably around $75,000."

"How many weeks a year do you actually work at selling?"

"52," I shot back.

"Not so fast." He shook his head. "You've got some vacation time, meetings, holidays, and you might even be out sick, so you are not going to be selling every week, are you?"

"Well, no, not exactly."

"Okay, so how many weeks will you actually be working?"

"When you look at it that way, maybe . . . 48?"

"Yep," he replied. "That sounds about right. And how many hours a day are you actually available for sales activities?"

With trepidation I answered, "I guess six or seven?"

"That's true when you take out lunch and breaks."

"So let's do the math: 6 hours a day times 5 days is 30 hours of selling time; $75,000 divided by 48 is $1,563 divided by 30 equals $52 an hour."

He let that sink in for a moment before going on.

"So you are worth $52 an hour when you are working. The repairs you did on your days off took you 12 hours. You did them yourself because you felt paying $150 was too expensive. But based on your math, it cost you $624 to do them yourself—had you been at the office selling rather than at home pretending to be a plumber. Don't you think your time would have been more wisely spent selling? Can you see why paying a specialist $150 was actually a bargain?"

I had no response. I'd never looked at things that way.

He went on to explain that most people don't take the time to calculate their worth, and because they don't understand what they are worth, they spend their time on activities that are far below their pay grade, and this holds them back.

It was one of the most poignant lessons I ever learned and one I have never forgotten. *Know your worth.*

When you know what you are worth, you become acutely aware of the damage that doing $10-an-hour work (like data entry) during $50-an-hour prime selling time has on your income.

The Law of Triviality describes the human tendency to waste time on unimportant activities while mission-critical tasks are ignored. It's why so many salespeople allow nonselling activities to become an excuse for their failure to focus on selling activities. It's not uncommon for salespeople to waste 50 percent or more of their time on low-value activities.

Understanding what you are worth helps you gain awareness of the cost of focusing on trivial things. Getting a bead on your worth is easy to do. Just take your annual income goal and divide it by the total number of Golden Hours in each year and you'll find what you are worth per hour.

$$(Annual\ Income\ Goal)/(Number\ of\ Working\ Weeks \times Golden\ Hours) = What\ You\ Are\ Worth\ an\ Hour$$

Use this per-hour number as a gauge to determine whether a given task, activity, or assignment is moving you toward your goals or away from them.

When you take time to gain a clear understanding of what each Golden Hour is worth, you will make far better decisions about how to spend your time.

Effective time management is about the choices you make. The bottom line is you've got roughly eight Golden Hours each day to sell and make a living, and you have a choice. You can either dawdle those hours away doing things that don't make you money, whining that "they" give you too much paperwork, there's too much reporting, admin, traffic, bad prospects, or whatever lame excuse you are using that day to justify that fact that you are wasting it. Or, you can plan effectively, block your time, and stick to your guns when others try to corrupt, interrupt, or usurp your time for their use.

9 | The Four Objectives of Prospecting

I don't focus on what I'm up against. I focus on my goals and I try to ignore the rest.

—Venus Williams

"If you don't know where you're going, you might end up someplace else." The great and oft-quoted Yogi Berra said those words. Sadly, this is how many salespeople approach prospecting— on a wing and a prayer.

From the get-go I've been clear that my objective is to teach you how to be both efficient and effective with prospecting. Another way to say this is balancing quantity with quality.

Knowing your objective for each call makes you more efficient because you are able to build prospecting blocks and group your prospecting channel touches around those objectives. This allows you to move faster and make more prospecting touches in less time.

We'll discuss this further in Chapter 10, "Leveraging the Prospecting Pyramid."

Developing a defined objective makes you effective because on each prospecting call, e-mail, social media touch, networking event, or referral request, you know exactly what to ask for and how to bridge to your prospect's problems to give them a compelling reason to accept your request.

The objective is the primary outcome you expect from your prospecting touch. There are four core prospective objectives:

- Set an appointment.
- Gather information and qualify.
- Close a sale.
- Build familiarity.

Your situation, industry, prospect base, product, and service are unique, as will be your prospecting objectives. Here are some quick rules of thumb to get you started when developing prospecting objectives:

- If you are selling a complex, high-risk, high-cost product or service, your primary objective will most often be an appointment with a qualified decision maker, influencer, or other stakeholder who can help you move the deal forward. Your secondary objective will be to gather information. Your tertiary objective will be to build familiarity.
- If you are selling a transactional, low-risk, low-cost product or service and you are in inside sales, your primary objective will be closing the sale and secondarily gathering information.
- If you are selling a transactional, low-risk, low-cost product and you are in outside sales and prospecting via any channel other than in person (phone, e-mail, text, social), your primary objective will be to set an appointment and secondarily to gather information. If you are prospecting in person ("knocking" on the prospect's door), your primary objective will be to close the deal.

- If you have a highly qualified database of prospects in your CRM, the primary objective of most of your prospecting calls will be setting appointments as the buying window opens to start the sales process. The secondary objective will be building familiarity to increase the probability that your prospect will engage when the buying window opens.
- If the product or service you are selling can only be purchased during specific buying windows, like when a contract expires or within a defined budgetary period, gathering information to qualify the buying window will be your primary objective and building familiarity your secondary objective with most calls. You don't want to waste setting an appointment with a prospect that cannot buy because of contractual or budgetary handcuffs. Once you have identified the buying window, your primary objective will shift to setting an appointment.
- If you are new in your territory or working for a start-up or new division, your primary objective will be gathering information so you can identify decision makers and qualify buying windows and budgets. The secondary objective will be to build familiarity.

Lots of salespeople stumble from unqualified prospect to unqualified prospect and wonder why, at the end of the day, week, or month, they sold nothing. This is why it is so important to have an objective for every prospecting touch.

Prospecting Is a Contact Sport

Prospecting, in many ways, is a brutal contact sport that shuns the nuance, art, and finesse of moving a deal through the sales pipe. To be effective, you've got to know what you want and ask for it. To be efficient, you've got to get in as many prospecting touches as possible during each prospecting block.

Prospecting is not for building relationships, selling, or chatting up your buyer. It is for setting the appointment, qualifying, building familiarity, and when it makes sense, moving into the sales process right on the spot. You don't need brilliant scripts. You don't need complex strategies. You don't need to overcomplicate it.

You have no time to waste on small talk, chitchat, or long-winded scripts (or e-mails) written by some dude in marketing who has never been within 50 feet of a prospect. You've got to get to the point, ask for what you want, and move on to the next touch.

Set an Appointment

The most valuable activity in the sales process is a set appointment—no matter where you are in the pipe: initial meeting, discovery meetings, presentations, closing meetings, and so on.

To be absolutely clear, an appointment is a meeting that is on your calendar and your prospect's calendar; in other words, they are expecting you to show up in person or by phone, video call, or web conference at a specific time and date.

Many salespeople confuse "Just stop by," "I'll be here anytime," and "Call me maybe" statements from their prospects to be a commitment for an appointment. Let's not mince words. "Call me maybe" and "Just stop by anytime" are not appointments. To believe that they are, and to put them on your calendar as such, is pure delusion, and, as we've already learned, in sales you cannot be delusional and successful at the same time.

It is only an appointment when you have a firm commitment for a specific meeting time. Consider how much time is wasted driving to or calling into prospects who are not there because they never had a commitment to be there in the first place. Consider the emotional cost of believing you have firm commitments only to discover that you don't.

Working with prospects who are not committed to moving to the next step—either an initial meeting or a subsequent meeting—is like pushing a rope. You expend a tremendous amount of energy and emotion trying to move the deal forward, but you never get anywhere.

Recently I was working with an outbound inside rep who sells capital equipment to midmarket buyers in the manufacturing space. I followed up with him a few weeks after he and his peers attended a training program we designed for his company. Our dialog:

Me: "Armando, tell me how things are going."

Armando: (Sighs) "I guess okay?"

Me: "Okay? How do you mean?"

Armando: "Well, this appointment thing is not working for me."

Me: "How come?"

Armando: "I can't get anyone to show up."

Me: "What percentage of your appointments are no-shows?"

Armando: "I don't know, I guess around 80 percent of them."

Me: "Okay, tell me about the last one that was a no-show."

Armando: "I had a meeting schedule with Jessica Thomson, a buyer at AmCorp International. She's never purchased anything from us before, and we had an appointment scheduled to review our line. When I called this morning at 10:00 AM she didn't answer the phone. I tried several more times until I got her assistant, who said she was traveling."

Me: "Did she accept the meeting request you sent via e-mail?"

Armando: "Well, um, I uh, didn't send one."

Me: "How come?"

Armando: "When I called her last week, she said she was super busy and would be happy to meet with me another time. She said she was usually available in the mornings and I could call anytime. I suggested 10:00 AM today and she said that would be fine, to just call her anytime."

Me: "Was that a real commitment to 10 AM on her part or more of a brush-off just to get you off of the phone?"

Armando: "I guess when you look at it that way, it was a brush-off."

Armando and I went through all the appointments he had on his calendar for the next seven days and not surprisingly, almost all of them were "call me maybe" noncommittal wishes he had accepted as real.

Delusion gets you nowhere. So here is a simple rule: It is only an appointment when it is on your calendar and your prospect's calendar and your prospect is expecting you to show up at a specific time, date, and place (physical or virtual).

Gather Information and Qualify

I'm a big fan of Little League baseball. It is a rite of passage that helps kids build character, hone their values, and learn how to win and lose.

Several years back, when my son played Little League, we were fortunate to be on a team with great coaches who invested their time to help our sons learn to love the game. Along the way, they helped our tight-knit group of parents learn a few lessons, too.

In one of our most intense games, we were in the bottom of the sixth inning with two outs and the bases loaded. The game was tied. With the winning run on third base, all we needed was a hit to win the game and advance to the play-offs.

As our next batter walked from the dugout toward the batter's box, Coach Sandro pulled him aside for one last pep talk. He kneeled in front of the 10-year-old young man, got a handful of his jersey near the collar, and gave him some sage advice.

"Whatever you do," Coach Sandro admonished, "don't swing at nothin' ugly."

As Coach Sandro walked back to his position on the third base line, it struck me how profound his coaching was when applied to sales and frankly, life.

If you've ever played baseball or softball or watched your kids play, you've no doubt witnessed a player chasing a wild pitch—too high, too low, or way outside of the strike zone. The awkward swing of the bat, swishing through thin air, leaves the player off-balance and embarrassed. It is sometimes funny to watch, but mostly the fans, coaches, and players just echo a collective groan and wonder why in the world the player took a swing at that pitch.

It is no different is sales. Each day salespeople waste time, energy, and emotion swinging at ugly deals. Deals that are unprofitable, unqualified, not in the buying window, don't have a budget, don't have an identified decision maker, or because of contracts don't have the ability to buy.

From the outside looking in, it is obvious that these low-probability, ugly deals will never close and will divert the salesperson's time and attention from better opportunities. Yet, in spite of the obvious signs, salespeople forge forward, either delusional or oblivious, placing these deals in their pipelines and projections, wasting endless hours working on ugly deals that will never close.

Sadly, the results are predictable. Almost all of these salespeople strike out.

Savvy sales professionals are super disciplined in qualifying prospects. They understand that time is money and it is a waste of time to work with prospects that are not going to buy. They know that qualified buyers are scarce, and a moment spent with a prospect who will never buy takes them away from their most important task—finding prospects that will buy.

It begins with gathering information during prospecting. While setting an appointment is your primary objective with prospects you have already prequalified as potential buyers, gathering information is your primary objective with prospects you have not qualified.

Here's what I mean. If we drew a bell curve from the statistical distribution of qualified prospects in your database/CRM or the potential customers in your market (if you are a start-up and have not yet built a database):

- A small percentage will be totally qualified and in the buying window (ready for an appointment or ready to buy, in the case of a transactional low-risk product).

- A larger percentage will be totally qualified—you know the decision maker, the key influencers, the size of the business, the budget, and your competitors. But, they won't be in the buying window due to budget restrictions or contractual obligations.
- A larger percentage will be semi-qualified—you will have some information, but there will be holes in your data.
- An even larger percentage will be potential buyers, but you will have almost no information about them or the information will be outdated.
- A small percentage will never be buyers or will be out of business, or the record in the database will be bogus.

Your drive as a sales professional should always be to spend your time with the most qualified prospects in your database. This means that you will want to:

- Set appointments with the prospects that are highly qualified and/or in the buying window
- Nurture the prospects that you've qualified but are not in the buying window
- Gather information on the prospects for which you have some or no data so you can qualify their potential and learn their buying windows
- Eliminate the prospect records that are bogus, out of business, too small, too big, or will never be buyers

There are some sales experts who will tell you to set an appointment with every prospect and qualify later. Many are adamant about it. I get their point. They've observed so many salespeople use qualifying as a reason to avoid making calls that they figure the best way to get them to prospect is to have them set appointments and do the qualifying once they're in the meeting.

Frankly it probably makes sense to just set the appointment regardless how qualified your prospect is if:

- You sell a product or service that is noncontractual
- There is a high probability that most of your prospects will be buyers because your product is something they use all of the time

- There is no set budgetary period for making these purchases
- The decision maker role is fairly consistent and usually a single person

However, when your product or service is complex, contractual (especially when the contract requires exclusivity with a single vendor or limited number of vendors), the sales cycle is long, decision making is done at a high level in the organization, there is a defined budgetary period, or budgets need to be approved in advance, your best bet is to qualify first, then set an appointment.

Define the Strike Zone

The first step in qualifying is to clearly define the strike zone. Far too many companies (especially start-ups and small businesses), sales organizations, and sales professionals fail to develop a profile of a qualified prospect. This includes the optimal time for engaging the prospect prior to the opening of the buying window.

Here is a blinding flash of the obvious: If you don't define the strike zone, you will waste a lot of time chasing ugly deals. This process shouldn't be difficult. If you work for a big company, just go sit down with your sales manager and some of the more successful reps. They'll likely have the information you'll need—decision-making roles, account size, buying windows, budgetary windows, contractual obligations—to build a profile of your ideal opportunity.

If you work for a small company or start-up, start by analyzing your product and service delivery strengths and weaknesses. Look for patterns and commonalities among your best customers. Analyze the deals you are closing and gain a deeper understanding of trigger events that open buying windows. Based on the information you know, gauge how soon you need to engage prior to the buying window opening. Uncover common buyer roles. Then develop a profile of the prospect that is most likely to do business with you and, over the long-term, be a profitable, happy customer.

Once you have developed the profile of your ideal customer, you can develop the questions you'll need to qualify your prospects and identify the best opportunities. Next, make a commitment to measure every prospect, deal, and customer against this profile. When they don't fit, develop the discipline to walk away.

I am not saying that every deal must fit your profile perfectly in order to enter your sales pipe. This is not how the real world works. In some cases, it makes sense to take some risk and swing outside of the strike zone. However, there is a difference in taking a calculated, data-driven risk and chasing an ugly deal.

The end goal is keeping your pipeline full of viable, qualified deals that have a high probability of closing. This is why fanatical prospectors use daily prospecting activity to systematically qualify their databases.

Heed Coach Sandro's advice: "Don't swing at nothin' ugly."

Close the Sale

When you are selling transactional, low-risk, or relatively low-cost products or services and prospecting via phone and in-person channels, your primary prospecting objective is closing the sale right on the spot. If you are prospecting via e-mail, text, or social channels, your primary objective is to convert that prospecting touch into a sales conversation that leads to closing the sale.

When closing the sale is your objective, the prospecting interaction gets a bit more complicated because you've got to engage, qualify, and ask them to commit to giving up their time for a sales conversation right on the spot.

On the phone or in person, where you have the highest probability of a one-call close, this means you have to quickly get past the initial reflex response or brush-off, ask one or two questions to qualify the opportunity, and gain agreement for an appointment on the spot that gives you the space to ask deeper questions, bridge to a solution, and close the sale.

It all happens in the span of a few minutes and it requires poise, confidence, and a fundamental mastery of the sales process.

The techniques for closing the sale on a prospecting call (one call close) are beyond the scope of this book. However, we'll discuss the techniques you'll need to get past the initial pushback and objections from your prospect and move them into a sales conversation in Chapters 15, 16, and 18.

Build Familiarity

Our data and data that we've gathered and analyzed from a diverse set of sources indicate that it takes, on average:

- 1 to 3 touches to reengage an inactive customer
- 1 to 5 touches to engage a prospect who is in the buying window and is familiar with you and your brand
- 3 to 10 touches to engage a prospect who has a high degree of familiarity with you or your brand, but is not in the buying window
- 5 to 12 touches to engage a warm inbound lead
- 5 to 20 touches to engage a prospect who has some familiarity with you and your brand—buying window dependent
- 20 to 50 touches to engage a cold prospect who does not know you or your brand

These are general averages. Depending on your overall brand recognition, geographic location, prospecting channel, product, service, sales cycle, and industry vertical, you may find that these numbers shift in or out of your favor.

The point, however, is not the numbers. It is the story these numbers tell us. Familiarity plays an important role in getting prospects to engage. The more familiar a prospect is with you, your brand, and/or your company, the more likely they will be willing to accept and return your calls, reply to your e-mails, accept a social media connection request, respond to a text message, and engage when you are prospecting in person. We're going to do a much deeper dive into the Law of Familiarity in Chapter 12.

Building familiarity is almost always a secondary or tertiary objective of a prospecting touch, though at times, especially with strategic prospecting campaigns, it may be your primary objective. Familiarity as a prospecting objective requires a long-term focus because it is improved through the cumulative impact of ongoing prospecting activity. This is why savvy sales professionals create strategic prospecting campaigns (SPCs) that cross-leverage prospecting channels to systematically build familiarity.

For example, let's say you have done some research and uncovered the contact names of 100 manufacturing operations managers—the most likely decision makers for your service. Problem is, they don't know you and you don't know them. Many of them may have no familiarity with your company.

In this scenario, it may take multiple touches over a long period of time to get one of these potential buyers to engage. To gain their attention you might develop an SPC that includes phone calls and voice mails, e-mail, social, targeted trade shows, and industry conferences. Your primary objective is to create enough familiarity that these cold prospects are more likely to engage.

- Each time you leave a voice mail, they hear your name and your company name and their familiarity with you increases.
- Each time you send an e-mail, they read your name and see your e-mail address, company name, and service brand, and their familiarity with you increases.
- When you connect with them on LinkedIn, familiarity increases.
- When you like, comment on, or share something they post on a social media channel, familiarity increases.

- When you meet them at an industry conference and put a face with a name, familiarity increases.

The bottom line is, if you don't have a plan and you don't know your objectives, your prospecting blocks will be far less effective and you will waste time. However, when you build more effective prospecting lists, with clear objectives, centered on specific prospecting channels, your prospecting blocks are easier, faster, more impactful, and generate far better results.

10 | Leveraging the Prospecting Pyramid

The only difference between a mob and a trained army is organization.
—Calvin Coolidge

When you get into the office in the morning and begin your prospecting block, which prospects do you call or touch first?

Last year I was hired by a company to develop a prospecting training program for their sales organization. The sales team was missing its number and the CEO was looking to my firm to help him reverse this trend.

My first step was to sit and watch the sales team make their morning prospecting calls. The team worked in a comfortable modern office environment and had a top-tier CRM that was packed full of prevetted prospects and contact records. They also had access to robust social media and business intelligence tools that offered deep insight into their prospective customers, and these tools were integrated into the CRM.

The director of sales expected his sales team to be on the phones qualifying and setting appointments starting at 8:00 AM. I introduced myself to the team and then took a seat in the corner and observed. In particular, I kept my eye on the sales rep in the cubicle closest to me.

After an hour of watching this rep, I asked him a simple question. "When you pick up the phone each morning, how do you know which prospect to call first?"

He looked confused by my question, and I could see the wheels turning as he searched for the "right" answer. Finally he replied, "I don't know. I just login to the CRM and start calling."

It was clear from the team's sales results that collectively they shared the same philosophy. There was no rhyme or reason to their prospecting pattern. They just showed up in the morning, opened up their CRM, ran a rudimentary filter to pull leads for a specific geographic location, and called the first prospect that popped up.

They were wasting a huge amount of time randomly dialing through their database. No plan. No objective. No qualifying methodology. The result was a miserable prospecting experience, a weak pipeline, and desperation appointments and demos set with poorly qualified prospects just to get any kind of win.

Following the phone block, I gathered the team together and drew a triangle (pyramid) on the whiteboard in the training room. I asked the question again to the entire group, "When you pick up the phone in the morning, how do you decide which prospect to call first?"

Blank stares, until one of the young reps said, "I usually pick a city or zip code in my territory, create a list, and start by calling the first prospect on that list."

I followed up with, "Is it possible to sort that list in a more meaningful way?"

Crickets.

"Okay, let me ask this a different way. Ideally, if you could call any list of prospects, which ones would you want on your list?"

They were thinking a little harder now. Finally someone blurted out, "The ones most likely to buy?"

"Bingo! That is exactly right. How might you identify the prospects that have the highest probability of buying?" I asked.

Someone blurted out, "Prospects who have a budget."

Now they were thinking.

Someone else, "Prospects who have expiring contracts with competitors."

From the back of the room, "Prospects who were referrals." "Large prospects." "Prospects with more than 50 employees."

Then more.

"Prospects who called us or filled out one of our web forms."

"Prospects who came to our booth at the last trade show."

"Prospects that are fully qualified but we've been unable to set an appointment with them."

They were finally getting it.

Walk Like an Egyptian: Managing the Prospecting Pyramid

Salespeople who struggle with prospecting view their prospect database as a square. In other words, they treat every prospect exactly the same. For this reason, they attack their database randomly—with no system and no objective.

There are several problems with this approach. First, it is statistically inefficient. When your first call and subsequent calls are made merely by chance, you might call a prospect who is ready to take action or you might not. However, because only a small number of your prospects will be in the buying window at any given time, the statistical probability that you will call poorly qualified prospects is high.

The result is ineffective prospecting blocks that make you feel like you are getting nowhere, far more rejection, and low productivity. Your sales results, income, confidence, and self-esteem all suffer.

Top performers have no interest in hunting and pecking for opportunities, so they design their lists to make prospecting blocks efficient and effective. They segment their prospects by potential or size of the opportunity and the probability the prospect will convert into a sale. They organize their prospecting block to get themselves in position to win with highly qualified prospects who are in the buying window.

Top performers view their prospect database as a pyramid.

- At the bottom of the pyramid are the thousands of prospects they know little about other than a company name and perhaps some contact information. They don't know if the information about the prospect is correct (and there is a good chance that it isn't).

  Action: The goal with these prospects is to move them up the pyramid by gathering information to correct and confirm data, fill in the missing pieces, and begin the qualifying process.

- Higher up the pyramid, the information improves. There is solid contact information, including e-mail addresses. There may be information on competitors, product or service usage numbers, the size of the budget, and other demographic information. There may also be contact information for decision makers and influencers.

  Action: The goal with these prospects is to identify the buying window and all potential stakeholders.

- Moving higher up, potential buying windows have been identified. There are complete contact records for decision makers and influencers, including social profiles.

  Action: Your focus at this level is to implement nurturing campaigns to stay in front of confirmed decision makers in anticipation of an identified future buying window.

- Further up are conquest prospects. This is a highly targeted list of the best or largest opportunities in your territory. There will be a limited number: 10, 25, 50, 100.

   Action: The focus for conquest prospects includes nurturing and regular touches, stakeholder identification, buying window qualifying, monitoring for trigger events, and building familiarity.

- Closer to the top are hot inbound leads and referrals.

   Action: These prospects require immediate follow-up to qualify and/or move them into the pipeline.

- At the tip-top are highly qualified prospects who are moving into the buying window due to an immediate need, contract expiration, trigger event, or budgetary period.

   Action: These are your highest-priority prospects and should be on the top of your daily prospecting list. The goals is to move them into the pipe.

The key to leveraging the prospecting pyramid philosophy is a systematic daily focus on gathering qualifying information that identifies buying windows and stakeholders and moves prospects up the pyramid based on that information.

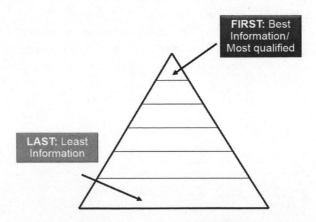

Figure 10.1   The Prospecting Pyramid (Organizing Prospecting Blocks)

Powerful Lists Get Powerful Results

Being a more efficient and effective prospector begins and ends with an organized, targeted prospecting list. A high-quality prospecting list is like a track for your prospecting train. It eliminates wasted time hunting and pecking for qualified prospects and helps you focus on a specific objective within a particular prospecting channel.

The sad fact is most salespeople are working off poorly constructed lists or, in many cases, no list at all. Some companies try to provide lists for their reps, but most don't, and the ones that do usually do it poorly.

Building effective and robust prospecting lists requires consistent effort and discipline, which is why salespeople don't do it. It's so much easier to open up the CRM and just start calling the first prospect record you find.

This is a wake-up call. The quality of list you work from during each prospecting block has a more significant impact on the success of the block than any other element except your mindset.

When you build powerful lists, you get powerful results.

Lists should be constructed based on the following filters (or other methodologies depending on your unique situation). Use these elements in combination to structure your prospecting lists for maximum impact.

- Prospecting objective: set an appointment, gather information, close the sale, build familiarity
- Prospecting channel: phone, e-mail, social, text, in person, networking
- Qualification level: highest qualified at the top of the list—least qualified at the bottom of the list
- Potential: largest opportunities at the top of the list—lowest potential at the bottom of the list
- Probability: highest potential probability to achieve your objective at the top of the list—lowest probability at the bottom of the list

- Territory plan: day of week, postal code, street, geographic grid, city
- Inbound leads
- Conquest prospects
- Decision maker/stakeholder role
- Industry or market vertical
- Customers that purchase a specific type of product or service
- Seasonal customers
- Inactive customers
- Leads from a recent trade show or conference

Some of these filters can be automated in your CRM, while others may require manual decisions. Automate the process as much as possible with preset filters, views, and reports to make it easy to pull lists based on your prospecting objectives.

There will only be a handful of prospects in your database at any given time that are in the buying window, and you've got to get in front of them before they buy or the window of dissatisfaction from a trigger event dissipates. Start each morning with a prospecting block focused on a list of these top-of-pyramid prospects while you are fresh, feeling your best, and motivated.

Because these prospects are in the buying window it will be much easier to convert them into an appointment, demo, or sale. Starting your day by calling the prospects on the top of your pyramid will deliver early wins. These wins give you confidence and motivation to attack the remainder of the sales day.

Once you have exhausted your high-potential prospects, focus your prospecting activity on qualifying and nurturing activities with conquest accounts. Follow that by focusing on qualifying the hundreds or thousands of prospects lower on the pyramid.

If each day you start at the top of the pyramid and set quality appointments early, you will have time left over to systematically qualify the other prospects in your database moving them to the top of your pyramid. Over time, you'll experience more successful prospecting blocks, a dynamic prospect database, and a full pipeline.

Tomorrow morning when you get ready to make your prospecting calls, take a look at the first name on your list and ask yourself, "Is this the best prospect to call?" Then, get familiar with the filters and sort tools on your CRM program and build your own prospecting pyramid.

11 | Own Your Database

Why the CRM Is Your Most Important Sales Tool

The most expensive thing you can do in sales is spend your time with the wrong prospect.

—Jeb Blount

I hate writing about or talking about CRMs. It's boring and tiresome. It is also a turnoff because I know salespeople have no love for the CRM. Honestly, it pained me to include this important but tedious subject. But, this is the brutal, and often ignored, reality:

There is no weapon or tool in your sales arsenal that is more important or impactful to your long-term income stream than your prospect database. Nothing. Your database of prospects is what helps you make a living now and in the future. It does not make a difference what you sell; a well-managed, living, breathing prospect database is a golden goose that keeps on giving.

Your CRM is the most important tool in your sales arsenal because it:

- Allows you to manage the details and tasks related to many different contacts without having to remember everything.
- Keeps you organized, manages your pipeline, and saves your deals and relationships from getting derailed. It makes life easier by doing work for you.
- Allows you to segment and sort your prospect database and build prospecting lists based on any field or group of fields in the database. This makes you exponentially more effective and efficient in your prospecting activities.
- Helps you systematically qualify prospects so that you move them up the prospecting pyramid.

When you peel all of the technology away, a CRM is just a software-based filing system that makes it easier for you to manage and access information because it does a very simple task: It remembers important things for you and reminds you when those things are important. Face it, you are moving fast and forget things. In sales the little things are big things and a well-managed CRM will prevent slipups that could cost you deals.

Own It Like a CEO

Here's the truth about the CRM: If you don't *own* it, you will never reach your true earning potential. Owning it means applying the CEO mindset we discussed earlier. It means:

- Being accountable for maintaining the integrity of your prospect database.
- Not waiting until your manager is screaming at you because you haven't updated a record in a month.
- Taking time to make copious notes following sales calls and logging those calls.

- Putting new leads in the system rather than carting around a pocket full of business cards you've collected from prospects.
- Rather than sitting around whining about how you don't understand the CRM, taking the time to learn it through trial and error and online learning tools.

Fanatical prospectors own their database. They own it because they get it. Their database is where targeted lists come from. Their database makes them more efficient and effective. It should be so important to you that you eat, sleep, and drink it.

I had a rep who worked for my company for nine months. This guy was talented and he could sell. But he could never keep his pipeline full and never even got close to his quota. When we finally started to dig into what was going on, we discovered that he had only logged into the CRM once the entire time he worked for us. Sad but true, and by then it was too late. We fired him.

Some salespeople don't see how the system benefits them personally. They've got a sales manager on their case about updating the CRM, but in their mind they're doing it for the company, not themselves. It's a mindset issue. These salespeople see themselves "working for the man," whereas fanatical prospectors believe that they are the CEO of their territory. They are working for themselves.

I can get on my soapbox and preach. I can warn you of the consequences. I can explain the benefits. But the only person who can motivate you to fully exploit your CRM and invest diligently in building a quality prospect database is you. If you choose not to invest in your database, as the saying goes, you can't fix stupid.

A Trash Can or a Gold Mine

More often than not, salespeople treat their database like a trash can rather than a gold mine. Call notes aren't inputted. Records aren't kept up to date. Calls are not logged. This inattention to detail causes the value and integrity of the database to be undermined, leaving salespeople struggling to set appointments and engage the right prospects, at the right time, with the right message because they don't know who to call.

Gathering information and qualifying is where managing and building your database really pays off. Over time, through relentless prospecting and research, you'll gain a clear picture that helps you fully qualify the opportunity. You'll know the key decision makers and influencers, what your prospects buy and how much, who your competitors are, potential trigger events, and most importantly, when the buying window opens.

Building a database is like filling in a jigsaw puzzle. It takes time, lots of work, and sometimes there is not much evidence that it is paying off. The key is recognizing the cumulative value of small wins. I'll often hear a sales rep bemoaning a call that he felt didn't go very well rather than celebrating the small nugget of information that they uncovered about a decision maker that added another piece to the qualification puzzle.

When it comes to building a powerful prospect database, my philosophy is simple: Put every detail about every account and every interaction with every account and contact in your CRM. Make good, clear notes. Never procrastinate. Do not take shortcuts. Develop the discipline to do it right the first time and it will pay off for you over time.

12

The Law
of Familiarity

*After seeing a lot of the world, I now tend to return to the same spots.
I enjoy the familiarity.*

—Louise Nurding

The more familiar a prospect is with you, your brand, and/or your company, the more likely they will be to accept and return your calls, open your e-mails, accept a social media connection request, respond to a text message, accept an invite to an event or webinar, download information from a link you sent them, engage in sales conversations, and ultimately do business with you.

That's the Law of Familiarity.

This is supported by data that indicates that it can take between 20 and 50 touches to engage a prospect with little to no familiarity with you or your company, but just 1 to 10 touches to engage an inactive customer, warm inbound lead, or prospect who has a high degree of familiarity with you, your company, or your brand.

The lack of familiarity is why you get so many objections to your requests for your prospects' time. When prospects don't know you, it's much harder to get in the door.

Prospecting Lubrication

This is why it's in your best interest to invest time and effort to build familiarity with your prospects. Familiarity lubricates prospecting because it makes the prospect's decision to give you their time feel less risky.

There even comes a point when a prospect will readily communicate and build a "first-name" relationship with you—even when they aren't interested in buying at the moment. Sean Burke, CEO of KiteDesk, calls this the Familiarity Threshold.

When you earn enough trust to cross the familiarity threshold, you also gain the ability to communicate more freely—including through social media inboxes and text messaging—without being considered intrusive.

You won't cross the familiarity threshold with most of your prospects because you'll never have enough time to make that level of investment with all of them. Crossing the familiarity threshold requires a significant investment of time, intellect, emotion, energy, and technology. This is why you must create your conquest lists and develop strategic prospecting plans so you focus your time and attention on building familiarity with your most valuable prospects.

The Five Levers of Familiarity

The familiarity threshold is also why the senior reps in your organization—the ones who've been in the same territories for years—make it look so easy. The years of investment they've made in building familiarity in their territory have paid off. If you were to take a closer look at their efforts, you'd discover that there were five levers that helped them build familiarity over time.

Persistent and Consistent Prospecting

The first step in creating familiarity is through persistent and consistent daily prospecting. Each time you call, e-mail, meet face to face, drop off a business card, and leave a voice mail, you create familiarity. This is one of the core reasons persistence pays off. The more times they see or hear your name, the more familiar you become to them and the gatekeepers that protect them. Simply put, the more you prospect, the more familiar you become to your prospect base.

Referrals and Introductions

"Ron, you mentioned that you still have close ties to your former company. Do you know who makes the decisions on sales training over there?" I was speaking with the decision maker at one of my top clients.

"Yep. That's Mary Walker. She used to work for me. Great lady, you'll like her." He looked down at his phone. "Let me get you her number."

A few seconds went by and he gave me her contact information. Then I asked, "Would you mind giving her a call and making an introduction?"

He looked up from his phone and said, "Sure, no problem." Then he dialed, got Mary on the line, and said, "I'm standing here with a guy named Jeb Blount. He's been helping us with developing our sales training curriculum. You two need to meet. He's going to be giving you a call."

The most powerful and direct path to familiarity is a referral or introduction. The referral gives you instant credibility because you get to ride on the coat tails of a person who is already trusted by your prospect. There are three basic types of referrals:

1. *Customer referrals* come from happy clients that trust you. The key to generating these referrals is developing a disciplined, systematic process for asking for referrals.
2. *Personal referrals* come from friends, family, and acquaintances. These are people who know you and are willing to send prospects your way. Take time to educate your personal connections on what you do and your ideal prospects so they know what to look for. Then (this is critical), keep reminding them so they don't forget about you.
3. *Professional referrals* come from relationships you've developed with other professionals in related industries or with salespeople who may call on the same type of prospects but don't compete with you. These are typically mutually beneficial relationships. To generate these referrals, you must seek out, form, and make an ongoing investment in these professional relationships. The wider your professional network, the more referrals you'll generate.

I've read dozens of books on referrals. These books offer excellent advice, techniques, and tips for generation referrals. For the sake of time, I'll give you a short synopsis of the core message that is common to every one of these books. The real secret to generating referrals is:

- Give a legendary customer experience.
- Ask.

That's it. Straightforward and simple. Yet, while standing in front of a group of B2B sales reps last month, I asked: "How many of you provide great service to your customers? Raise your hand."

Every hand in the room went up.

"How many of you asked for at least one referral last week?"
No hands went up.

"How about in the last month?"

Again, no hands.

"How about in the last quarter?"

One hand went up.

"How about the last year?"

Three hands up out of a hundred salespeople.

Shocking? Not really. I ask this question to groups of salespeople regularly. The response is always the same. I'm not going to waste your time discussing why salespeople don't ask because that answer is more than obvious: They either fear getting turned down or they just don't think of it.

It's relatively easy, low key, and low risk to ask a happy client for a referral. It goes like this:

"Patricia, thank you again for your business. I'm glad to hear you are happy with us. I'm working hard to add more customers like you. Would you be able to introduce me to other people in your network who might want to use our product?"

Yes, there are more strategic and powerful ways to ask. Yes, there are ways to make it easier for your customers to help you with referrals. What's most important, though, is the discipline to ask.

Networking

There are opportunities to network in your community or in your territory every week. The first place to check with is the chamber(s) in your territory. Then Google or Bing the calendars of other business and civic organizations in your area. Finally, ask your prospects and customers which events, conferences, and trade shows they attend.

Then *go!* Can I make this any clearer? Go shake hands. Go meet people. Go learn about them. You'll get leads and referrals, and nothing builds familiarity better than face-to-face contact. We'll talk about social prospecting and social media in the next chapter, but networking is the real social prospecting.

To be successful at networking, refrain from becoming a walking, talking marketing brochure and get it through your thick skull that nobody cares about you or what you have to say. They want to talk about themselves.

You don't go to networking events to sell. You are not there to set appointments, get leads, or close business. You are there to create connections with other people. You get those other things after the connections are established. There should be no quid pro quo attached to your conversations.

You create connections when you ask questions, listen, and become genuinely interested in other people. Maya Angelou said, "People will forget what you said or did, but they will always remember how you made them feel." Take this to heart as you invest time in networking events.

Following up after networking events is the key to anchoring your new relationships and familiarity. Use handwritten notes to remind the other person of your conversation by referencing something you spoke about. I make it a habit to keep a stack of prestamped envelopes and thank-you notes in my car. I write my notes while the conversations are still fresh.

When I've had a positive conversation, I will also send a short text to thank the person for taking time to speak with me, followed by a LinkedIn connection request to further anchor familiarity.

Finally, I log any leads in my CRM no later than the next morning. If I promised to send something, schedule an appointment, or introduce them to someone else, I schedule a task and take action within 24 hours of the event.

Then I follow up on a regular basis until I move my networking prospects into the pipeline.

Company and Brand Familiarity

Here's the good news. If you are lucky enough to work for a well-known company or sell a recognized brand, prospecting is exponentially easier than it is for the rep selling for a start-up or small, unknown company. In some cases, all you need to do to strike up a conversation or set an appointment is to mention your company's name or product.

The large company marketing machine is always at work, driving brand recognition and generating leads through traditional advertising, social media, content marketing, trade shows, and conferences. This gives the rep who works for a big company with a big brand a decided advantage in the war for their prospects' attention.

If you work for a start-up, emerging brand, or a small, unknown company without a sustained marketing strategy, you are almost always at a disadvantage. It is much harder to get people to meet with you when they are not familiar with your company. For this reason, small company and start-up sales teams are intrinsically an integral part of the brand-building and market-awareness process. In conjunction with (or in some cases in spite of) limited marketing resources, you must actively participate in getting the word out.

You may be called on to—and I suggest, volunteer to—write and post relevant blogs, be an active part of trade shows, build and leverage your social media network, contribute to white papers and e-books, create podcasts, and host webinars. And when it comes to social media, you can generate massive brand awareness to a targeted audience by committing to being active, growing your network, and sharing content.

The bottom line is, when you are in a small organization, it is almost always all hands on deck and it is a given that sales and marketing are a mash-up rather than separate silos.

For reps who work for a well-recognized brand, the key is staying out of the gears of the marketing machine and allowing marketing to do its job.

Personal Branding

Familiarity is also built through personal branding—making a direct investment in improving the awareness of your name, expertise, and reputation.

This is the ultimate way to build familiarity because people buy *you*. They buy you and trust you because they believe that you are the only person who can solve their unique problem.

Never in the human experience has it been easier to build familiarity through personal branding. Today distributing content is easy. Just jump on your favorite social network and go to town. Point, shoot, write, click, and publish—it's all at your fingertips. You can get your name and reputation out there fast and for very little cost.

There is, however, a personal branding methodology that is so little used, I consider it a secret weapon in the war for familiarity. It has an extraordinary track record for producing results and creates instant familiarity, credibility, and leads.

The secret: Speak in public, regularly.

Public speaking is a powerful method for meeting people and developing business relationships because it creates an environment where prospects seek you out.

When you speak in public, at least for a moment, you are considered a minor celebrity who people want to meet. After you give your speech, people walk up to you, engage you in conversations, freely reveal their business issues, and voluntarily hand over their contact information.

You can easily get speaking gigs. Organizations like the chamber of commerce, Rotary Club, trade organizations, and other business and civic groups are always in need of guest speakers. All you really have to do is call and volunteer and they will happily put you on the schedule. If you attend trade shows and association meetings, just call the meeting planners and tell them you would like to be a speaker or deliver a workshop. These folks are on the lookout for subject matter experts to add value to their programs.

Although less effective, you can also speak on webinars and live streaming events put on by industry trade associations and your own company.

Speaking allows you to showcase your knowledge. It also gives you tremendous visibility and credibility. And because so few of your competitors do it, it will set you apart, enhance your personal brand, and create a greater sense of familiarity with your prospects.

Warning

The information in this chapter comes with a warning. It is easy to spend all of your time creating familiarity. If you do this in place of other prospecting activities, you'll wake up a month from now with an empty pipe and a screaming, pissed-off boss.

Like everything in sales, building familiarity is about balance. You've got to balance the need for sales today with an investment in the future.

13 | Social Selling

Sales is a blend of art and science. The art is influencing people to make commitments. The science is influencing the right people.

—Jeb Blount

The influence of social media in today's society is inescapable. Millions of people are linked together on social media sites—constantly checking and updating their status. As a business tool, social media has moved from cutting edge to ubiquitous.

As I write this book, *social selling* is one of the hottest buzzwords in the sales profession.

There is no doubt that the social selling (sometimes called social prospecting) channel is a critical component of a balanced prospecting methodology.

I believe that for the sales profession, social media is the most important technological advancement since the telephone.

There has never been a time in sales when so much information about so many buyers was so easy to access. And not just contact information, but context. Through the social channel, we gain glimpses into our prospects' behavior, desires, preferences, and triggers that drive buying behavior and open buying windows.

The social channel gives us the ability to easily and economically build familiarity through low-impact, nonintrusive techniques. We can easily map the buyers, influencers, potential coaches, and other stakeholders at our prospective accounts and strategically uncover buying motivations and interests that lead to more impactful and robust in-person conversations. We can monitor our competitors and industry trends in ways that were not possible or economically feasible in the past.

Technology that allows us to easily tap into, analyze, and use this endless stream of data is emerging at a lightning pace. Which is both good news and bad news. The good news is technology will make it even easier for you to utilize the social channel to build your pipe and accelerate the sales process.

The bad news? As the data pool morphs and options for tapping into that data increase, the social ecosystem is becoming more overwhelming and the expense of tapping into this data is rapidly rising.

The owners of the social channels—LinkedIn, Google, Facebook, and Twitter—are keenly aware that they hold all the data and all the cards. The companies that build software that unlocks this data are having to pay up to gain access to it. To make a profit, those costs are being passed on to you. In other words, in the future, to get the most out of social selling, you're going to need to bring your wallet.

Yet, social selling is inextricably woven into the fabric of fanatical prospecting. Top performers know this, and that's why they are rapidly adopting social selling tactics for prospecting and are willing to pony up to pay for access.

What I am going to focus on in this chapter is giving you a framework for becoming more effective and efficient with social media in your prospecting routine. I'll help you understand the core objectives and the five Cs of social prospecting along with the five categories of social selling tools that help you become more efficient and effective in your efforts.

Five Objectives of Social Prospecting (Outcomes)	The Five Cs of the Social Prospecting Process (Effective)	Social Prospecting Tools (Efficient)
Personal branding and building familiarity	Connecting	Engagement tools
Inbound prospecting via education and insights	Content creation	Creation tools
Trigger-event and buying-cycle awareness	Content curation	Curation tools
Research and information gathering	Conversion	Distribution tools
Outbound prospecting via direct engagement	Consistency	Intelligence and data tools

Because the social selling landscape is changing so rapidly, though, I am going to avoid diving into the specific features/tactics of the major social media sites and tools. Frankly, because the social media sites are so feature rich, it would require several more books to give you everything you'd ever need to know, and by the time those books were published, they'd be out of date.

So, instead of trying to cram everything you ever need to know about social prospecting into this short chapter, I've created a rich set of resources that are constantly being updated. You'll find virtual training modules, tutorials, articles, comprehensive e-books, and videos on social prospecting at www.FanaticalProspecting.com.

Social Selling Is Not a Panacea

Along with the increased awareness of the power of the social channel, there has been a disturbing trend of newly minted "social selling" gurus proclaiming that social selling will solve all of your sales problems.

I recently witnessed one of these "gurus" pronounce all other forms of prospecting dead and advise sales people to focus all of their energy on social selling (of course using his complicated nine-step system that he was offering at a special discount). Ironically and hypocritically, his pitch was made via a cold e-mail.

Another expert cold-called my VP of Sales at Sales Gravy on the telephone to pitch her social selling program as an advanced lead generation program that would eliminate cold calling forever. He challenged her: "If your program is so good, why are you cold-calling me? Shouldn't I be calling you?" That abruptly ended the call.

Social selling is not a panacea. Contact and conversion rates from phone and e-mail dwarf conversion rates on social media. The social channel enhances, elevates, and sometimes accelerates your prospecting efforts. It certainly impacts familiarity. But it is not a replacement for focused and deliberate outbound prospecting efforts.

The Social Selling Challenge

From time to time, though, I'll hire a new sales rep who will challenge me on this premise. Last year one of my new reps walked into my office and declared the telephone dead. He'd read an article by a social selling "expert" and then attended one of his webinars. My rep claimed that he'd learned how to eliminate cold calling (which meant *all* calling) with a more powerful LinkedIn strategy.

"Besides," he told me, "no one answers the phone anymore. Buyer 2.0 wants to talk to salespeople on their terms." (I remember thinking to myself, "Buyer 2.0? WTF!")

He even uttered the words "old school" as we debated his position on calling versus LinkedIn and I pointed to the phone and insisted he pick it up and start dialing.

So I challenged him. He could employ his "new school strategy" for a week, and I would go old school and open up our database of prospects, get on the phone, and interrupt "Buyer 2.0s" day.

At the end of the first day, he proudly came into my office beaming that his contact requests had been accepted by seven people—"Good prospects," he said.

"Awesome! So how much did you sell?" I asked.

"You don't understand, Jeb. It doesn't work that way," he replied. "This takes time."

I looked down at my call sheet. I'd completed 73 dials, made 19 contacts, and sold two deals for which I'd collected credit cards—real money in the bank.

We repeated this exercise for four more days. At the end of the week, I'd closed 17 new accounts and collected payment on all of them. He'd been successful in getting a whole lot of people to accept his connection requests, liked and commented on lots of posts, followed company pages, joined groups, posted a bunch of content, and . . . sold nothing.

To be sure, I used social media too. I sold two deals when the prospects called me back after I left a voice mail, sent an e-mail, and then pinged them on LinkedIn. I also sent connection requests to the prospects I sold and the ones I'd had conversations with on the phone but was unable to close. While building my call lists, I scanned LinkedIn profiles for data points that might make my calls more relevant. In other words, I wove social media into a balanced prospecting effort rather than making it my exclusive channel.

Following our exercise, the exchange of a $10 bet, and a coaching conversation that included a calculator on which I introduced him to how much commission he would have earned if he'd made those 17 sales, my new rep agreed that he'd fill up his bank account faster with a balanced approach that included interrupting people rather than hanging out on the social channel all day waiting for them to interrupt him.

Before running headlong into this brutal reality, my new rep had adopted a methodology from a "guru" who promised an endless stream of prospects who were ready to buy, along with minimal effort and no rejection.

If you decide to buy into this crap, you might want to keep your resume warmed up, and if you think social selling is the new magic fairy dust that will turn you into the next sales superstar, you are in for a rude awakening.

Social selling will not solve your pipeline woes or provide an endless stream of inbound leads with little effort. It takes far more than a LinkedIn connection, content curation, and hope to move today's buyers to take action. Social Selling is time consuming and intellectually draining, and it requires a long slog of consistent daily effort to see any results.

So perhaps the best place to start is with what social selling is not.

Social Selling Is Not Selling

Let's get this straight from the get-go. Social selling is *not* selling. If you are trying to sell your stuff on LinkedIn, Twitter, Google+, or Facebook, you are likely selling nothing while irritating your soon to be ex-connections and causing major damage to your reputation and relationships.

The bottom line is people don't want to be pitched or "sold" on social media. They prefer to connect, interact, and learn. For this reason, the social channel is better suited to building familiarity, lead nurturing, research, nuanced inbound prospecting, and trigger-event awareness.

With the exception of the social inbox that can be a supplement and alternative to the traditional e-mail inbox, social prospecting is about nuance, tact, and patience. With complex and enterprise prospects, the social channel becomes a core part of a strategic chess game designed to influence the key stakeholders and deftly move these deals into the pipe at just the right time. (I will address prospecting into the social inbox when we discuss e-mail prospecting.)

Social selling is a collective term that encompasses a variety of activities—all designed to enrich the sales process and fill the pipe with more qualified and motivated prospects. These activities include:

- Social research
- Social networking
- Social lead generation
- Social inbound marketing
- Social prospecting
- Social trigger-event monitoring
- Social competitive intelligence
- Social customer relationship management (CRM)
- Social account management

With that said, it is critical that you include social selling in your sales arsenal and work to become a master at leveraging the social channel. No matter what you are selling, integrating social into your prospecting and sales process is no longer an option.

Choosing the Right Social Channels

Question: Why do people rob banks?
Answer: Because that's where the money is.

On which social channels should you be active? Where should you invest your limited time? The simple answer: Go where your prospects hang out.

LinkedIn, Facebook, Twitter, Google+, Pinterest, Instagram, Tumblr, Foursquare, Swarm, Ello, SoundCloud, YouTube, Snapchat, WhatsApp, SlideShare—the list of social media sites is long (I'm sure I missed a few), and new social channels will keep coming. It's enough to make your head spin. The social media landscape is complex. The task of mastering and getting engaged on social media is daunting and, frankly, overwhelming—so much so that most companies have an individual (small companies) or entire team (large companies) assigned to manage social media. That's how much effort it takes.

As an individual sales professional, there's no way you can keep up with them all and still have time to sell. Should you try to develop a presence on all of these channels, you'll find that it is exhausting.

This is why you shouldn't try. I've found that I can effectively manage three to four major channels at a time, and I'm much better when I'm only working two. Beyond that it gets tedious and my efforts are diluted. Take a step back and answer these two questions:

1. On which social channels will I find my customers and prospects?
2. On which social channels do I feel most comfortable?

The first question is, by far, the most important. If your customers aren't on Twitter, for example, don't worry about it. But if your customers are on Twitter, you'd better figure it out. The ROI on your social selling investment (time, money, and emotion) will increase significantly if you are playing in the same sandbox as your prospects. For example, if you sell cloud-based software to financial services companies, you wouldn't attend a trade show for farmers. Same goes for social.

It's also important to engage in channels you're comfortable with and enjoy. For example, I spend a lot of time on Twitter because I love it. My audience spans almost all of the major channels, but Twitter is by far my favorite, and it shows in my follower base (follow me @salesgravy).

If you don't enjoy a particular channel, you'll tend to ignore it and your activity won't be consistent. But let's keep it real, if your prospects are on a channel that you detest, I suggest you figure out how to like it so that it becomes part of your sales day.

For most salespeople, though, LinkedIn will be the primary social channel. First, you need to have a presence there because LinkedIn is the social channel for professionals. Second, if you are in B2B or high-end B2C sales, LinkedIn is where your prospects hang out. Third, LinkedIn has a robust set of tools and capabilities that are designed for salespeople and will help you across all of your prospecting channels.

(I have included a comprehensive social channel guide on FanaticalProspecting.com that is updated regularly and will help you choose where and how to spend your time.)

Five Objectives of Social Prospecting

Do you hear that giant sucking sound? That is social media stealing Golden Hour time from salespeople across the globe. Hours upon hours of prime selling time wasted with heads stuck in laptops, tablets, and smartphones—"social selling."

The social channel is mesmerizing and addictive. It is designed to be that way, to hook you so you keep coming back for more. That's why those likes, shares, stars, notices, and little numbers on the social apps on your phone exist. They trigger your curiosity and competitiveness.

Social media is a big, money-making machine that devours your data and time and sells it to advertisers. To do that, it needs you to be hooked. When you spend your entire day on social media, don't think for a minute that it is any different than parking yourself in front of a TV screen.

Of course, the difference between the TV channel and the social channel is you can actually accomplish something on social when you gain the discipline to focus your time on creating specific outcomes that help you identify prospects and move them into the pipeline. These outcomes include:

- Personal branding and building familiarity
- Inbound prospecting via education and insights
- Trigger-event and buying-cycle awareness
- Research and information gathering
- Strategic prospecting campaigns
- Outbound prospecting

You must learn to use social media the right way so it is a good use of time. *Efficient* and *effective* are the name of the game. Your time investment in the social channel must be focused on increasing the size and viability of your pipeline. Otherwise, you're just wasting it.

Personal Branding

Here are two questions you must constantly be asking yourself as you engage in social prospecting:

1. Does my presence online support my efforts to build my reputation as a sales professional who solves problems and can be trusted?
2. Does it help people become familiar with my name and brand in a positive way?

If the answer to either of these questions is "no" or "I'm not sure," it's time to make an adjustment in your strategy. The primary, top, number-one reason why you should engage in social selling is to improve familiarity and build trust. You want to be seen and heard, and you want to be viewed as a credible resource for potential buyers.

At a basic level, prospects will look you up online in an effort to get the gist of who you are and what you are all about prior to meeting with you. What they find will cause them to make instant judgments about you. Those judgments will impact your ability to influence and persuade them to make commitments to give up time, resources, and money. You want your professional presence online to position you as the one person who is most capable of bringing solutions to the table.

Like most people, you make quick judgments or build quick impressions about others when you are introduced for the first time. It is just how we operate as human beings. With so much incoming data attacking our nervous system, our brains have evolved to quickly grab available information about others (how they look, talk, act) and compile that information into a snapshot of that person. Those first impressions—regardless of how valid they are—influence our feelings towards the other person.

True, in the physical world, you sometimes get a second chance to make a good first impression. In the virtual world, however, you have zero chance of changing first impressions that are made about you online. When potential customers view the "online you" and don't like what they see, they just move on.

Of course, the vast majority of sales professionals have the good sense not to berate their boss, post inflammatory political or religious commentary, or toot their horn about how drunk they got the night before on online venues. Instead, they create poor first impressions online in more subtle ways.

I'm constantly shocked at the shameful way some salespeople manage their social media image. The most common mistakes are:

- Poorly written profiles
- Incomplete and outdated profiles
- Unprofessional photo or no photo
- Extremely opinionated political or religious postings and discussions
- TMI—too much information about personal issues

Your social media profiles are a direct reflection of your personal brand. These profiles are the tip of the social selling spear. Until your prospect meets you by phone or in person, who you are online is who you are. So you must invest time in developing and perfecting your social profiles.

Today, not tomorrow, take action to ensure that your online image casts you in the best light. We have a comprehensive guide to building winning social media profile pages at FanaticalProspecting .com that provides detailed instructions and tips for each of the major social media networks.

Here are some of the basics:

Headshot

According to PhotoFeeler.com, a website that helps people choose the right photo for online profiles, "Profile photos are so essential to modern communication that a good one's become a basic necessity. And that couldn't be truer than for those of us whose professional lives are tied to social media profiles."

Ensure that you have a professional headshot on all your pro-files—including Facebook. Professional means you leave your cat, dog, kids, vacation, college buddies, cool sunglasses, and bottle of beer out of the picture. Make sure the picture is taken in good light and at a flattering angle and has a neutral background. Lose the cheesy poses—like with your arms crossed, hand on your chin, or cocking your eyeglasses. You don't want to come off looking like a schmuck.

Instead, smile and put a pleasant look on your face. In a study[1] based on over 60,000 ratings, Photo Feeler found that a genuine smile has a significant impact on other people's perceptions of your competence, likeability, and influence based on your profile picture.

A best practice that I highly recommend is posting the same headshot on all of your social media profiles. Your image is like your logo. You want it to stick.

Cover Image

Inbound marketing and CRM juggernaut HubSpot.com says that "having a social media profile without a cover photo is like having a brick-and-mortar business without a store sign."

Most social media sites allow you to upload a cover image to your profile. This is usually a background placed on the header, but sometimes it can be the background for the entire page. It is a free way to let an image tell your story.

Make sure you have a professional cover image on all of your social profiles. The image dimensions and specs for each social network are different and have a tendency to change. You'll find dozens of resources online that provide detailed information on cover images. If you are not a graphic artist, creating your own professional cover image can be daunting. The good news is there are many experts online who will help you create professional covers at a nominal cost. I suggest you look to Fiverr.com first for help. For a low-cost self-service option, I recommend Canva.com.

Summary/Bio/About You

Personal branding expert William Arruda says that "an effective LinkedIn summary makes people want to know more about you and, ultimately, connect with you one-on-one." This is also true of the "about you" and bio sections on each of your social media profiles. You can go long form on LinkedIn, Facebook, and Google+ and get creative with short and sweet descriptions on Twitter and Instagram.

Writing a perfect summary that connects with the reader requires thoughtfulness and effort. It's your story, and it should make people want to meet you.

It should be well written, compelling, and truthful. Write in the first person and make it conversational. Your bio should explain who you are, what you are all about (values), what you do best, and why customers and clients count on and trust you to solve their problems.

Contact Information

Privacy? Forget about privacy. You are in sales. The very best thing that can happen is a prospect calls and interrupts you. If you make it hard for them, they won't. If you don't provide contact information, they can't. So make it easy. Put your contact information, including phone, e-mail, and website on your social media profiles.

Media and Links

Ensure that you are cross-linking each social profile page to your other profile pages along with any place you are blogging or contributing content. In the case of LinkedIn, you have the opportunity to add rich media including documents, photos, links, presentations, and videos. Take the time to add information that will be interesting to your prospects, educate them, and give them a reason to connect with you. (Be sure to check with your marketing department to get permission to add content related to your company brand.)

Custom URLs

Most social media sites will allow you to create a custom URL for your page. A custom URL makes it easier for people to find you and to share your profile.

History

Be sure to complete your entire profile. Don't leave gaps, holes, or partially completed profiles. This sends the message that you cannot be trusted.

Update Your Profiles Regularly

Make a commitment to manage your online presence by reviewing, updating, and continuously improving all of your online profiles at least once a quarter. Things change. Make sure your profiles are changing with you and that they stay fresh. As you review your online profiles, answer this question: Would *you* buy you?

Building Familiarity

The social channel is the most efficient and effective way to build familiarity. To build familiarity, you must be present and consistently engaging with prospects online so they see you often and over time become more comfortable with you.

Engaging means liking, sharing, and commenting on their posts as well as content they are commenting on and sharing. You also need to post content that is of interest to them, congratulate them on achievements, and be present in groups where they participate.

Be aware that you are always onstage. Everything, from your profile picture to the things you post, like, share, and comment on, is being watched by potential customers, so it's critical that you manage your message.

We live in a hypersensitive world. People are easily offended by the smallest things. Political correctness has run amuck. The wrong words, wrong like, wrong comment can make it impossible for your prospect to do business with you and in extreme cases can go viral and ruin your career. You want people to know your name and face, but in the sales profession, "all publicity is *not* good publicity."

Familiarity is a two-edged sword. When impressions of you are positive, familiarity can cut through a lot of friction and help you gain appointments and enter sales conversations with prospects. When prospects have a negative impression of you, they will erect walls to keep you out.

Think before you post.

Inbound Prospecting Through Insight and Education

The very best outcome of the investment you make in social media is to entice prospects to contact you. An inbound lead is much easier to convert into an appointment, sale, or qualifying information than an outbound prospecting call.

Familiarity plays a key but passive role in inbound prospecting. When you are well known to prospects, from time to time they will contact you as they move into the buying window for your product or service.

Sharing and publishing relevant content that is intriguing to prospects and helps them solve problems, answering questions in groups, and posting thoughtful comments can also open the door to prospects contacting you for more information or to ask you questions—especially when these posts position you as an expert.

A more active way to generate inbound leads is to directly share white papers, e-books, and reports that require prospects to enter contact information to get the content. This direct approach on social media, however, can come off as pitchy or spam, and can be perceived as overt self-promotion—which may not create the best impression of you.

I use a more subtle method. When I publish original content or link to a blog page, I include links to white papers and reports embedded in the content. That tends to generate leads without hurting my reputation. You can use a similar tactic with content that has been generated by your marketing team.

Leveraging Insight and Education to Power Up Strategic Prospecting

Providing insight and education to prospects is also a brilliant way to nurture high-value prospects as part of a strategic prospecting campaign (SPC). Strategic prospecting is a long-term, comprehensive effort that spans multiple prospecting channels. SPCs are designed to warm up and nurture contact relationships in anticipation of a future buying window. The core objectives of strategic prospecting are:

- Decision-maker and influencer mapping
- Warming up and nurturing the right contacts
- Identifying and developing relationships with potential coaches
- Creating personal and brand familiarity
- Generating goodwill and tapping into the Law of Reciprocity by offering value first
- Getting invited in by the prospect when the buying window opens or reducing friction when you make contact to set the initial appointment(s)

For most sales professionals, SPCs will be limited to a handful of conquest opportunities, primarily because SPCs are time consuming and require ongoing attention.

With the right focus and tools, you can leverage social channels to cover more ground and connect with and nurture more contacts than ever before. When you combine social with phone, in-person, e-mail, networking, and trade shows, you build a robust strategic prospecting machine that is almost impossible to beat.

A complete dissertation on developing effective SPCs is beyond the scope of this book. However, you may download the *Ultimate Guide to Strategic Prospecting* at FanaticalProspecting.com. This comprehensive ebook gives you the tools and techniques for launching and managing effective SPCs that get results.

Trigger-Event and Buying-Cycle Awareness

Trigger events are disruptions in the status quo that open buying windows and compel buyers to take action. For some prospects, buying windows are predictable because they're based on set budgetary or contractual time frames. With other prospects, buying windows are unknown and random and can be triggered by internal issues or external industry, economic, environmental, safety, employment, and other market-based trends. Additionally, when people you have sold to in the past move to other companies, the door is opened for you to step in.

Most social networks give you the ability to follow people without being directly connected to them. Twitter and Google+ go a step further and allow you to create lists and circles, respectively, that make it easy to monitor segmented groups. LinkedIn also offers tools (some free, some paid) that provide updates on the people you are following. It is important to consistently monitor your news stream, lists, update alerts, and discussions in the groups where your prospects hang out for trigger events.

Research and Information Gathering

Social media is a smorgasbord of data. You can gather an impressive amount of information about prospects that can be plugged into your CRM, used to develop prospecting messages, and leveraged for decision-maker mapping and precall planning. LinkedIn, Facebook, Google+, and Twitter offer powerful search capabilities that give you access to detailed information about prospects. You can also keep tabs on your competitors.

For social search shortcuts, I highly recommend picking up a copy of Sam Richter's book, *Take the Cold Out of Cold Calling*. Sam's book is the bible on using online and social resources to gather information.

Outbound Prospecting

The social channel also allows you to directly engage prospects to ask for appointments or gather additional information. You can message them directly through the platform—for example, in a

LinkedIn mail, Facebook message, or a direct message on Twitter—or just pick up the phone and call. A surprising number of people include phone numbers and e-mail addresses on their profiles.

The Five Cs of Social Selling

There are five behaviors/activities that define social selling. Mastering these behaviors and activities makes the time spent on social channels effective.

Connecting

There is one question I ask at every Fanatical Prospecting Boot Camp:

How many of you send a LinkedIn connection request each time you meet a new prospect, potential customer, or someone who might be a valuable addition to your professional referral network?

Rarely do more than 10 percent of the hands go up.

For centuries, highly successful people have understood the power of connections and how to leverage these connections to accomplish their goals. Connections get you in the door and in front of the right people faster. When your connections introduce you to people inside of their network or company, your message has immediate relevance.

Everything on social media begins with a connection. When you meet prospects by phone and in person, you've opened the door to familiarity. At that moment, after they've just met you, you have the highest probability of them accepting your social connection request. By sending them the connection request just after they've met you, they see your name again, anchoring familiarity. (Follow that connection request with a handwritten thank-you note and you're a superstar in their eyes.)

On LinkedIn, once a person connects with you, you gain the ability to see all of their connections, which helps you develop a more detailed buyer and influencer map and determine if they are connected and engaged in conversations with your competitors, or connected to contacts at other companies you are trying to penetrate.

This is why it is in your best interest to send a LinkedIn connection request every time you meet a potential customer, new contact at a prospect, and people who have the potential to become a core part of your professional network. Your professional network can be more powerful than any other means of prospecting.

LinkedIn offers both free and paid tools that give you the ability to tag, add notes, add contact information to profiles, organize, search, label the contact source, and manage your connections. LinkedIn is becoming a CRM on steroids. With LinkedIn's mobile apps, you have a massive and very powerful contact database in the palm of your hand.

There are three ways to create connections:

- *Direct:* On both LinkedIn and Facebook you may initiate a direct request for a connection. On Facebook, the process is straightforward: You just click "Send a Friend Request."

    On LinkedIn, you have the option of sending a standard, generic connection request (you may be asked to say how you know the person) or you may customize your connection request. I highly recommend sending a personalized note with each connection request that references any past meetings or conversations and gives a reason for your connection request.

    Though Facebook has primarily been an entertainment tool for keeping up with family and friends, I'm finding I'm having more business conversations on Facebook and through Facebook Messenger than ever before.

- *Reciprocal:* With Twitter and Google+, you can gain connections by simply following people because when you follow, people will reciprocate and follow you back. The probability that they will reciprocate is determined by their level of familiarity with you, so it makes sense to follow or circle people as soon as you meet them.

- *Passive:* When you publish original or curated content that connects with your audience and is shared, people will connect with and follow you. This is the most powerful way to build connections because the person connecting with you is making a conscious choice to add you to their network because they believe you add value to their career or life.

Content Creation

Creating and publishing original content that is relevant to the issues and problems your prospects are facing is the most powerful way to build trust and credibility with your prospect base. Original content will typically be in the form of:

- Articles
- Videos
- Slide presentations
- Podcasts
- Infographics
- White papers
- Case studies
- E-books (and traditional books)

Publishing original content positions you as an expert. It makes you a valuable resource. It draws prospects to you and entices them to engage with you or share your message with others in their organization. When people that were previously unknown to you like or share your content, it reveals new prospects and develops additional contacts within organizations you are working with.

You also gain insight into trigger events and buying windows. When people like, comment on, or share your information, you learn about the problems they are facing, their emotions, their urgency, and opportunities to help them.

Creating high-quality content is powerful, but is very, very difficult. It requires a significant investment of time and intellectual resources. If you work for a large organization with a robust marketing and branding team, there is also a very good chance that they will discourage you from creating content without their express approval and oversight.

I highly recommend investing the time to create and publish original content because the benefits to your reputation and career are massive. But if developing original content is not your thing, an easier way to leverage content is through curation.

Content Curation

Intuitively, we know that salespeople who can educate, offer insight, and solve problems are far more valuable than those whose primary sales strategy is to pitch products and services. However, to add value, you must *be* valuable.

Trust me on this: Salespeople who lead with self-promotional company, brand, product, or service plugs on social media get banned, blocked, reported as spam, and ignored. Don't do it!

In the social channel, the primary way you provide value is through content that educates, builds credibility, anchors familiarity, and positions you as an expert who can solve relevant problems.

The right content shared at the right time with the right prospects can create important connections and convert passive online relationships into real-time conversations.

The challenge is that the social channel is a voracious and insatiable beast that devours content. It must be fed daily for you and your message to remain relevant and present. Even if you had the time to create loads of original content, it would never be enough to keep up. So, the solution is something called curation.

A simple analogy for curation is the act of clipping articles from magazines and newspapers and sending them to someone. Except that on social, you are doing this digitally and amplifying the impact by going from a one-to-one analog footprint to one-to-many digital distribution.

Instead of publishing your own original content, you leverage the content that is being created and published by others. Essentially, you become a maven who aggregates the most relevant content for your audience and shares it through your various social media newsfeeds.

Sharing can either be a direct link that you post or a share/retweet from a source you follow. The beautiful thing about sharing content is even though you didn't produce it, some of the credit for the content rubs off on you.

There are three pillars of content curation:

- *Awareness:* You need to be aware of what is happening in your industry—trends, competitors, and movers and shakers. Have your eyes and ears open, pay attention to what is going on around you, and consume industry-specific information. Discover and follow the thought leaders who are shaping the dialog in your industry and know where great content is being published.
- *Intent:* When you curate with intent, you begin linking together relevant content based on an overall strategy, rather than just randomly and disparately sharing. You take time to read and understand what you are sharing, which allows you to add comments and insightful takeaways to the shared content, which further burnishes your expert status.
- *Tools:* Content curation is extremely time consuming, so you'll want to leverage tools that deliver relevant content to you and automate the distribution of the content you wish to share.

Conversion

Let's get real. You want the time and effort you invest in social prospecting to produce real, tangible results. You want more deals in your pipeline, to close more sales, and to increase your income. Otherwise, what's the point?

The social channel leveraged the right way can and should generate inbound leads. Although it is somewhat an oversimplification, social prospecting is like building your own little inbound marketing machine. This is where intent comes into play. You have to actively plan for and work to generate leads and engagement that opens sales conversations.

Consistency

Social prospecting is a grind. It takes work. It is not easy, simple, or automatic. Getting value from and adding value to the social channel requires consistent, focused, and regimented discipline. Consistency is crucial. Social doesn't work if you show up some of the time. You dilute your efforts if you are random and hit-or-miss.

Time blocking and the deployment of tools that automate some of the activity are the keys to being efficient. You must block 30 minutes to an hour each day (preferably before or after the Golden Hours) to engage in planned, intentional social prospecting activities. Have the discipline to limit your activity to the block of time you have set aside for your social selling activities and no more.

You may feel that you are not accomplishing much in short daily social prospecting blocks, but the cumulative impact of daily activity is enormous over time.

Social Media Prospecting Tools

Leveraging the right tools for social prospecting allows you to work the channel while remaining focused on high-value activities. There are myriad tools that automate social selling activity for you. Some tools are as close as your CRM, some are embedded in the social channels themselves, and there are dozens of apps that can easily be loaded onto your phone or Chrome browser.

What you may want to brace yourself for is cost. While most tools offer some level of free access, that access has a tendency to shrink as the tool gains popularity. The developers of these tools are not building them for altruistic reasons. They are keenly aware of the high cost in time and resources to fully and effectively leverage social for prospecting. They know that time is money, and as long as you are willing to part with money, they promise to save you time.

The good news is almost all of these tools, with the exception of enterprise level-solutions, allow you to try or use a limited number of features for free. And, your company may provide some of them for you.

As I write this chapter, new tools are emerging and others are being discontinued, rebranded, or acquired and rolled up into other tools. Yesterday one of my very favorite tools was made unusable because the social channel it helped me manage cut it off from its API. This is happening more often as the major social channels are intent on limiting access and charging more.

Because of the dynamics at play, I am providing a limited list of tools in this section. You'll find a comprehensive, regularly updated *Guide to Social Selling Tools* and reviews at FanaticalProspecting.com.

Tools for social prospecting fall into five basic categories.

- *Content curation:* These tools help you easily find and/or bank new content to distribute on your social channels. Tools like Feed.ly, Google News, and Sprout.it make it easy to identify the type of content that you want to share, aggregate that content from multiple sources, and deliver it to your desktop or smartphone. Tools like Pocket (one of my absolute favorite apps) allow you to bank content you find online to share at a later time.
- *Content creation:* Tools that help you create your own content abound. LinkedIn Pulse is a fantastic publishing tool that allows you to post full-length articles directly on LinkedIn. Likewise, Tumblr is an easy-to-use social blogging tool. For video, YouTube, along with a host of mobile apps, offers an array

of editing and publishing tools. SlideShare allows you to post presentations and is owned by LinkedIn, so you can post them directly to your LinkedIn profile. Canva.com is an outstanding tool for editing images and creating infographics.

- *Distribution:* Posting content you create or curate to multiple social sites many times over each day is extremely time consuming and tedious. Distribution tools like HootSuite, Buffer, and HubSpot (very expensive) allow you to load the content you wish to share during nonselling hours and automate the distribution of that content on a set schedule. Set it and forget it.
- *Engagement:* Tools like HootSuite, HubSpot, Bit.ly, and TweetDeck, along with the analytics tools embedded in the major social channels, allow you to view and analyze how people are engaging with your content and if that content is effective.
- *Intelligence:* These tools help you gather information about companies, people, trigger events, and buying windows. My absolute favorite is Google alerts. You will also find a growing suite of intelligence tools being built by and embedded into the major social networks.

Social Prospecting + Outbound Prospecting = A Powerful Combination

The problem you face is, in the ocean of content flooding the social channel, it's getting more and more difficult to stand out and get noticed (which is why the social channels are making so much money selling sponsored posts). If you are starting from the ground up with no followers or a small audience on established social platforms like LinkedIn, it can take from six months to two years to create enough gravity to pull prospects in to you.

That does not mean that a targeted and narrowly focused social selling strategy can't be effective. It just means that it will require more and more effort and money to get a reasonable return on your investment.

This is why even HubSpot, the granddaddy of the inbound marketing movement, and LinkedIn, the grand pooh-bah of the social selling movement, combine inbound and outbound prospecting strategies.

Outbound prospecting and inbound social prospecting go together like mashed potatoes and gravy. Social selling impacts familiarity, is an excellent for research and trigger-event awareness, and will generate inbound leads. It is, however, a long-term, passive strategy that requires patience and nuance and is unlikely to produce immediate results or to ever scale to a size that generates enough inbound leads to allow you to reach your sales and income goals.

Outbound prospecting, on the other hand, is an active approach to filling the pipe by engaging prospects in person, by phone, by e-mail, through social inboxes, or by text. It is the art of interrupting your prospect's day, opening a conversation, setting an appointment, or gathering information.

Combined with social prospecting, outbound becomes enormously powerful. The combined benefits include:

- Amplifying familiarity, which increases the probability that your prospect will engage
- More targeted prospecting lists focused on the highest-qualified prospects and individual buyers
- Leveraging trigger events to open or walk through buying windows at just the right time
- Nurturing and educating prospects ahead of expected or projected buying windows
- Research to gain contact information
- Buyer-influencer-coach (BIC) mapping
- Qualifying
- Refining and making your outbound prospecting message relevant

Once again, it comes back to balance—balancing your prospecting channels, methodologies, and techniques to be efficient and effective with your scarcest resource: time.

14 | Message Matters

"What do I say when I get them on the phone?"

"What do I write?"

"How do I approach this type of prospect?"

"How do I respond if they ask . . . ?"

We all want those magic words that will roll off our tongue like sugar and wow our prospect into complete submission. I know that salespeople secretly fantasize about having the perfect pitch that gets prospects to swoon and say yes to their request every time.

The bad news is, that's not going to happen.

The good news is, with some introspection, diligent effort, and practice, you can craft impactful messages that move prospects to take action and deftly turn around reflex responses, brush-offs, and objections.

As we've already established, the thing that makes prospecting so hard is you are interrupting someone's day and that interruption creates immediate resistance and, sometimes, not-so-pleasant responses from your prospect. Words and how you use those words—no matter which prospecting channel you are leveraging—can either increase the severity of that reaction and subsequent rejection or reduce resistance, break down emotional walls, and improve the probability that qualified prospects will respond positively to your request for their time.

In our crazy-busy world where everyone, is in a state of near-constant stress, asking for your prospect's time is the most difficult request you will make during the entire sales process—including asking them for a buying decision. This is one of the primary reasons why prospecting calls meet such stiff resistance.

Many salespeople freeze up at the first hint of rejection, spout nonsensical or cheesy pitches that turn prospects off, and say things like: "I would love to have a few minutes of your time to tell you about my company."

Messages like this add no value and generate instant resistance because subconsciously the prospect hears: "I would love to come by your office and waste an hour of your life talking all about me, my products, and my wants. Won't it be awesome for you to spend your valuable time listening to my pitch?"

Salespeople are making egregious messaging mistakes on the phone, in person, via e-mail, and social media because they don't realize that prospects are not going to give up their time for:

- A product and service features dump
- An enthusiastic pitch about their company being "number one this" or the "biggest of that"
- Regurgitated lists of generic facts and figures

- Marketing brochures
- Information that is not relevant
- Or any of the other mindless crap that spews from the mouths and keyboards of salespeople

No one wants to be pitched. You hate it, I hate it, and prospects hate it. Pitching leaves prospects feeling that you don't listen and makes them feel unimportant. This is the primary reason you face so much resistance getting prospects to give up their time.

Prospects resent you interrupting their day to tell them about how you are going to waste more of their time talking about you and your generic kitchen-sink data-dumps. They would rather get a root canal than spend an hour listening to a mouthy salesperson.

Prospects meet with you for their reasons, not yours. You must articulate the value of spending time with you in the context of what is most important to them. Your message must demonstrate a sincere interest in listening to them, learning about them, and solving their unique problems. This is how you break down initial resistance so that you earn an appointment, gain the opportunity to gather qualifying information, or engage in a sales conversation right in the moment.

What I want to make clear is prospecting messages are not complex. Be careful not to overcomplicate things. Your prospecting message is designed for one purpose: to quickly persuade your prospect to give you their time.

What You Say and How You Say It

In most prospecting interactions, you have mere seconds to get your prospect's attention. In those precious few moments, message matters. What you say (the words you use) and how you say it (nonverbal cues) are critical to your success.

I've spent most of my life around horses. Horses have an innate ability to sense fear, and they will take advantage of riders the moment they sense that the person is afraid or lacks confidence. Horses have a 5-to-1 weight and size advantage over the average person. If the horse doesn't believe that you are in charge, it can and will dump you.

Prospects are no different. If they sense fear, weakness, and lack of confidence, they will shut you down or bulldoze right over you. Delivery matters. Fanatical prospectors exude confidence, which is why they are so successful at opening doors that others believed were nailed shut.

One of the truths about human behavior is people tend to respond in kind. If you are relaxed and confident, you'll transfer that emotion to your prospect. If you want prospects to be enthusiastic about meeting you, be enthusiastic about meeting them. A relaxed, confident, enthusiastic demeanor and tone will open doors when nothing else will. Nonverbal communication includes:

- Voice tone, inflection, pitch, and speed
- Body language, facial expressions
- The way you dress and your outward appearance
- Sentence structure, grammar, punctuation, and the words used in written communication—e-mail, text messaging, and social messaging

Enthusiasm and Confidence

Confidence and enthusiasm are the two most powerful and persuasive nonverbal messages you send to prospects.

A simple definition of confidence is "a feeling or belief that you can do something well or succeed at something."[1]

Enthusiasm is defined as "a strong excitement about something; something inspiring zeal or fervor."[2]

Being enthusiastic and feeling confident in the face of rejection can be very difficult. This is why it makes sense to develop techniques for building and demonstrating confidence and enthusiasm even when you don't feel confident and enthusiastic.

This begins with developing your mindset and mental toughness to allow you to regain focus and bounce back from rejection
and fatigue. Even the best of us, those who have experience
and success, struggle with enthusiasm and confidence from time to
time.

Studies on human behavior from virtually every corner of the
academic world have proven time and again that we can change
how we feel by changing our facial expressions, the words we use,
our self-talk, and our physical posture. In other words, what is
happening on the inside of you manifests itself in your outward
confidence and enthusiasm.

This is not just a psychological response.[3] It's physiological.[4]
Studies are coming in from across academia that the hormones
cortisol and testosterone play a significant role in confidence. Work
by researchers, including Harvard University's Amy Cuddy, reveal
that your posture and body language can shape your emotions—
including enthusiasm and confidence.

Cuddy's research demonstrates that "power posing," physically
standing in a posture of confidence, even when you don't feel
confident, impacts testosterone and cortisol levels in the brain, and
that influences confidence.[5]

This isn't something new, though. Thought leaders, self-help
experts, teachers, and moms have been giving us this same advice for
years. *Sit up straight and you'll feel better. Keep your head up.* Most inside
sales trainers teach salespeople that putting a smile on their face will
transfer that smile to their voice. Some trainers suggest that you
should put a mirror by the phone when you are prospecting so you'll
be aware of your facial expression.

We know that when you dress your best, you feel your best.
When you put your shoulders up and chin up, you look and feel
confident. Tell yourself that you will succeed and your chances of
success go up. Use assertive and assumptive words, phrases, and
voice tone and you will be more powerful and credible—and more
likely to get a yes when you ask for what you want.

Act enthusiastic, think enthusiastic thoughts, and use enthusiastic language and you will begin to feel enthusiastic and eventually become enthusiastic. Even the simple act of saying "I'm awesome!" when someone asks you how you are doing can lift your mood and cause you to feel awesome—even if you don't.

What You Say

Prospecting is primarily designed to quickly engage a prospect and persuade them to give up their time. You don't need to craft elaborate pitches or come up with complicated scripts. In fact, this is where most prospecting goes wrong.

You are interrupting your prospect's day. If a salesperson were interrupting your busy day, what would you want? Think about it.

- You'd want them to be quick and get right to the point so you could get back to your day.
- You'd want them to be clear and transparent about their intentions—to tell you want they wanted.
- You'd want the interruption to be relevant to your situation, problems, or issues.

Your prospecting message must be quick, simple, direct, and relevant. The relevant part is the critical element. Prospects are going to agree to give up their valuable time for their reasons, not yours. The lower the risk to them for giving up their time, the more likely they'll be willing to give it up.

This is why, for example, it is more difficult to get a yes when requesting an hour-long meeting to do a full demo than when asking for a 15-minute discovery meeting to determine if there is enough interest and reasons to move to a next step.

You lower the risk for your prospect by answering WIIFM—the most important question on their mind:

What's in it for me?

Of course, it is not always possible to know which reason will lower the risk enough for your prospect to say yes to your request. Sometimes you've got to make an educated guess.

In his book *Smart Calling*, Art Sobczak calls these assumptions about WIIFMs "Possible Value Propositions." He suggests that for each class of prospect and decision-maker role, you should take time to define the possible reasons that would create enough WIIFM for them to give up their time to spend it with you.

Jill Konrath, author of *SNAP Selling*, says that in our current business environment, where potential decision makers are crazy busy, being able to deliver powerful value propositions is the way to "pique curiosity and open doors."[6] Jill defines a value proposition as "a clear statement of the tangible results a customer gets from using your products or services. It's outcome focused and stresses the business value of your offering."[7]

Konrath suggests that there are three key parts to a winning VP:

1. *Focuses on a business objective that is measured:* You'll get their attention when you focus on a metric that impacts their performance.
2. *Disrupts status quo:* The status quo is powerful. People abhor change and will only move from the status quo when they feel they can significantly improve their current situation—increase sales, reduce costs, improve efficiency, reduce stress, and so on.
3. *Offers proof or evidence:* When you can provide information about how much you have helped prospects in similar situations, you gain instant credibility.

The higher the risk for your prospect to give up time to meet with you, the more powerful and convincing your value prop must be. For example, if you are asking a C-level executive to give up their time, you have to bring a damn good reason for them to do so because their time is incredibly valuable. You'll want to craft a well-laid-out case that is specific and germane to your prospect. For example:

"I've helped multiple companies in your market segment reduce time to profitability on new product launches by as much as 50 percent. In fact, Aspen Systems' IDEK SaaS launch was the fastest ramp to ROI in the history of the company. With our system, they made a 41 percent improvement over their last launch."

On the flip side, if you work for a well-known brand and are meeting with small business owners who regularly use products like yours, asking for a few minutes to "learn more about their business" can work like a charm. Why? Because small business owners like to talk about themselves and the risk of taking a few minutes to meet with you is low.

For example: "I'm helping several restaurants in town with significant savings on supplies. I thought we could meet so I can spend time learning about you and your restaurant to see if what we offer might be a fit."

I'm a fan of Mike Weinberg's Power Statements and sales story development process, detailed in his book *New Sales. Simplified.* Mike does a masterful job of laying out the process for building compelling stories that get your prospects' attention. Mike says your Power Statement must answer:

- The prospect's issues
- Your offerings that address these issues
- Competitive differentiators

Weinberg says you need to answer the question, "Why do my customers choose to do business with me?" This is how you define why you are truly different from your competition—not just your company, product, or service, but *you*. Like Weinberg says, "Differentiation gets the attention of your prospect."

WIIFM—The Power of Because

According to Robert Cialdini, author of *Influence*, "A well-known principle of human behavior says that when we ask someone to do us a favor, we will be more successful if we provide a reason. People simply like to have reasons for what they do."

I don't use the term *value proposition* very much. Honestly, I don't like the phrase. It sounds complicated. I like simple and straightforward. In prospecting, all you really need to do is give your prospect a good enough reason to meet with you and they'll say yes. It doesn't need to be perfect—just good enough to get in the door.

I'm also realistic. To be efficient at prospecting, you must pack lots of prospecting touches into a short period of time. In most cases, you will be prospecting to a similar group of prospects who share a common set of issues. Stopping to craft a perfect, unique value proposition for each one of these prospects is inefficient and impractical.

Instead, you need a compelling message that works most of the time with most of your prospects. It has to be quick, direct, and persuasive, but it cannot sound like a cheesy script. It's got to be natural and authentic.

Of course, if you are calling a C-level contact or high-potential prospect, it's critical to craft something specific and relevant that answers their unique WIIFM question.

Let's get real, though. For most salespeople, most of the time, you won't be in this situation. You need a message that can be delivered in 10 seconds or less and gives your prospect a reason or a "because" that's good enough to get them to say yes.

In a landmark study on human behavior, psychologist Ellen Langer and a team of researchers from Harvard demonstrated the raw power of *because*. Langer had her team of researchers cut in line in front of people waiting for access to photocopiers.

She discovered that when the researcher politely asked to jump in front of the person waiting for the copier without giving a reason— "Excuse me, I have five pages. May I use the copier?"—the person would say yes about 60 percent of the time. However, when the researcher qualified the request with a valid reason—"because I'm in a hurry"—the person said yes, on average, 94 percent of the time.

Here's where the research became interesting. When the researcher gave a nonsensical reason like, "Excuse me, I have five pages. May I use the copier? Because I have to make copies," the person still said yes 93 percent of the time. It was a truly stunning finding. Saying the word *because*—giving a reason—was more important and powerful than the reason itself.

Now, I want to be absolutely clear that I am not advising you to make up nonsense and use that while prospecting. What I am saying is that focusing on a simple, straightforward *because* works, and spending hours agonizing over some complex value prop is unlikely to give you anything more effective in prospecting than a simple, direct *because*.

For example, just saying, "I'd like 15 minutes of your time because I want to learn more about you and your company" works surprisingly well with many prospects.

What we learn from Langer's copy machine study[8] is when we ask people to do something for us, like give up their time, they are more likely to do so when we give them a reason.

Bridging to the *Because*

Bridges connect.

Bridging solutions to your prospect's problems using their language, not yours, is one of the core disciplines of sales. In the context of the sales process, bridging helps you advance deals through the pipe and close the sale.

In the context of prospecting, your bridge is the *because* that gives them a good enough reason to give up their time to spend it with you. There are two types of bridges you'll use when prospecting: targeted and strategic.

Targeted bridges are bridges that are common to a large group of similar prospects—decision-maker roles, industry vertical, product or service application, and so on. Targeted bridges are most appropriate when you have little information about a specific prospect and the cost/benefit of doing reams of research is not worth it.

For example, if you work in business services and have a prospect database of 10,000 SMBs, taking time to research every prospect before calling them would make no sense. It is a better use of your time to make as many calls as possible to engage and qualify as many prospects as possible, in the least amount of time as possible.

When you don't have specifics about their problems, issues, or concerns, you'll need to infer problems based on economic trends or your knowledge of what other businesses are experiencing in the same industry, geographical area, or market segment, or with a certain competitor's product.

You'll naturally iterate and refine your message as you engage in more conversations with these prospects. Here is an example:

"Hi, Candace, this is Jeb Blount from Sales Gravy. The reason I am calling is to schedule an appointment with you to show you our new sales onboarding automation software. Many of my clients are frustrated because it takes too long to get new salespeople ramped up to full productivity and find that it's holding their business growth back. Our software typically cuts onboarding time and costs for new sales reps by 50 percent, and makes it super easy to manage new rep onboarding, giving you the peace of mind that your new hires will start selling fast. I have 2:00 PM on Thursday open. How about we get together for a short meeting so I can learn more about you and see whether it makes sense to schedule a demo?"

You'll notice that I implied that Candace is frustrated because it is taking too long to get her new salespeople up to speed and selling. I don't know for sure that this is her issue, but it is a high-probability educated guess because most executives experience anxiety when new salespeople aren't selling.

Strategic bridges are unique to a single high-value prospect and specific individual (decision-maker role) at that prospect. You will typically craft strategic bridges for enterprise level, conquest prospects, and C-level executives. Strategic bridges require research so that your bridge or *because* is specific and relevant, reduces risk, and gives them a compelling reason to give you their time.

Developing bridges specific to a single prospect is time consuming and can seriously limit the activity you are able to accomplish in a day—especially if you are doing this during the Golden Hours. However, if your target prospect database is limited or you are trying to engage a large conquest prospect in your territory, developing a specific bridge is risk/reward positive. In some cases, you may only get one shot at a C-level executive and you'll want to make it count.

To develop a bridge specific to your prospect, you will first need to determine the objective of your prospecting touch:

- Are you attempting to get more information to further qualify the opportunity, decision-maker role, or buying window?
- Do you want to set up an initial meeting?
- Are you seeking an introduction to another person?

Defining your objective in advance, so you know what you are asking for, will help you develop a bridge that gives your prospect a reason to take that step.

Next, research your prospect. Set up Google alerts to have information about the company or individual sent directly to your inbox. Review notes and history in your CRM. Research the company/division/location through online searches, visiting their website, press releases, and company pages on LinkedIn, Google+, Twitter, and Facebook. Visit your contact's social media profile pages. Review posts for jargon, core values, PR, awards, trigger events, initiatives, changes, and problems that you can solve. Research industry trends and read the most recent trade articles.

Craft your message to demonstrate that you can relate to their specific situation. Bridge to a specific problem they are facing using their language (gleaned from your research). An example:

"Hi, Windsor, this is Jeb Blount from Sales Gravy. The reason I am calling is to set an appointment with you. I read in *Fast Company* that you are adding another hundred sales reps to keep up with growth. I imagine that it has got to be a bit stressful to bring on that many reps and get them producing.

"I've worked with a number of companies in your industry to reduce ramp-up time for new reps. At Xjam Software, for example, we cut ramp-up time to ROI for their new reps by 50 percent. While I don't know if our solution would be a fit in your unique situation, I've got some ideas and best practices I've seen work well for companies like yours and thought you might be interested in learning more about them. How about we get together for a short meeting on Thursday at 2:00 PM?"

The Secret to Crafting Powerful Bridges

Frustration. Anxiety. Stress. Fear. Peace of mind.

What do these words have in common? They describe emotions. Emotional words demonstrate empathy and connect with how your prospect is feeling. The real secret to crafting prospecting messages that convert into meetings, information, or sales is staring with a simple but powerful premise:

People make decisions based on emotion first and then justify with logic.

This is why pitching logic—features—doesn't work. Trust me. Your prospects abhor a pitch. This, by the way, is why you get so much resistance with those long scripts your marketing department writes for you.

Prospects want to feel that you get them and their problems (emotional and logical), or are at least trying to get them, before they'll agree to give up their time to meet with you. They only give their up time because you offer them:

- *Emotional value:* You connect directly with them at the emotional level—typically by relating to painful emotions like stress, worry, insecurity, distrust, anxiety, fear, frustration, or anger and offering them peace of mind, security, options, lower stress, less worry, or hope.

- *Insight (curiosity) value:* You offer information that gives them power or leverage over other people. Most prospects worry about maintaining their competitive edge—either as a company or an individual. They're anxious that there may be something in the marketplace that they are not privy to. Unknowns are disconcerting—especially if a competitor has a best practice, information, system, or process that they don't.
- *Tangible (logic) value:* Executives and contacts in technical and data-centric roles will value data and case studies. How much, how many, and what results can you deliver, have you delivered, will you deliver—specific to their unique situation?

The most effective way to craft the right message is to simply stand in your prospect's shoes. Look at things through their eyes and use your God-given empathy to sense their emotions and to consider what might be important to them. Consider how you might feel in their situation. Start by answering these questions from your prospect's perspective:

- What would cause you stress? When do you feel stress?
- What makes you worry? When do you worry? Why do you worry?
- What creates anxiety? When do you feel anxiety?
- How do you feel when you run out of time for important things?
- How do you feel when you don't have enough money to accomplish your goals? When does this happen?
- How do you feel when you don't have enough resources to accomplish your goals? When does this happen?
- How do you feel when you don't have the knowledge to accomplish your goals? When does this happen?
- How do you feel when you fail to accomplish your goals?
- When do you get overwhelmed, and how does it feel?
- What impacts your peace of mind or sense of security?
- How would it feel to have limited options?

- What is causing you to feel frustrated or stuck?
- What makes you mad?
- What causes you to feel distrust?
- What causes you fear?
- What causes you anguish?
- How do you feel when _____ happens?
- What might you want to know?
- What unknown would make you worry?
- What information would you fear getting into your competitor's hands?
- What might a competitor be doing that would make you want to do it, too?
- What information would you believe might give you a winning edge?
- What would cause you to be curious?
- What might be stealing your time, money, or resources?

Analyze your product and service delivery strengths and weaknesses. Review or define your competitive advantages and the value you bring to the marketplace. Look for commonalities among your best customers. Analyze the deals you are closing and gain a deeper understanding of trigger events that open buying windows.

Think about how you might be able to relate to your prospect's unique situation and how you can express this through the words you use, tone and inflection of voice, and body language.

And, before moving forward, answer the most important question. The one question that will keep you from getting shut down on prospecting calls:

What would cause your prospect to say, *"So what?"* to your message?

Ask For What You Want

The most important element of any prospecting touch is the *ask*— what you are asking the prospect to do or give up. It really doesn't matter what else you say or do. If you fail to directly ask your prospect to take action, everything else is just academic.

The primary reason prospecting gets overcomplicated, companies create long moronic scripts, and salespeople beat around the bush with passive "Maybe if it would be okay and if you are not too busy we could kinda maybe get together for a few minutes, what do you think?" statements, is to avoid directly asking, which carries with it the potential for rejection.

Fear is why so many people seek the easy way out and look for shortcuts and silver bullets rather than just biting the bullet and asking for what they want.

It's the reason I get so many questions from salespeople that begin with "What's the trick," or "Can you tell me the secret?" It is also why so many salespeople are duped into buying into seminars and products that promise to deliver the secret to prospecting only to find that there really is no secret.

Here is the brutal truth: There is only one technique that really works for getting what you want on a prospecting touch.

Ask.

That's it. Just ask. Ask for the appointment, ask for information, ask for the decision maker, ask for the next step, ask for the sale. Ask for what you want. Ask.

The fact is, if you are having a hard time getting appointments, getting to decision makers, getting information, or closing the deal, 9 out of 10 times it is because you are not asking.

Why? Because 9 out of 10 times you are afraid to hear "no."

Starting with prospecting and all the way through the close, you must constantly be asking for what you want. Otherwise your deals tend to stall and die or you never get into the door in the first place. There are three steps to asking:

1. Ask with confidence and assume you will get what you want.
2. Shut up.
3. Be prepared to deal with reflex responses, brush-offs, and objections.

Assume You'll Get What You Want

We've tracked thousands of calls across a diverse set of industries. When salespeople demonstrate confidence and ask assertively for what they want, prospects say yes about 70 percent of the time. Nonassertive requests have about a 30 percent success rate. When you pair an assertive request with a *because*, the probability of getting a yes goes up even higher.

Jeffrey Gitomer, author of the *Little Red Book of Selling*, says that "the assumptive position is the strongest selling strategy in the world."[9]

Assuming you'll get what you want begins with your belief system and self-talk. When you tell yourself you are going to win and keep telling yourself so, it bolsters your internal belief system. Assuming you will get what you want is a mindset of positive expectation that manifests itself in your outward body language, voice inflection and tone, and the words you use.

Because an assumptive ask has a higher success rate, you'll get more wins, and with more wins your confidence grows to greater heights.

Whether on the phone, in person, or communicating via e-mail or social, the words you use and how you structure those words send the message loud and clear that you assume you will get a yes or assume you'll get a no.

Nonassumptive, Passive, and Weak	Assumptive and Confident
"Is this a good time?"	"The reason I'm calling is . . ."
"I was wondering if . . .?"	"Tell me who—how—when—where—what . . ."
"I have the whole day open."	"I'm super busy bringing on new clients, but I do have a slot available at 11:00 AM."
"What do you think?"	"Why don't we go ahead and get that set up?"

"What's the best time for you?"	"I'll be visiting a client not far from your office on Monday. I can pick you up for lunch."
"I kinda, sorta, was wondering if maybe you have time to answer a few questions, if that would be okay?"	"A lot of my customers are telling me that they're having problems with XYZ. What do you feel is your biggest challenge?"
"Would this be a good time for you?"	"How about we meet at 2:00 PM?"

With e-mail, social messaging, and text messages, direct, assumptive words and sentence structure are the body language of the written word. When you choose weak, passive words, it sends the message that you lack confidence.

On the phone and in person your words and how you deliver those words must match. Your prospect is subconsciously assessing whether your words, voice tone, and body language are congruent. If they are not, your prospect will not trust you and will put up resistance.

Most importantly, you must directly, quickly, and concisely get to the point. Asking directly for what you want makes it easy for your prospect to say yes.

Voice Tone and Inflection and Body Language

When you are facing the potential of rejection, the fear you feel is real. It is a physiological response that is driven, in part, by an almond shaped structure in your brain called the amygdala, which triggers the fight-or-flight mechanism. This part of your brain is designed to keep you alive, but unfortunately, it doesn't distinguish between threats—rattlesnake coiled and hissing at you or a prospect about to tell you no.

To the amygdala it all looks the same. So it prepares your body and mind to fight or run, begins shutting down nonessential parts of your body to conserve energy, and directs that energy to your muscles. Essentially, it is preparing you for peak performance so you stay alive.

This is why you feel physically anxious before you ask. Your mind reels, palms sweat, stomach tightens, and muscles become tense as you subconsciously prepare for "no." This is the root cause of your feeling of fear.

Getting past the fear of "no" isn't easy. I've been selling my entire life and have been incredibly successful at it, yet today I still have to remind myself that "no" won't kill me. That, by the way, is the key. You have to teach your rational brain to tell your amygdala, or "reptilian" brain, that the threat isn't real.

Start by learning to anticipate the anxiety that comes right before asking for what you want. Then practice managing your internal self-talk and outward physical reaction to that fear. Courage, by the way, is just like a muscle. The more you exercise it, the stronger it gets.

This awareness helps you manage your body language, voice inflection and tone, and words despite the volcano of emotions that may be erupting below the surface. Like a duck on the water, you appear calm and cool and project a relaxed, confident demeanor on the outside even though you're paddling frantically just below the surface.

Demonstrates Lack of Confidence, Insecurity, and Fear	Demonstrates a Relaxed, Confident Demeanor
Speaking with a high pitch of voice.	Speaking with normal inflection and a deeper pitch.
Speaking really fast. When you speak too fast you sound untrustworthy.	Speaking at a relaxed pace with appropriate pauses.
Tense or defensive tone of voice.	Friendly tone—smile in your voice.
Speaking really loud or soft.	Appropriate voice modulation with appropriate emotional

	emphasis on the right words and phrases.
Frail or nervous tone of voice with too many filler words, "ums," "uhs," and awkward pauses.	Direct, properly paced tone and speech that gets right to the point.
Lack of eye contact—looking away. Nothing says "I can't be trusted" and "I'm not confident" like poor eye contact.	Direct, appropriate eye contact.
Hands in your pockets.	Hands by your side or out in front of you as you speak. Note: This feels uncomfortable but makes you look powerful and confident.
Wild gesticulations or hand motions.	Using hand gestures in a calm and controlled manner.
Touching your face or putting your fingers in your mouth—clear sign that you are nervous or insecure.	Your hands in a power position—by your side or out in front of you in a controlled, nonthreatening manner.
Hunched over, head down, arms crossed.	Straight posture, chin up, shoulders straight and back. This posture will actually make you feel more confident.
Shifting back and forth on your feet or rocking your body.	Standing still in a natural power pose.
Stiff posture, body tense.	Relaxed, natural posture.
Jaw clenched, tense look on face.	Relaxed smile. The smile is a universal language that says "I'm friendly and can be trusted."
Weak, limp, sweaty palm handshake. (Yuck!)	Firm, confident handshake delivered while making direct eye contact.

Shut Up

The hardest part of asking is learning to ask and shut up. When you've asked for what you want, you've put it all out there and left yourself vulnerable to rejection. And what happens when you feel vulnerable? You try to protect yourself.

In that awkward moment after you ask, your head starts spinning, rejection flashes before your eyes. The split second of silence is unbearable. It feels like an eternity.

When you fail to manage the disruptive emotions that are triggered by silence, your call turns into a train wreck. Your mouth starts moving. You attempt to overcome objections that have not even surfaced, overexplain yourself, offer your prospect a way out, and start blabbing on and on about your product's features and benefits, your company, your dog, and where you went to school. Until the prospect who was ready to say yes gets talked into saying no by *you*.

This is why, despite all of the alarm bells going off in your adrenaline-soaked mind, you must *shut up* and give your prospect room to answer. Here's why:

The faster you get to an answer, the faster you'll be able to move on to the next prospecting touch or deal with a no or maybe. It's governed by a simple rule of thirds.

- *Get to yes fast.* About one-third of the time they're going to say yes just because you asked. Your goal is to get these yesses on the table and avoid talking yourself out of them. This makes you super-efficient. They say yes to your request. You get what you want. Both of you quickly move on to the next thing on your list.
- *Get to no fast.* About one-third of the time the prospect will say no and mean no. Sometimes this is a phone hung up on you, a door slammed in your face, or a deleted e-mail. Sometimes it is a string of expletives. Most times it is the prospect giving you a very direct and uncertain *no!* Although it sucks to hear no, it is

also a blessing. It allows you to quickly move on to the next call—again, making you more efficient.

■ *Get to maybe fast.* About one-third of the time the prospect will hesitate, say maybe, negotiate, or give you a false objection just to get you off of the phone. This is where the rubber meets the road in prospecting—it's where you have a chance to turn a maybe into a yes with effective RBO tunrarounds.

When you are prepared, you know exactly how to handle reflex responses, brush-offs, and objections (RBOs), and you gain the confidence to shut up and manage silence. We're going to dive headfirst into techniques for turning around RBOs in Chapter 16.

15 | Telephone Prospecting Excellence

"Mr. Watson—Come here—I want to see you." [First intelligible words spoken over the telephone]

—Alexander Graham Bell

Question: "How do you get a salesperson to stop working?"

Answer: "Put a phone in front of him."

That's a little joke that elicits nervous laughs at keynotes and seminars.

For thousands of salespeople, picking up the phone and calling a prospect is the most stressful part of their life. Many of these reluctant salespeople stare at the phone, secretly hoping that it will disappear. They procrastinate, get ducks in a row, and work to ensure that everything is perfect before they dial. Any excuse—and I mean *any* excuse—to do something else takes priority.

They work over their leaders, too. Whining that no one answers the phone anymore. Arguing that it is a waste of time. Complaining that people don't like to be contacted by phone. Labeling any outbound phone call a cold call—even when they are calling back inbound leads—while gravitating toward so-called experts who pontificate that cold calling is dead.

Last month a top-five insurance company hired me to deliver a Fanatical Prospecting Boot Camp. The executive who bought me in said that the single biggest challenge facing their new agents was prospecting. His words: "We are having such a hard time getting them to just pick up the phone and talk to people."

When I arrived on the morning of the training, he pulled me aside and said, "I hope I haven't put you in a bad spot. We didn't spend time discussing the new reality in our industry, but no one answers the phone anymore. I realize you are going to do live phone blocks, but I wouldn't expect too much out of them." (This is the guy paying me big bucks to teach his agents to prospect effectively on the phone, and on the morning of the training he is already making excuses for why it won't work.)

We did three live phone blocks that day using targeted lists the agents brought with them. Over the course of the day, we had a whopping 51 percent contact rate—actual live prospects answering their phones. This was not a statistical anomaly. It was generated by 19 agents who made 1,311 outbound dials.

At the end of the day I sat down with my contact and showed him the numbers. He was both thrilled—as in "when can we get you to come back and do this again" thrilled—and bemused. "I don't understand how you got those results. Everybody tells me that people don't answer the phone anymore."

"Who is telling you that?" I asked.

"The agents," he responded.

"The same people that you say won't make calls?" I asked.

He slowly nodded his head as the weight of this realization sank in.

Nobody Answers a Phone That Doesn't Ring

The myth that the phone no longer works—because people don't answer—is disproven daily in our Fanatical Prospecting Boot Camps. The myth is disproven by our sales team at Sales Gravy and with thousands of sales teams across the country that survive and thrive on the phone.

The statistics don't lie. We see between a 15 percent and 80 percent contact rate on the phones depending on the industry, product, and role level of the contact. For example, in the business services segment, contact rates are consistently between 25 and 40 percent.

This, by the way, is far higher than response rates with e-mail and light-years higher than those of social prospecting. All of our real-world evidence flies directly in the face of the myth that gets repeated over and over again that the telephone has a low success rate.

It gets better. We have stats on phone prospecting going back to the early 1990s, and we are seeing clear trends that contact rates via phone have actually risen by around 5 percentage points. We don't know the exact reason why more prospects are answering their phones, but we suspect three drivers:

1. *Phones are anchored to people, not desks.* It is common for prospects to answer their mobile phone when you call them—either because their mobile line is their only line or because their office line rolls over to their mobile line.
2. *No one is calling.* Because so much sales communication has shifted to e-mail, social inboxes, and text, phones are not ringing nearly as much as in the past. Because of this, salespeople who call are standing out in the crowd and getting through.
3. *Prospects are getting burned out on impersonal, irrelevant (and often automated) prospecting e-mails.* E-mail and social inboxes are being flooded with crap. Prospects are hungry for something different—a live, authentic human being.

Think about it. If the phone did not work, why are so many teleprospecting companies springing up across the globe—and thriving? Companies are spending tens of thousands of dollars on outsourcers who use the phone to prospect—because there is no other viable way to keep the pipe full, and they've allowed their salespeople not to do it.

The Telephone Is, Has Always Been, and Will Continue to Be the Most Powerful Sales Prospecting Tool

Listen to me! The phone is your most powerful sales tool. Period, end of story.

Let me say this one more time slowly. There is no other tool in sales that will deliver better results, fill your pipe faster, and help you cover more ground in less time than the phone.

So stop looking at it like it's your enemy or an alien being covered in slimy tentacles. And no, it is not going to dial itself.

Here is the brutal truth: Salespeople who ignore the phone fail. They deliver mediocre results and cheat themselves out of hard cash.

Tonya, an outside sales rep, wrote me with this question:

"My manager is always trying to get me to use the phone for prospecting. I'm terrible on the phone and I've tried to explain to him that I'm much better in person. How can I convince him to let me get on the street and knock on doors?"

Many outside salespeople when faced with telephone prospecting will say, "But I'm way better in person."

My answer: Of course you are better in person. That is why you were hired to be an outside sales rep. But here's the deal: In sales, time is money, and you can cover far more ground, qualify more opportunities, and set more appointments in a one-hour targeted phone block than in an entire day of driving around in your territory randomly knocking on doors.

Think about it this way: How many prospects could you qualify or set appointments with face to face in an eight-hour period? Even on the busiest city street, 20 would be a stretch. In most territories, with travel time and parking, it would be closer to 10. If it is hot, raining, snowing, or freezing out, the numbers go down further.

How about one hour on the phone, with a list of targeted prospects? How many phone calls could you make? Averaging one to two minutes per call, you could make 25 to 50 calls. So if you are touching twice as many prospects in about a tenth of the time, in a climate-controlled environment, which do you think will yield better results? The answer is an obvious no-brainer.

The phone is the most efficient prospecting tool because when you are organized, you can reach more prospects in a shorter period of time than through any other prospecting channel—even e-mail. Because you have many more things to do in your sales day than prospect, it is in your best interest to use the most efficient method for contacting lots of prospects. The most efficient, cost-effective way is the telephone.

The telephone is also more effective than e-mail, social, and text because when you are actually speaking to another human being, there is a higher probability that you'll set appointments, sell stuff, and gather qualifying information. Yet, many salespeople find it awkward to use the phone for prospecting because:

- They don't know what to say, say stupid things, or read awkward, cheesy scripts that generate resistance and rejection.
- They don't have an easy-to-execute telephone prospecting process that actually works.
- They don't know how to deal with reflex responses, brush-offs, and objections.
- They are afraid of rejection.

Nobody Likes It; Get Over It

While I was working on this book, Dave, a sales rep from North Carolina, hit me up with this question:

"Jeb, I need your advice. The first call to a prospect proves very difficult for me, and I know it's all in my head. I'm like that kid in seventh grade who is calling a girl to go to a school dance and then gets scared when her dad answers the phone. I'm normally very confident, comfortable with product knowledge, and I can close business. But, when I'm on the phone with a new prospect, it's a different story. I know that if I can overcome this my monthly goals will get knocked out quicker than a fixed prizefight. Please help."

What I love about this question is that it is honest and reflects accurately how many salespeople feel about telephone prospecting.

Dave, like most salespeople, heads into the office each morning with every intention of getting on the phone and engaging new prospects. As he reluctantly dials that first number—after wasting an hour piddling around in an effort to avoid the inevitable—his palms sweat, his heart pounds, and he secretly prays that no one will answer. Then, the prospect or a gatekeeper answers and he forgets what to say. He stumbles over his words, stuttering and sputtering. The prospect quickly brushes him off:

"I'm not interested!"

"We're happy!"

"I don't have time to talk."

He feels rejected and embarrassed and the motivation for calling evaporates. To avoid making more calls, he shuffles papers and wastes time doing anything but dialing again. So he sends e-mails, takes a spin on social media, wastes time digging through the CRM, and whines to his manager that he has no time to call because there is so much admin work to do.

I'm not going to sugarcoat it. Telephone prospecting is the most despised activity in sales. Calling and interrupting people you don't know is uncomfortable. You get a tremendous amount of rejection.

It will always be uncomfortable picking up the phone and calling people you don't know. It is just not a natural thing to do. There will always be calls and even days when you fumble your words and become embarrassed. You will always get more rejection than acceptance (but that is true for every prospecting channel).

That's why it is called prospecting, not order taking. Look at it this way: If telephone prospecting were easy, everyone would be in sales and we'd all be making minimum wage and living with our parents.

Most Salespeople Have Never Been Taught How to Use the Phone

What I find across the board, though, is that most salespeople don't know how to use the phone for prospecting or sales. They've never been taught and/or they have a bias toward communicating via e-mail or text.

This problem is exacerbated by the fact that at most companies there is deficient to nonexistent telephone prospecting training—both outside sales and inside sales. When companies do provide telephone prospecting training, it is usually complex, contrived BS developed by people who've never even used the phone successfully for prospecting. This crap never works in the real world with real prospects, giving salespeople another excuse for avoiding the phone.

Then there are the companies and sales organizations that task the marketing department (or worse, the HR department) with developing phone scripts for the sales team and training the salespeople to deliver the scripts. The marketing people who develop these scripts have never had to interrupt the day of a prospect on a live call and most would rather slit their wrists than actually make one.

Some of the stuff I find sales teams using leaves my head spinning. Just this month while at a conference, I ran into an HR manager who had been tasked with building the sales prospecting training for the company's sales organization. I asked her if she had ever made a prospecting call or conducted a sales call.

She responded, "No."

"If you've never sold anything, how will you be able to build a sales training curriculum?" I asked.

"I built the new-hire orientation curriculum and my boss liked that, so they want me to take a shot at the sales training program."

"But I don't understand how you can teach people how to sell if you don't know how to sell."

Her response: "Well, I've had people try to sell things to me, and I know what I don't like, so I'm going to start there."

"I'm just curious, how do you feel about telephone prospecting?"

"I could never do that!" Her response was emphatic.

My prediction for her sales training is more crap created by a person who has no understanding or appreciation of the sales profession.

Finally, there are throngs of sales leaders who have no clue how to coach their people to develop and master phone prospecting skills. They know that the pipeline is more robust and performance improves when their people are actively and consistently prospecting by phone. They just don't know how to lead their people down that road.

My goal with this chapter is to set things straight and give you the tools to leverage the phone to drive qualified deals into your pipe and crush your numbers and competitors.

- You'll start by learning how to leverage the telephone to maximize your sales day. I'm going to teach you how to double or even quadruple the number of dials you make in a much shorter period of time so that you can get your phone block knocked out and move on to other things that are far more enjoyable.
- Then I'm going to teach you what to do and say when you get prospects on the phone. You will learn how to reduce resistance, increase the probability that you will achieve your defined objective, and mitigate rejection.

- Finally, in the next chapter, you will learn how to effectively deal with and get past reflex responses, brush-offs, and objections (RBOs) to more effectively set appointments, gather information, and qualify.

Before moving forward, though, let's stipulate a few things:

- You are going to get rejected a lot on the phone because statistically you will generate more real-time interactions with prospects than through any other prospecting channel.
- Most of your calls will go to voice mail. Depending on your industry, prospect base, and targeted list you'll connect with between 20 percent and 50 percent of your prospects on average during phone blocks. This is why you must be effective when you get a prospect on the line.
- Most of the reason that you are frustrated with the phone and find making telephone prospecting calls abhorrent is because you or the people who taught you how to prospect are overcomplicating the living stew out of a very simple, straightforward process.
- Nobody really likes telephone prospecting. No matter what I teach you, you are probably going to still hate the phone. That doesn't negate the fact that to reach peak sales performance, you must master telephone prospecting.

If you want to earn big bucks and stand tall on top of your team's ranking report, you've got to accept that telephone prospecting sucks and get over it.

The Ultimate Key to Success Is the Scheduled Phone Block

Fanatical prospectors set up daily telephone phone blocks of one to two hours. During this time they remove all distractions—shutting off e-mail and mobile devices, and letting those around them know that they are not to be disturbed. They set clear goals for how many calls they will make. This call block is a booked appointment on their schedule and it is sacred. Nothing interferes.

Some people choose to break call blocks into small, manageable chunks and set goals for those chunks. It is much easier to set a goal to make 10 calls than 100 or to dial for 30 minutes rather than two hours. It is much easier to overcome your initial fears and trepidations a few calls at time. You can wrap your mind around these small chunks.

Some people set an overall goal for each daily phone block. For example, they will decide in advance to make 50 dials. Next, they'll set smaller, 10-dial blocks. Then they'll pump themselves up for these small blocks. When they finish, they give themselves a small reward and move to the next 10 calls.

I observed a software sales rep who listed the numbers 50 to 1 on a piece of paper. With each dial she put a strike through the number, starting with 50. She said it was much easier for her to get her prospecting calls done using this technique.

At Sales Gravy we do Power Hours (and sometimes Power Half Hours). During Power Hours, we put everything aside and focus on making as many dials as possible in a short period of time. Putting the time limit on it helps us stay focused and on track.

Have fun. You are likely a competitive, creative person. If you weren't, you wouldn't be in sales in the first place. Set up challenges for yourself. For example, some people count nos. They play a game to see how many nos they can get. It sounds a little sick and twisted, but I've done it and it is actually motivating since you will always get more nos than yesses.

No matter what you do, though: Schedule that block. Make the appointment with yourself. Keep it sacred and don't be late.

The Five-Step Simple Telephone Prospecting Framework

Few things in sales have been more overcomplicated than the simple telephone prospecting call. Efficient and effective telephone prospecting should get you to yes, no, or maybe as fast as possible, in the least intrusive way, using a relaxed, confident, professional tone that reduces resistance. That way you get the yesses on the table fast and deal with RBOs directly without the painful dance around the bush.

When you pick up the phone and call a prospect—cold, warm, hot, referral, follow-up, inbound lead, even existing customer—and they are not expecting your call, you are an interruption.

Consider how you feel when your work day is interrupted by someone calling you unannounced. It can make you feel irritated, angry, or resentful because in most cases, the call comes when you are right in the middle of something else.

Let's step into your shoes. What would you want?

Okay, your first response is probably, "I wouldn't want to get the call in the first place." I'll give you that. No one wants to be interrupted, not me, not you, not your prospect—even if the call is something we welcome.

But let's get back to reality. As a salesperson you've got a choice to make: Interrupt or start a new career at your local coffee shop making minimum wage. Salespeople who don't interrupt prospects have skinny kids.

So if you're going to get interrupted, what would you want?

You would want the caller to get right to the point and get off the phone quickly so you could get back to posting your cat videos on YouTube.

Now try standing in your prospect's shoes. They are people just like you who resent having their day interrupted by an unscheduled caller. Your goal is to make the call quick and to the point so that you achieve your objective and they can get back to what they were doing.

To do this effectively, your call must be structured so that you get to the point fast—in 10 seconds or less—and sound like an authentic professional rather than a scripted robot or a stereotype of the cheesy sales guy so often portrayed in movies.

You also need a process that is consistent and repeatable. A consistent, repeatable structure takes pressure off of you and your prospect. Because you are not winging it each time you call, you won't have to worry about what to say. And, because you are focused and deliberate, it is respectful of your prospect's time.

Shorter, more impactful calls mean you complete phone blocks faster, which in turn keeps your pipeline full and gives you more time to spend engaged in the activities that make sales fun. An effective telephone prospecting call might sound like this—a simple five-step framework:

1. Get their attention by using their name: "Hi, Julie."
2. Identify yourself: "My name is Jeb Blount and I'm with Sales Gravy."
3. Tell them why you are calling: "The reason I'm calling is to set up an appointment with you."
4. Bridge—give them a *because*: "I just read an article online that said your company is going to add 200 new sales positions over the next year. Several companies in your industry are already using Sales Gravy exclusively for sourcing sales candidates and they are very happy with the results we are delivering."
5. Ask for what you want, and shut up: "I thought the best place to start is to schedule a short meeting to learn about your sales recruiting challenges and goals. How about we meet Wednesday afternoon around 3:00 PM?"

Figure 15.1   5-Step Telephone Prospecting Framework

One point I want to be sure you get: There are no pauses. The moment you pause you lose control of the call. As soon as my prospect answers the phone, I walk through the five-step framework without stopping. My goal is to respect their time by getting to the point and getting an answer—yes, no, or maybe—fast.

Here is another example. My objective is to gather information:

"Hi, Ian, this is Jeb Blount with Acme Restaurant Supply. The reason I'm calling is I read in the paper that you are building a restaurant over on the 44 bypass and I want to learn more about your process for purchasing kitchen equipment. I realize I'm calling a little bit early in the game; however, I've found that when we get our design team working with your team before you make critical decisions about kitchen layout, you'll have more options and can often save a ton of money in construction costs and future labor with a more efficient and streamlined kitchen layout. Can you tell me how you make those decisions and when the selection process will begin?"

Here is another example where my objective is to qualify and move them directly into a sales conversation:

"Hi, Corrina, this is Jeb Blount from AcmeSoft. The reason I'm calling is you downloaded our white paper on creating more effective landing pages for lead generation and I'm interested to learn what triggered your interest. I work with a number of marketing executives who've been struggling to bring in enough quality leads to meet their growth objectives, and I've got a few best practices that my clients are using to generate more and better leads that I'll be happy to share with you. Can you tell me more about your situation?"

When you use this framework, you'll find that you stumble over your words less and achieve your objective more often.

A framework is a guide. It makes you agile and adaptive because it can be leveraged across different situations, freeing you to focus on your message rather than the time-consuming effort of rethinking your process each time.

Telephone prospecting should be professional and straight to the point. There is no reason to overcomplicate it with cheeseball scripts that piss off prospects, create resistance, and make you look foolish. Let's take a closer look at the elements of the Five-Step Simple Teleprospecting Framework.

Get Their Attention

Once your prospect answers the phone, you have a split second to get their attention. The easiest, fastest way to get someone's attention is to use the most beautiful word in the world to them—their name.

Anywhere, anytime, when you say another person's name, they will sit up and look up. For that split second you have their attention. The same dynamic is at play when telephone prospecting, and it is important to use this to your advantage. Just say: "Hi, Julie."

Important point: Notice that I didn't ask Julie, "How are you doing?"

There is a reason for this. When you interrupt a prospect's day, you get resistance. This resistance hits a peak as soon as they realize that you are a salesperson and that they made a big mistake by answering their phone.

This realization happens right after you say something like, "Hi, this is Stephen from the widget company. How are you today?" Then you pause.

That's when your prospect's instinct to get off the phone and back to whatever they were doing kicks in. They immediately hit you with a reflex response like "I'm not interested" or ask, "Who is this?"

Your prospect was going about her morning happily when her phone rang, interrupting her day. Then she realized her mistake as soon as you said "How are you doing?" Suddenly her get-away-from-this-salesperson-fast mechanism kicked in. As soon as you paused, she hit you with an objection and a stern tone of voice. That's how your prospect is doing and that's how you lose control of the call.

Don't ask, "How are you doing?" and don't pause or leave any awkward silence. Say their name and keep moving.

Identify Yourself

Get right down to business. Say your prospect's name, then tell her who you are and the reason you called. Transparency has two benefits.

1. It demonstrates that you are a professional and that you have respect for your prospect's time—save the idle chitchat until you have established a real relationship.
2. By telling them who you are and why you are calling, you reduce their stress because people are more comfortable when they know what to expect.

The one thing that I know to be true is prospects are people just like you. They don't want to be tricked, they don't want to be manipulated, and they don't want to be interrupted. What they want is to be treated with respect. The best way you can show your respect is to be truthful, relevant, and to the point.

Bridge—Give Them a Because

We've already learned that when we ask people to do something for us, like give up their time, they are more likely to do so when we give them a reason—or a *because*. The bridge connects the dots between what you want and why they should give it to you. You've interrupted their day, told them why you are calling, and now you must give them a reason to give up more of their precious time to you.

The person you are calling could not care less about your product, service, or features. They don't care about what you want or what you would "love" or "like" to do. They don't care about your desires, your quota, or that you are "going to be over in their area."

They only care about what is relevant to their problems and they will give up their time to you for their reasons, not yours. This is why message matters. What you say and how you say it will either generate resistance and objections or it will pull the wall down and open the door to a "yes."

Avoid saying things like:

- "I want to talk to you about my product."
- "I'd love to get together with you to show you what we have to offer."
- "I want to tell you about our new service."

These statements are all about you and the words *talk*, *tell*, and *show* send a subtle message that what you really want to do is pitch. I assure you the last thing your prospect wants or has time for is you talking at them.

Using the bridging and messaging frameworks from the "Message Matters" chapter, craft a short, compelling message that connects emotionally with what is important to your prospect. Use phrases and emotional words like:

- Learn more about you and your business
- Share some insights that have helped my other clients
- Share some best practices that other companies in your industry are using to . . .
- Gain an understanding of your unique situation
- See how we might fit
- Flexibility
- Options
- Peace of mind
- Save
- Frustrated
- Concerned
- Stressed
- Waste
- Time
- Money

These statements and words are all about them. Prospects want to feel that you get them and their problems, or are at least trying to get them, before they'll agree to give up their time for you.

The most effective way to craft the right message is to simply stand in your prospect's shoes. Look at things through their eyes and use your God-given empathy to sense their emotions and consider what might be important to them.

Ask For What You Want and Shut Up

The most important step is asking for what you want.

- If you are qualifying, ask for the information you need to determine your next step.
- If you want an appointment, ask for a day and time.
- If you want to engage in a sales conversation, ask an open-ended question that gets them talking.

Your goal is to get to yes, no, or maybe fast. Don't waste any time here. Don't talk in circles. Don't use passive, limp language and phrases like "maybe if it would be okay and if you are not too busy, we could kinda maybe get together for a few minutes, what do you think?"

Be confident, direct, and smooth—and don't pause. Get to the point. Ask and assume.

Then shut up. The single biggest mistake salespeople make on prospecting calls is they keep talking instead of giving their prospect the opportunity to respond to their request. This increases resistance, creates objections, and gives your prospect an easy way out.

So shut up and let your prospect respond. Will there be an RBO when you ask for what you want? Absolutely. This is reality—in sales there are always objections. However, because you wasted no time getting to the objection, you will have more time to respond, which in turn will give you a better chance of achieving your objective.

We're going to dive headfirst into techniques for tuning around reflex responses, brush-offs, and objections in the next chapter. What I want to impress upon you, though, is just how many prospects will say yes when you are straightforward, confident, and assume through your words and tone of voice that they're going to say yes.

Ask for what you want, and shut up.

Leaving Effective Voice Mail Messages That Get Returned

No matter how proficient you become with the teleprospecting framework, no matter how targeted your prospecting list or focused your phone block, no matter how well you time your dials, the majority of your calls are still going to go to voice mail.

I know that voice mail drives you crazy, because it drives me crazy. Most of the time it feels like you are wasting your time. There are always these little questions floating around in the back of your mind:

When should I leave a voice mail message?

Should I even leave a voice mail message?

If I do leave a message will I get called back?

While there are no definitive answers to any of these questions, knowing how to leave voice mail messages is important because prospects do listen to and return voice mail. An effective voice mail should help you achieve at least one of two objectives:

1. Get a callback from a high-value qualified prospect
2. Build familiarity with a high-value prospect

When salespeople ask me when they should leave a voice mail, I always answer, "When it matters."

For example, if you are dialing a list of prospects for which you have little qualifying information, it might not make sense to leave a voice mail for those prospects. You don't know them, nor how qualified they are, and they don't know you. The probability that you will get a callback from one of these prospects is low. For this reason, you'll be more efficient and effective just dialing as many of them as possible in your allotted block rather than wasting time leaving voice mails.

Leaving a voice mail is inefficient. It takes time to work your way through the phone prompts. At around 20 to 30 seconds per voice mail, you can easily spend 10 to 15 minutes of an hour-long phone block just leaving voice mail messages. The callback rate on voice mail messages is very low. As in single-digits low. This makes voice mail both inefficient and ineffective for across-the-board application on all calls.

This is why when you leave voice mail, it has to count. For instance, when you are working a list of conquest prospects, you'll want to leave a voice mail on every call. The same goes with a prospect that you know or suspect is moving into the buying window. With these prospects, it is critical that you get in front of them, so leaving a voice mail that generates a callback or builds familiarity makes sense and has a reasonable risk/reward.

Since there is no tried-and-true rule for when to leave voice mails, though, it's up to you to decide when to make an investment of time in voice mails based on your objectives, list, time availability, and unique situation. However, if you are going to leave a voice mail, leave one that will give you the highest probability of getting a callback.

Five-Step Voice Mail Framework to Double Callbacks

As I reluctantly trudge through voice mail messages from sales-people, there are three kinds that drive me crazy:

- *No contact information:* These messages are automatically deleted.
- *Long-winded:* Somewhere in the middle of their droning on and on, I usually hit "delete."
- *Garbled contact information:* When I have to listen to a message more than once, it wastes my time and I delete it.

Here's the deal: To get more of your messages returned, you must make it easier for your prospects to call you back. There are five steps to leaving effective voice mail messages that get returned. This process deployed consistently will double your callback rate.

1. *Identify yourself.* Say who you are and the company you work for up front. This makes you sound professional.
2. *Say your phone number twice.* Prospects can't call back if they don't have or you garbled your number. Give your contact information up front and say it twice—slowly. After they hear your name and company, they may not care about the rest of your message because based on their situation, they can infer what it is about.
3. *Tell them the reason for your call.* Tell them why you have called. There is nothing more irritating to a buyer than a salesperson who is not honest about their intentions. After you give your personal information just say, "The reason for my call is . . ." or "the purpose of my call is . . . ," then tell them why you are calling and what you want. Transparency is both respectful and professional.
4. *Give them a reason to call you back.* Prospects call back when you have something that they want or are curious about. Curiosity is a powerful driver of behavior. When you have knowledge, insight, information, special pricing, new or improved products, a solution to a problem, and so on, you create a motivating force that compels your prospect to call you back.
5. *Repeat your name and say your phone number twice.* Before you end your message, say your name again slowly and clearly and always, always say your number twice.

Figure 15.2   5-Step Voice Mail Framework

Bonus tip: Keep voice mail messages to 30 seconds. When you hold yourself to 30 seconds, you are forced to be clear, succinct, and professional.

"Hi, Rick, this is Jeb Blount from Sales Gravy. My phone number is 1–888–360–2249, that's 1–888–360–2249. The reason I am calling is you downloaded our white paper on cold calling and I want to learn more about your situation and what triggered you to seek out this information. I also have some additional resources on voice mail messages and phone prospecting I thought you might be curious to learn about. Let's get together this week. Give me a call back at 1–888–360–2249, that's 1–888–360–2249."

I am aware that it feels awkward to say your phone number four times on the same voice mail message. Your goal is to make it easy and pleasurable for them to call you back, not more comfortable for you.

By hearing your phone number twice up front, they don't need to listen to the entire message to get your phone number if they are ready to call you back. If your message intrigued them and they want to call you back, you also gave them your number twice at the end, so they don't have to replay the message. Making it easy increases the probability that you'll get a callback.

Timing Teleprospecting Calls Is a Losing Strategy

The most frequent question I get about telephone prospecting is:

"Jeb, what is the best time to call? I mean, is there a time when people will be more receptive to my calls? You know, like is it better to contact a prospect during the morning than the end of business day? Or are there some days of the week that are better than others?"

This is followed by a longing expectation that I will reveal the secret code that will open them up to a utopian world where prospects always answer the phone, are always in chipper moods and receptive to sales pitches, agree to appointments without rejection, and close themselves.

I get this question from salespeople across all industries and all experience levels—all the time. There are several reasons salespeople ask this question:

- They are truly interested in timing their calls.
- They are frustrated and just venting, in which case my answer falls on deaf ears.
- They are seeking a way out of making calls—an excuse.

Timing calls is the greatest excuse and cop-out for salespeople who don't want to prospect by phone (or frankly, prospect at all). Here are some timing excuses from salespeople looking to escape the phone:

- "I can't call on Monday because people are getting ready for the week and it will disturb them."
- "I can't call on Friday because people are getting ready for the weekend and will probably be leaving early."
- "I can't call in the morning because people won't answer the phone when they are getting ready for the day."
- "I can't call before lunch because people are getting ready to go to lunch and I don't want to disturb them."
- "I can't call after lunch because people are just getting back in the office and probably checking e-mail."
- "I can't call in the afternoon because people are probably in meetings and not in their offices."
- "I can't call at the end of the day because people are getting ready to go home."
- "No worries, I'll just do my dials tomorrow when prospects will be more likely to answer my calls."

What really happens is teleprospecting is put off day after day until pipelines are dead empty. Then these desperate salespeople end up in front of me looking for the top-secret call-timing technique that will make everything okay.

A great analogy for timing your calls is investing. The investor who attempts to time the market has historically failed to beat the investor who uses a dollar-cost-averaging strategy—making incremental investments on a regular schedule over time.

If you think about prospecting in the same vein, salespeople who prospect daily on a regular schedule are always more successful over time than those who make the attempt to time their prospecting. Like investing, statistics are always in the favor of the salesperson who does a little bit of prospecting every day.

Yes, there is plenty of data from dozens of studies that validate that there are particular days and times of days that are best for calling. If you go looking, you will find article after article, study after study, and opinion after opinion on the best time to call. A simple online search will also yield hundreds of anecdotal insights about the best time to call: Wednesdays at lunch, in the morning at 10:12 A.M., Friday afternoons, and so on. You'll find lots of justification for this reasoning. Some of it is on target. Some of it is bunk. Some of it is contradictory.

Most of it is meaningless. For example, Insight Squared produced a study[1] on call timing that indicated that Tuesdays between 10:00 AM and 4:00 PM are the best times to call. Of course, their best day to call was only 1.3 percent better than their worst day to call.

Just Eat the Frog

Most of what has been written about call timing is just confusing noise that provides less-than-eager-to-prospect salespeople with an easy excuse to put off telephone prospecting until tomorrow or this afternoon or anytime other than now.

So, forget about timing your calls and commit instead to a daily, first-thing-in-the-morning call block.

Frenchman Nicholas Chamfort advised people to "swallow a toad in the morning if you want to encounter nothing more disgusting the rest of the day." In his book *Eat That Frog*, Brian Tracy says that your "frog" is "the hardest, most important task of the day. It is the one task that can have the greatest positive impact on your life and results at the moment."[2]

Telephone prospecting is the most important activity in sales. It is the one activity that will have the greatest positive impact on the health of your pipeline, career, and income. It also sucks. It's frustrating, uncomfortable, and covered with slimy green frog warts.

Tracy writes that staring at the frog will not make it more appetizing. When "you have to eat a frog, it doesn't pay to sit and look at it for very long." The same with prospecting. Thinking about it, pushing it off, or trying to time it will not make it any more appetizing.

The longer that frog sits there, the more foul it gets. That's when the bargaining starts happening. Instead of just eating it and getting it over with, you start making deals with yourself to "double up" on your frog eating tomorrow.

It never works, though. Once you start procrastinating, you'll never catch up. As you push prospecting off, more tasks, problems, and burning fires move in to take its place.

This is why you should block your first two hours every day for telephone activity. Set the appointment with yourself and keep it. Your energy level, confidence, and enthusiasm will be at their peak at the beginning of the day. Plus, prospects will have fewer things on their plate as they begin their day, which makes for less resistance and more *yesses*.

The best way to avoid becoming a statistic is to embrace the suck and eat that frog.

16 | Turning Around RBOs

Reflex Responses, Brush-Offs, and Objections

Everybody has a plan until they get punched in the face.
> —Mike Tyson

They say that public speaking causes the most fear in people, but in my experience, given the choice between giving a public speech and making a prospecting call, you'd have a line for the speech.

Rejection is a powerful de-motivator. For millions of salespeople, picking up the phone and calling a prospect is the most stressful part of their day. Sadly, these reluctant salespeople stifle their earning potential, get fired, or fall into financial ruin.

Prospecting, especially telephone prospecting and in-person prospecting, conjures up our deepest fears of vulnerability. Vulnerability, according to Dr. Brene Brown, author of the *Power of Vulnerability*, is created in the presence of uncertainty, risk, and emotional exposure (read: potential to be rejected).

This is why so many salespeople hate prospecting. They cannot control the situation and therefore feel vulnerable and uncomfortable.

The feeling of rejection happens the moment you get a reflex response, brush-off, or objection (RBO). You feel like you've been punched in the gut. Your brain turns off and you stumble over your words. You feel embarrassed, small, and out of control. Feeling that you lack control is an awful, sometimes debilitating emotion.

Yet, it's right here, at this very inflection point of rejection, that the rubber meets the road in prospecting and sales. It's the skill and poise to deal with RBOs and turn them into *yesses* that will give you the biggest wins and get you in front of the high-value prospects that every salesperson in your territory is chasing.

My objective with this chapter is twofold:

1. I'm going to give you a framework for dealing with prospecting objections that increases your probability of getting to yes. Once you master this framework you'll gain the confidence to take anything that is thrown at you by a prospect.
2. You'll learn to manage rejection and know that you can quickly gain control of the conversation when your prospects throw RBOs at you.

These techniques will be used primarily for telephone and in-person prospecting. However, the same techniques can be used with e-mail and social prospecting responses.

Rejection Won't Roll Off Your Back

When I was growing up in sales, I consumed sales training, books, audio programs, and seminars the way some people devour chocolate. My appetite was insatiable (and still is). I saw all of the greats on stage and worked for companies that provided a steady dose of sales training.

When it came to objections and rejection in sales there were consistent themes and clichés proffered by these trainers and experts. I continue to see these same themes today:

- "If you want to be good in sales, you've got to learn to let rejection roll off your back."
- "They aren't rejecting you; they're just objecting to your proposition."
- "When you get rejected by a prospect, it's not personal."

"Don't take it personal." That's my favorite one.

Let's see. You've poured blood, sweat, and tears into your efforts to contact the prospect. You are competitive and driven. You hate to lose. You take your job seriously. You work hard to be a professional. Your income and security is directly tied to your success throughout the sales process.

I've got news for you. It feels personal and it is personal. If rejection just "rolls right off your back," like so many drops of water and you feel nothing, you are probably a psychopath.

Let's begin with a basic premise: The feeling of rejection is real. When a prospect tells you *no*, your brain doesn't know the difference between the prospect rejecting your proposition or rejecting you. To your brain, it is one and the same. We learned in a previous chapter that the fight–or–flight response triggers the physiological reaction to fear. The psychological and neurochemical response is generated by your innate and insatiable need to feel accepted, important, and in control, which is why rejection carries such a powerful sting.

Sales trainers and experts say things like, "Just let it roll off your back" because it's easier to offer platitudes and intellectualize the pain of rejection than to acknowledge that it's real and teach people how to deal with it. I believe it is completely disingenuous to tell you that you can just snap your fingers, detach from rejection, and let it roll off your back. I can't do it, and I'm as fanatical as they come.

I'll walk in any door, call any prospect, at any time. I dive into prospecting like it's my best friend. When I'm told no, I still feel rejected.

What I've done, though, is develop a framework that allows me to gain control of that disruptive emotion so that when I get objections, my feelings don't run amuck and cause my prospecting call to become a train wreck.

Reflex Responses, Brush-Offs, and Objections, Oh My!

Learning how to manage the disruptive emotions that are triggered by rejection begins with a deeper understanding of where your prospect is coming from when you interrupt their day.

Reflex Response

I was traveling and realized that I'd left the cord for my iPad at home. There was an office supply store within walking distance of my hotel, so I strolled over to get one.

As I entered the store, a nice young man walked up to me and asked, "Can I help you?"

I responded, "I'm just looking."

As I walked away, I caught myself. I did need help finding a cord. So I went back and he walked me over to the shelf where the cords were hanging, saving me a ton of time "just looking."

Why did I respond this way when it clearly wasn't the truth? It was automatic, something I'd said hundreds of times. It was habit and part of my *buyer script* when I get approached by salespeople.

"We're not interested."

"We're happy."

"We're all set."

"I'm busy."

"I'm in a meeting."

"I'm just running out the door."

"I'm not interested."

These are all examples of things that prospects reflexively say when they are interrupted by a salesperson. Your prospect doesn't think about the response. The response may not be true. But there isn't a conscious intent to deceive you. It is just the script they have been conditioned to use when confronted by salespeople.

Brush-Off

The brush-off is all about avoiding conflict.

"Call me later."

"Get back to me in a month."

"Why don't you just send over some information?" (The greatest brush-off of all time.)

A brush-off is your prospect telling you to bug off nicely. "Call me later," they'll say when they want to avoid confrontation and be kind enough to let you down easy. They have learned that sales-people, for the most part, are willing to accept these falsehoods and go away because salespeople want to avoid conflict too, and the brush-off doesn't feel as much like rejection.

Why do prospects lie—consciously or subconsciously? One of the most cogent explanations I've heard comes from Seth Godin.[1] He says that prospects lie because salespeople have trained them to, and "because they're afraid." They have learned that when they tell the truth, "the salesperson responds by questioning the judg-ment of the prospect. In exchange for telling the truth, the prospect is disrespected. Of course we [prospects] don't tell the truth—if we do, we're often bullied or berated or made to feel dumb. Is it any surprise that it's easier to just avoid the conflict altogether?"

Objections

Objections on prospecting calls tend to be more truthful and logical rebuttals to your request. They typically come with a *because*.

"There is really no reason for us to meet right now because we just signed a new contract with your competitor."

"We're busy implementing a huge project and I can't take on anything else at the moment."

"I can't meet you next week because I'm going to be at CES in Las Vegas."

"I'd love to talk, but our budgets have been locked down and I think it would be a waste of your time."

These types of responses are rare. When you get them, though, it opens the door to turning around the objection and setting up a meeting anyway, or changing gears and gathering qualifying information that will help you in the future.

Planning for the RBO

The real secret to gaining control of the conversation when faced with an RBO is planning for them in advance. This is contrary to how the average salesperson approaches prospecting calls. Instead of planning in advance, they wing it on every call and treat each RBO as if it were a unique event.

But RBOs are not unique. There are a finite number of ways a prospect will tell you no. Most RBOs will come in the form of:

- Not interested
- Don't have the budget
- Too busy
- Send information
- Overwhelmed—too many things going on
- Just looking (inbound leads)

Prospects don't always use these exact words. For example, instead of saying, "We're happy," they may say, "We've been with your competitor for years and they do a good job for us." The words are different, but the intent is the same—we're happy. Just look for the patterns and you'll know in which category the RBO fits.

To master and become effective at turning around RBOs, you simply need to identify all of the potential RBOs and use the Three-Step Turnaround Framework to develop simple, repeatable scripts that you say without having to even think about it.

Why a repeatable practiced script for RBOs? A practiced script makes your voice intonation, speaking style, and flow sound relaxed, authentic, and professional.

Turnaround scripts free your mind to focus on your prospect rather than the words you use. Scripts work so well with RBOs because you tend to get the same ones over and over again. When you have a script, you never have to worry about what to say and that puts you in complete control of the situation.

If you really want to observe the power of scripts, just notice the difference when a politician is speaking off script when confronted by reporters as opposed to giving a speech with the aid of a teleprompter. Onstage the politician is incredibly convincing. But without a script he often stumbles on his words, and makes many of the same mistakes we make when winging it with RBOs on prospecting calls. Scripts are what make politicians and public figures compelling personalities.

The worry for most salespeople, though, is that "I won't sound like myself when I use a script." The concern about sounding canned is legitimate. If actors and politicians sounded canned, TV shows and movies wouldn't be entertaining and speeches wouldn't be believable.

That's exactly why actors, politicians, and top sales professionals rehearse and practice. They work and work until the script sounds natural and becomes their voice. Scripts are a powerful way to manage your message in an emotionally tense situation, but they must be rehearsed.

I won't feed you a line and tell you this will be easy, because it is not. Writing and practicing RBO scripts will require contemplation and will be time consuming. The good news is, you already have the habit of saying certain things certain ways when you run into RBOs. The first step is to analyze what you are already doing and formalize what is working into a script that can be repeated with success, time and again.

As you prepare your scripts, practice and perfect them. Use a recorder, a role-play buddy, or a coach to help you rehearse.

The Turnaround Framework

Traditionally, sales trainers have taught salespeople to "overcome objections." The phrase "overcoming objections" is widely used in the sales profession to describe how to convince prospects that what they are saying is wrong.

Overcome means to defeat or prevail over an opponent.[2] Scores of salespeople try to argue their prospects into changing their minds—to prevail with debate. This is why, as we learned from Seth Godin earlier, prospects lie to us. They expect when they say no that they'll face a battle and be disrespected. The sales profession and the many movies that create ugly caricatures of salespeople have conditioned them to feel this way.

Overcoming doesn't work. There is a universal law of human behavior: You cannot argue another person into believing that they are wrong. The more you push another person, the more they dig their heels in and resist you.

It has never worked. Even when salespeople do manage to get prospects to say yes this way, it is in spite of the argument, not because of it, that they prevailed.

The act of overcoming creates animosity, exasperation, and frustration for both the prospect, who gets bulldozed with a pitch about why they are wrong, and the rep, who actually creates even more resistance and harsher rejection with this approach.

Disrupt versus Defeat

There is a better way. Rather than attempting to overcome—defeating or prevailing over your prospect—you should disrupt their expectations and thought patterns when they push back with a *no*. The key is a disruptive statement or question that turns them around so that they lean toward you rather than move away from away from you.

Disrupters work on humans because when we encounter something that isn't what we expected, we stop and pay attention. It's a pull versus push process.

Judo, a Japanese word that translates as "gentle or yielding way," is a martial art form that focuses on winning without causing injury. Similarly, when facing RBOs on prospecting calls, you want to achieve your objective—a commitment of time or information—without fighting or causing injury.

RBOs on prospecting calls happen in a split second. You have to be nimble, adaptive, and quick on your feet. It's verbal Judo at 100 miles an hour.

To be agile, you need a framework for both managing your emotions and pulling your prospect toward you so that it becomes easier for them to say yes. Three elements of the RBO Turnaround Framework are: Anchor. Disrupt. Ask.

Figure 16.1   3 Steps to Turning Around RBOs

Anchor

We've established that the initial physiological and emotional reaction (fight or flight) to rejection is involuntary. You can, however, gain control of the disruptive emotions that are triggered by rejection. The secret is giving your logical brain (neocortex) a chance to catch up.

If you were hiking in the woods and a bear suddenly walked out onto the path in front of you, the physiological reaction to the threat the bear posed is the exact response you feel when you get rejected. Your "reptilian brain" or amygdala, through millions of years of evolution, is hard-wired to prepare you to survive. The problem is, it cannot tell the difference between a bear and a prospect telling you no.

But your logical brain (the neocortex) can. The problem is fight or flight kicks in before logic. So you need a millisecond for your logical brain to wake up and tell the amygdala that there is no threat.

The purpose of the anchor statement, sometimes called a ledge, is to give yourself an anchor or something to hold on to until your logical brain catches up, takes over, and manages the disruptive emotions generated by rejection. That's how you regain your poise and control of the conversation.

Disrupt

Your prospect is conditioned. They expect you to act just like every other salesperson. When they tell you no, they expect a fight. The secret to turning around your prospect's RBO is delivering a statement or question that disrupts this expectation, "takes away" the fight, and pulls the prospect toward you. For example:

- When they say they're happy, instead of arguing that you can make them happier if they just give you a chance, say,

"Awesome. If you're happy, you shouldn't even think about changing!" This is completely unexpected.

- When they say they're busy, instead of arguing them into how you will only take a little bit of their time, say, "I figured you would be." Agreeing with them disrupts their thought pattern.
- When they say, "Just send me some information," say, "Tell me specifically what you are looking for." This calls their bluff and forces engagement.
- When they say, "I'm not interested," say, "That makes sense. Most people aren't." Their brain isn't ready for you to agree with them.

It is also important to avoid using words that only salespeople use. As soon as you do, you play right into their expectations. One phrase you want to avoid is "I understand." When you use the phrase "I understand," you sound just like every other schmuck who uses this phrase as insincere filler so they can get back to pitching. It demonstrates zero empathy and tells your prospect that you are not listening and don't care.

Ask

You may deliver the perfect turnaround, but if you don't ask again for commitment, you won't get what you want. You must ask confidently and assumptively for a specific commitment of time or information, without any hesitation or awkward pause, directly following your turnaround script.

About half of the time when you ask they'll throw out another RBO—one that tends to be closer to the truth. You will want to be prepared to handle it and ask again. What you should never do is fight. It isn't worth it. When you get two RBOs and still can't turn your prospect around, graciously move on and come back at them another day.

Putting It All Together

It is essential that you avoid overcomplicating this process. You need turnaround scripts that work for you and sound natural coming from *your* lips. They need to make you sound authentic, real, and confident. Keep them simple so that they are easy for you to remember and repeat. Here are three examples that put it all together:

1. *Prospect: "Look, Jeb, I'm busy."*

"Nancy, that's exactly why I called."

(Anchor: This is a simple statement that gives my logical brain just a moment to take control of my emotional brain. By agreeing with her, I immediately disrupt her expectation that I will try to talk her out of being busy.)

"I figured you would be, so I want to find a time that is more convenient for you."

(Disrupt: It also acknowledges that she is busy right now and disrupts that pattern by asking her to think about a more convenient time.)

"How about we get together next Wednesday at 3:00 PM instead?"

(Ask: This makes an assumptive, direct, and specific request.)

2. *Prospect: "We're not interested."*

"You know, that is what a lot of my current clients said the first time I called." (Anchor)

"Most people say they aren't interested before they see how much I can save them. I don't know if my service will be a good fit for you and your company, but doesn't it make sense for us to at least get together for a short meeting to find out?" (Disrupt)

"How about Friday at 2:00 PM? (Ask)

3. *Prospect: "We're really happy with our current provider."*

"That's fantastic!" (Anchor)

"Anytime you are getting great rates and great service, you should never think about changing. All I want to do is come by and get to know you a little better. And even if it doesn't make sense to do business with me at the moment, I can at least give you a competitive quote that will help you keep those other guys honest." (Disrupt)

"How about I come by on Tuesday at 11:30 AM?" (Ask)

I'd love to hear about turnarounds that are working for you. To share your scripts and pick up tips from other sales professionals, join the RBO discussion forum at FanaticalProspecting.com

When the Horse Is Dead, Dismount

Sometimes, no matter how good you are, the person on the other end of the line will tell you to "go screw yourself" or slam the door or phone in your face. Or scream—"Don't ever call me again!" or "It will be a cold day in hell before I ever buy something from you or your company!"

Because you are interrupting people, they'll be rude, short, and ugly, and sometimes take shots at you that are very pointed and personal.

Sometimes it's because you caught them at a bad time—the boss just dropped last quarter's numbers on their desk and told them that they are a loser with no future—and you called just in time to be a convenient human piñata for their frustrations and self-loathing. Sometimes they are just miserable assholes.

When you get treated this way, you have a tendency to dwell on it. You stop prospecting. Complain to a peer and play the conversation over and over again in your head. You feel embarrassed, angry, revengeful, and a whole host of other emotions that invade your mind and steal your joy. You log a note in your CRM to NEVER call them again, just for good measure.

You project your feelings on your prospect and make up a story in your head about what they said, did, or thought after they hung up the phone, pressed "send" in response to your e-mail, or watched you walk out of their door. In your mind's eye, you see your prospect laughing at you or fuming because you annoyed them.

Meanwhile, the prospect doesn't even remember you. They moved on the moment you hung up the phone and haven't given you another thought. You were just a blip—a momentary and meaningless interruption in their day. Trust me. I've had prospects scream at me on Tuesday and treat me like I'm their best friend on Wednesday. Completely oblivious to my previous call. That's why, when people tell me to "never call them again," I call.

It's like when kids learn to ride horses. If the kid falls off, they make them get back on. No matter if the kid is crying, shaking in fear, and saying they won't or don't want to get back on the horse. No matter—the instructor forces the kid to get back on. They know if that kid doesn't, they'll play the fall over and over again in their head, blowing their fear up to the point that they will never get on a horse again. Courage is developed in the presence of fear, not in spite of it.

It is difficult to regain your focus and keep moving when a prospect is horrible to you. It hurts. It's all you can think about and talk about. You fantasize about calling them back up and telling them to *f@*& off!* Anger invades your thoughts and keeps you up all night stewing. At times, you completely shut down your life as you dwell on your anger, angst, and anxiety.

I meet salespeople every day who are reliving these transgressions over and over again. In our Fanatical Prospecting Boot Camps, all they want to talk about is that "one time a prospect said __ to them." They've made thousands of prospecting touches but dwell on the one call that went bad.

They waste precious time, energy, and emotions beating a dead horse. No matter how hard they beat and kick it, the horse will not move. They are living in the past, unable to focus on anything else, and they seek company for their misery. Beating a dead horse is self-destructive. Dead horses don't trot, they rot.

Here's my advice: When the horse is dead, dismount.

Of course, letting go is easier said than done. So is the secret learning to turn the other cheek? Well, yes, but there is more. The real secret to moving on is understanding that anger is just energy and when you harness that energy, you tap into a powerful force. In fact, one of the enduring qualities of highly successful people is the ability to turn disappointment, defeat, and anger into unmovable determination.

When someone hurts you, your body, and mind fill with energy and adrenalin for revenge. Take advantage of that gift of energy to get better, because achievement is the ultimate revenge.

Over the years I've developed a simple trigger designed to shake me out of my self-pity when I've been slighted or find myself astride a dead horse. Behind my desk is an old index card taped to the wall. The paper has yellowed and the words faded just a bit because I've carried that card around with me for 25 years. On the card are four letters:

N E X T

17 | The Secret Lives of Gatekeepers

I am the Keymaster . . . Are you the Gatekeeper?

—Ghostbusters

Last week while I was training my new assistant and reviewing her responsibilities, she asked me how she should handle calls from salespeople. The look on her face told the story. Dealing with salespeople was a task she didn't consider pleasant.

It made me think about the ongoing tug-of-war between sales professionals, who are trying to get in the door, and the gatekeepers assigned the duty of keeping them at bay.

The reason I have a gatekeeper is there are so many people vying for my time, if I didn't have one I would never get my job done. Her most important job is to protect my time. Unfortunately, that puts her in the unenviable position of saying no to salespeople.

Salespeople hate gatekeepers. Sometimes to the point that they become so frustrated with gatekeepers that they experiment with tricks that, too often, make them look foolish. These schemes, regrettably, negative impact both parties, which is why so many gatekeepers, like my assistant, would rather have their teeth pulled than deal with a salesperson.

The reality, though, is you are going to have to deal with gatekeepers often. There is just no way to avoid it. So is there a secret? I know you are hoping I'll say yes, but the answer is no. There are no secret techniques that will get you past gatekeepers. There are, however, strategies that will give you an edge when dealing with gatekeepers.

To leverage these strategies, it is critical to understand that gatekeepers are people just like you. Step into their shoes. They have emotions, worries, and motivations and, like you, a boss and a job to do. Because of this, your success in getting through the gate depends on a combination of good manners, likeability, and people-savvy.

Seven Keys for Dealing with Gatekeepers

1. *Be likable.* Project a positive, cheerful, outgoing personality. Be polite and respectful. You are guaranteed to fail with gate-keepers if you are rude, pushy, and ill mannered. Always leave them with a positive impression of you and your company.

2. *Use please, please.* In his book *The Real Secrets of the Top 20 Percent*, the author, Mike Brooks, advises that the "single most powerful technique" to get past gatekeepers is to use *please* twice. For example, when a gatekeeper answers the phone you might say, "Hi, this is Jeb Blount from Sales Gravy. Would you please connect me to Mike Brooks, please?"

3. *Be transparent.* Tell the gatekeeper who you are—your full name and the name of your company. Full disclosure makes you sound professional and worthy enough to pass through to the boss.

4. *Connect.* Gatekeepers are people just like you. And like you, they like people who are interested in them. If you speak to a particular gatekeeper often, be sure to ask about how they are doing. Learn to listen to their tone of voice and respond when you hear something amiss. Ask questions about their family and their interests. There are gatekeepers I deal with on a regular basis who I know better than the boss. When I call, I will often spend more time talking to them than to my client. Because of these strong relationships, they take care to ensure that I get on calendars.

5. *Hold the cheese.* Never use cheesy schemes or tricks. Tricks don't work. They harm your credibility and you'll end up on the gatekeeper's do-not-talk-to list, which means it will have to snow at the equator before you get through. Be honest about who you are and why you are calling and ask for what you want. You may not get through the first time, but your honesty will be appreciated and remembered, which will play a huge role in opening the gate in the future.

6. *Ask for help.* Sometimes an honest and authentic plea for help will get a gatekeeper on your side. Sprinkling in a little humor can also make a difference. Once I walked into a business, attempting for the umpteenth time in a row to get an appointment.

    The receptionist looked up at me and said, "Are you back again? I thought I told you that we are not interested!"

    I responded with a smile, "I just came by to see you because I hadn't gotten quite enough rejection today to fill my quota."

    With that she laughed. It opened up a conversation where I was able to explain that I really needed some help. She made a call to the DM and I got a meeting.

7. *Change the game.* Sometimes the best strategy is to sidestep the gatekeeper. This can be accomplished in several ways:
    - *Call early or late.* The boss tends to be in the office earlier than the gatekeeper and stays later.
    - *Leverage social.* Few people allow their gatekeeper to have access to their social inboxes. Sending a LinkedIn InMail, for example, allows you to move right past the gatekeeper.

- *Meet them in person.* Attend conferences, networking events, civic clubs, charity events, and trade shows where your prospect hangs out—no gatekeepers there.
- *Send an e-mail.* An e-mail may allow you to skip past the gatekeeper.
- *Send a handwritten note.* In today's digital culture, hand-written notes sent via snail mail get through. If your note is sincere and funny, and if you add something of value (note: a brochure is not value) or congratulate your prospect on an achievement, there is a very good chance that you will get a response.

If the gatekeeper, usually a receptionist or lower-level blocker, is unwilling to give you the name and contact of the decision maker and you are unable to find the person through an online or social search, try these three hacks.

The Calling-Other-Extensions Hack

Evan was at a loss. He needed to contact a high-level buyer located in the headquarters of one of the largest U.S. grocery store chains. He faced two major challenges: He didn't know the buyer's name (or have any contact information other than the main phone number), and he didn't know the title of the person.

All he knew was that there was "someone in corporate who made those decisions."

He'd tried calling and asking for the "person who makes decisions on broadband services," but that had gotten him nowhere. No matter how many times he asked or how much he pleaded, he hit a wall over and over again. "I'm sorry, sir, we don't give out that information," "No, sir, I cannot connect you if you don't have a name."

Frustrated but determined, he kept at it. He called stores, did online searches, combed LinkedIn, and slowly but surely began to string small clues together. He narrowed his search down to a handful of possible titles but was still missing a name.

He finally got a break when, out of desperation, he started calling random extensions. On one of those calls, a friendly person gave him a hand. That yielded another clue:

"Yeah, I think a guy named Jack over in IT handles that."

"Thanks for the information. Do you know his last name or extension?"

"Sorry, I don't, but I can transfer you back to reception and maybe they can help you?"

Evan's heart sank. So far reception had been his Waterloo. He'd crashed and burned on every call.

When reception answered, he said, "Hey, I was talking to Dale Jones in purchasing and he was transferring me to Jack in IT, but somehow I ended up with you. Would you mind sending me over?"

"Hmmm," said the receptionist, "I'm not seeing a Jack. Did you mean Zack Freedman?"

Boom! He had a name.

"Yes, sorry about that. I thought I said Zack."

"Okay, no problem. I'll send you over now."

"Before you do, would you mind giving me Zack's extension just in case we get disconnected?"

"Sure, it's 5642. I'm transferring you now."

Evan ended up in Zack's voice mail but eventually got through and established a relationship and a beachhead with what became his largest customer.

The Salespeople–Help–Salespeople Hack

Two weeks ago I ran across a prospect that was a perfect fit for my business. I'd learned that they were hiring 30 new sales reps.

They were going to need someone to help them source, hire, and train all those new salespeople, and I figured it should be Sales

Gravy. Unfortunately, I had no idea who the decision makers were at the company. I called the phone number on the website and after finally getting past the lengthy automated message, I ran headfirst into a rude and brutal gatekeeper who refused to give me any information.

I did a search on LinkedIn and Google but came up empty. I tried once more to plead my case to the gatekeeper, and after she hung the phone up in my face—mid-qualifying question—I was right back where I started: basically nowhere.

That was when I used one of my favorite sales hacks for reaching hard-to-reach prospects.

I dialed the main number again. The automated message said, "Press 1 for the sales department."

I pressed 1.

Two rings later an enthusiastic voice answered the phone:

"This is Mike. Can I help you?"

I responded, "Hi, Mike, my name is Jeb Blount. The reason I'm calling is I'm trying to reach the person in your company who buys training programs. I wasn't having much luck going through the switchboard and I figured as a fellow salesperson you could relate and might give me a hand."

Mike was instantly empathetic. He replied, "I know what that's like. I've been having the same problem all morning. The person you are looking for is Jean. She's our VP of Sales. The best way to get her is on her mobile phone. Hold just a second and I'll get it for you."

Mike and I shot the breeze for a few more minutes, commiserating about gatekeepers. He also gave me the scoop on why they were growing, the sales role they were hiring for, and complained about the nonexistent sales training program.

My very next call was to Jean, who answered the phone on the second ring. Mike's information proved very powerful in helping me relate to Jean's issues. After a 15-minute conversation, Jean agreed to a next appointment and promised to include her company president. That meeting went well and opened the door to a formal proposal.

The salespeople–help–salespeople hack is an awesome secret weapon. It has worked for me time and again when I've had a hard time getting to the right people in prospective accounts. It's effective for several reasons:

- Most sales organizations pick up their phones, so there is a high probability that you will have the opportunity to speak to a live human being.
- Salespeople tend to know who's who in their organizations and how to get in contact with those people.
- Salespeople help other salespeople because they have stood in your shoes. They know what it is like to hit a brick wall.

If you are honest, polite, and respectful and bring a little humor and humility with you, they'll often open doors that would have been very difficult to open on your own.

The Go-Around-Back Hack

If you are prospecting in person and the receptionist refuses to give you any information, try going around back. Often there are people there loading and unloading, on breaks, or walking to their cars.

If you approach them in a transparent, nonaggressive way, sometimes they will give you information or even walk you in to meet the decision maker. Note: Do not try this if there are security guards or other measures present with the express objective of keeping unauthorized people, like you, out.

Persistence Always Wins

There are always going to be decision makers and contacts who are hard to reach. Always. Very often these are conquest, strategic, and high-value prospects. The prospects that every sales rep in your industry wants to set an appointment with. The more valuable the business opportunity, the more likely that the prospect will be walled in by gatekeepers.

These prospects drive you crazy. You can't seem to find the name of the right person to talk to. They don't answer the phone, are always in meetings, don't return calls, don't respond to e-mails, don't accept connection requests on LinkedIn, and never fill out lead forms.

These hard-to-reach contacts always seem impossibly elusive. Welcome to the real world. It takes hard work and a whole lot of persistence to get to some contacts and decision makers.

Just remember. In sales persistence always wins. Always.

18 | In-Person Prospecting

Nothing replaces being in the same room, face-to-face.

—Peter Guber

Kelly is a rental uninform services sales representative. His primary role and responsibility is selling new accounts. He is the top rep in his region and has been awarded a president's club trip each of the last six consecutive years. According to his sales manager, what sets Kelly apart from his peers is relentless prospecting.

Each day Kelly invests an hour prospecting by phone; his goal is to set two to three appointments with qualified prospects. Once Kelly has his appointments set, he researches his database for three to five additional prospects that are nearby each those preset appointments. Then, using the mapping tool embedded in his CRM, he creates an efficient route to each of the prospects in relation to the preset appointment.

Finally, he does a little research on each of these prospects to gain an understanding of what they do and remind himself of previous conversations. He also uses the social channel (usually LinkedIn) to gather information on and download pictures of the key players at the location. This research helps him develop and refine his approach before calling on these prospects in person— before or after his preset appointment.

Since most of his prospects are located in industrial parks or close to other businesses, he also leverages a technique called a T-Call. When he goes to his preset appointments and planned in-person prospecting calls, he makes a T by looking to the right, to the left, and behind him for other opportunities, newly opened businesses, or businesses that are not currently in his database. He walks into those doors as well.

This strategy of mapping his in-person prospecting (IPP) calls around his appointments and leveraging T-Calls maximizes his day. He's able to go to high-value planned appointments while making 10 to 20 face-to-face prospecting touches.

He says he is able to convert about 30 percent of his IPPs into future appointments, gets information on most of them that allows him to update his database, and once or twice a week he meets a decision maker who is ready to sit down immediately and begin a sales conversation.

Kelly told me he also uses IPPs to move past gatekeepers who block him on the phone. "Many times when I go in face to face I can either appeal directly to the gatekeeper to give me a chance or walk in the back door and act like I'm lost. It's harder for them to turn me away when I'm there in person."

Limited Application of the In-Person Prospecting Call

In-person prospecting is part of a balanced prospecting approach for outside sales reps. It works best for residential and B2B reps who work in a local territory and sell transactional to semicomplex products and services primarily to small and medium-sized businesses where it is easy to walk in without bumping into a wall of security.

I've leveraged IPP calls at large plants and companies, but primarily for information gathering by pumping the security guards or gatekeepers for information about decision makers and my competitors.

Of all the prospecting channels, in-person prospecting is the least efficient. Driving around in a car knocking on doors takes a ton of time. Done incorrectly and randomly (the way far too many outside sales reps do it), you can burn an entire day, make very few calls, and accomplish little more than wasting gas. On the scale of hot to cold, they're mostly cold.

This is why the IPP call should only be used to supplement and complement the other forms of prospecting. With the exception of T-Calls and when driving by a new business in your territory you've never seen before, they should be planned in advance. Yet, there are scores of outside salespeople for whom in-person prospecting is their primary and sometimes only prospecting channel. This is mostly due to:

- A false belief that driving around in their territory aimlessly is somehow working
- Managers who believe that the only good salesperson is a salesperson they can't see
- And, the most common, a fear or inability to use the phone— justified with "I'm just better in person"

When I confront salespeople who justify not using the phone with how they are "so much better in person," I ask this question:

"It is the middle of winter and snowing or the middle of summer and blazing hot and humid. You get started in the morning doing IPPs. Being honest, how many calls do you think you'll make?"

The truthful answer is somewhere between 10 and 20 before they would give up and go home for the day.

Then I ask: "If I give you a printed list of prospects, how many teleprospecting calls could you make to those same businesses in an hour?"

The truthful answer is usually somewhere between 25 and 50.

This usually gets their attention long enough for me to show them how to leverage IPPs within a balanced prospecting routine to maximize and get the most out of their sales day. To be both efficient and effective.

The Five-Step Hub-and-Spoke Technique

Kasey sells supplies to restaurants. Because competition in her segment is so fierce, maintaining relationships with her accounts is critical to driving repeat purchases. Each day, she is required to visit at least four existing accounts in person.

Like Kelly, from the previous story, once Kasey sets the appointments to visit her existing accounts, she uses the CRM to identify prospects close to those appointments and maps out a route that allows her to call on those prospects in conjunction with her appointment as efficiently as possible.

She typically maps out three to five calls around each appointment, which gives her 15 to 20 in-person prospecting touches a day with new opportunities. She is also able to leverage her existing relationships in the "neighborhood" to convince new prospects to give her a chance.

Casey explained, "Before I started using the hub-and-spoke process I was all over the board. I'd just drive around with no plan. I spent way too much time in my car looking for the 'perfect' prospect to call on rather than systematically working my territory."

The hub-and-spoke process has helped her open more new accounts than any account manager in her company.

The Five-Step Hub-and-Spoke System for IPPs:

1. Plan IPPs around preset appointments. Start with appointments you set during your phone block.

2. Leveraging your CRM, develop a list of prospects close by. A zip code search is often the best means to do this.
3. Plot three to five prospects on a map around your preset appointments.
4. Develop the most efficient driving route to call on these planned IPPs with the least amount of windshield time.
5. Give yourself time between appointments—before or after—to call on these prospects face to face. Don't stop until you reach your goal.

Leveraged effectively, IPPs will help you squeeze every drop of opportunity out of your sales day.

Preparing for Effective In-Person Prospecting

Develop your objective for each call in advance and then, if possible, personalize your approach to each prospect. This is accomplished through preplanning. The key objectives of in-person prospecting include:

- *Qualifying:* In many cases, people will give you more information in person than they will over the phone. Plus, you get to look around to see where your product or service will help them and gain insight on your competitor.
- *Making appointments:* If you've got the right person in front of you, but the timing isn't right for a sales conversation, set an appointment to come back.
- *Sales conversations:* You are there, the decision maker is there, and a problem or need exists. Sometimes your timing is perfect and an IPP turns into a full-fledged sales call. Be prepared to close.
- *Building familiarity:* By putting a face with a name with both gatekeepers and decision makers, it becomes easier to get an audience in the future when the buying window opens.
- *Maximizing your sales day:* The biggest benefit of in-person prospecting is you get the most out of your sales day by

     reducing windshield time and increasing the number of pros-
     pecting calls you can make.
- *Learning your territory:* IPPs help you learn, know, and own your
     territory.

The primary objective of the IPP is to gather qualifying information. You will use this information to further develop your database and create targeted lists for your phone, e-mail, and social prospecting blocks.

In the best-case scenario, you'll start the conversation right on the spot if the opportunity to potentially close a deal exists.

This past summer I was riding with Carl, a business services sales rep. We'd just walked out of a scheduled appointment and he decided to call on the other four businesses that were in the same industrial park (T-Calls).

The first two calls were quick. We gathered some basic information about the decision makers and the competition.

On the third call, the owner of the business overheard Carl speaking with the receptionist and came out of his office. He shook our hands and explained how he had just fired the rep's competitor and was happy that we had come by. He ushered us back to his office and started tossing out questions. He wanted to see a presentation.

If he'd had a neon sign over his desk that said "Close Me," the buying signals could not have been stronger. Unfortunately, Carl was not prepared to close. In an awkward moment, he had to explain that he didn't have the material needed to make the presentation.

Carl asked to come back later, but the gentleman said he was leaving for a conference and then would be out on vacation. He said, "Just call me in a couple of weeks and we'll get things set up then."

But when Carl called two weeks later, the business owner broke the news that he'd signed a contract with another company that had beaten Carl to the punch.

When you walk through your prospect's door, you've got to be ready. Have an objective for each call, pump yourself up so you walk and talk with confidence and enthusiasm, and carry everything in that you will need to close the sale in the event that your timing is right.

I realize that it is a pain to haul your sales material in on each call—especially when you know that the chance of closing a deal is small. What you can never forget, though, is sometimes you only get one chance with a prospect. Make sure when that happens you are ready.

There are five steps to planning for effective IPPs:

1. *Research.* With planned IPPs, do your research in advance to get decision-maker name(s), learn about the history of their business, visit their website, look for recent press releases, and review your CRM for notes and other insights. For T-Calls, grab your smartphone and do a quick scan of their website and social media sites to pick up any information that may help you ask better questions and refine your approach.

2. *Personalize your approach.* Personalize your approach to make it unique to each prospect. Develop relevant questions about their business, compliment them on recent accomplishments, or offer insights you have that may help them solve a particular problem. It is also a good idea to leverage the relationships you have with nearby customers to gain instant credibility: "We've been doing business with Billy next door for five years and he loves our service."

3. *Develop an objective for every call.* Before you walk into your prospect's door, make sure you have clearly defined what you want to accomplish.

4. *Be prepared to close.* Be ready! Make sure you have everything you need to close the deal with you—sale sheets, order forms, contracts, presentation material, and so on.

5. *Log calls, notes, and set follow-up tasks in your CRM.* It does you absolutely no good to go on IPPs and gather information if you don't log the information in your CRM and set follow-up tasks for additional research and callbacks. Take the time to log each IPP and enter copious notes before the close of each day. If you have time, do it on the spot.

Figure 18.1   Planning Effective IPPs

The Five-Step In-Person Prospecting Call Process

The in-person call process is similar to the five-step telephone prospecting framework. The main difference between the in-person framework and the phone process is the IPP will move along at a slower pace and there will typically be more dialogue.

1. *Approach with confidence.* As we've discussed in previous chapters, there is no substitute for enthusiasm and confidence. These are the two emotions that sell. You must approach IPPs with absolute confidence. Be bold—even if you have to fake it. I've found that there are two keys to confidence:
   - *Expect to win.* Walk in like you own the place and ask direct questions that help you gather information and get in front of decision makers.
   - *Plan questions in advance.* The research you do in advance helps you plan the questions you want to ask about problems, issues, decision makers, and competitors. Having a plan gives you an extra boost of confidence as you walk in the door.
2. *Identify yourself and say why you are there.* Don't beat around the bush, don't hesitate, and never use cheesy lines designed to trick gatekeepers. You are a professional, so be straightforward

and transparent about your purpose for being there. For example:

- "Hi, my name is Jeb Blount, I'm with XYX Company. The reason I'm here is ABC Company next door is one of my customers and they said I should stop in and introduce myself to your owner, Mary."

- "Hi, my name is Jeb Blount, I'm with XYX Company. The reason I stopped by is I provide my service to several of the businesses in this industrial park and I wanted to learn more about your company and situation to see whether or not working with you might be a good fit."

- "Hi, my name is Jeb Blount, I'm with XYX Company. The reason I stopped by is to speak to Jerry Richards. I've been following your Facebook page and noticed that you are doing regular promotions. We have a tool that can help you improve the impact of those promos and generate more leads. I want to ask Jerry a few questions to see if our solution might be a fit."

3. *Gather information.* Engage in a conversation rather than an interrogation. Eighty percent of human communication is visual. IPPs are powerful because unlike most other prospecting channels, you use all of your senses to communicate. You'll be most effective when you relax, are yourself, ask open-ended questions that encourage others to talk, listen, and engage in meaningful conversations.

Avoid the temptation to pitch. You will quickly lose the attention of your prospect if you begin talking about you, your company, your product, or your service. As soon as you start pitching, your ears turn off and so does your prospect.

Sales trainer Kelly Robertson says, "It may sound simple, but most sales people don't get it. They still believe that selling means talking at great length about their company, their product, or their service. However, truly effective salespeople understand that it is all about asking the prospect the right questions and demonstrating that you can help them solve a particular problem or issue. That means you need to direct *all* of your attention on their situation and resist the opportunity to talk about your company or your offering."[1]

Consider what it feels like to be on the other end of a conversation where someone is just talking about themselves. It's boring. As soon as you start pitching, you look and sound just like every other salesperson who walks through your prospect's door. Your prospect can tell that you care about nothing other than getting what you want, and that is why they zone out, make you feel uncomfortable, and put up emotional walls.

However, when you get them talking about themselves, show interest, give them your complete attention, and listen, they will engage, give you information, and look for ways to help you.

Before every IPP call, make the conscious decision to focus your attention on your prospect. Tell yourself to listen instead of pitch. Make a commitment to slow down and ask questions, really listen to the answers, and ask relevant follow-up questions.

4. *Ask for what you want.* If you don't ask, you won't get. Decide what you want to ask for before you walk in the door, and be prepared to bridge to something else—like closing the deal—if the opportunity presents itself.

5. *Turn around objections.* Because you are interrupting, you're going to get RBOs. Develop and prepare turnarounds in advance. Review the previous chapter on turning around RBOs for techniques that will help you get past objections and into sales conversations.

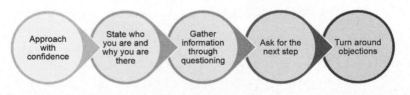

Approach with confidence — State who you are and why you are there — Gather information through questioning — Ask for the next step — Turn around objections

Figure 18.2   5-Step IPP Framework

Put Your Sales Goggles On

Madison left her appointment with Dr. Roberts, walked straight to her car (with me following), got in, and drove away. "What about all of the other doctors in that complex? Why didn't we call on those too?" I asked.

Sales reps like Madison walk out of appointments and right past what might be their next sale without blinking an eye. They usually mumble something about not having enough time or lunch or some other lame excuse. But the real truth is they are oblivious. They are myopic and blind to the opportunities that are often right next door to their prospect.

That's why you've got to put on your "sales goggles" so you can see these opportunities. This is how fanatical prospectors do it. They train themselves to be acutely aware of the opportunities around them. They are always on—looking around every corner, behind every bush, and in every window for their next prospect.

Look to the left, the right, and behind you every time you go into or come out of an appointment, and make it a point to walk through those doors and gather information.

Likewise, remain aware as you drive from place to place in your territory. New prospects and opportunities are everywhere. When you see a new business, new construction, or a company you've never noticed before, put your sales foot on the sales brake, get out of your sales car, and walk through the door.

Look for the names of businesses on delivery trucks and signs. If the trucks are parked, stop and quiz the drivers. You'll be amazed at how much information they will give you about the business, decision makers, buying windows, and your competitors.

Personally, I make it a practice to speak to every person I meet who is wearing a uniform or logoed shirt with the name of their company on it. I ask them about their company and who makes decisions there. They can almost always tell me who the decision makers are at their company and often know where my competitor is failing. I also talk to the person next to me when I'm waiting in line, sitting in waiting rooms, on trains, buses, and airplanes. Over the past five years, I've generated more than a half-million dollars in business from these conversations.

Keep your eye out for business cards pinned to gas station and restaurant bulletin boards. When I see cards that match my sales vertical, I grab them, call them, qualify, and add the information to my database.

If you don't have time to stop and walk into a business or chat up a delivery driver, use that amazing tool in your pocket called a smartphone. When you are driving down the road and you see the name of a potential prospect on a sign or truck, just record a voice memo or note to yourself. Use your camera to take pictures of signs, new business locations, and the sides of trucks. When you get back to the office, do a little bit of research, create a prospecting list, and reach out to qualify or set an appointment.

Remain alert for businesses and people that are using a product or service similar to yours. Recently when working with a group of mobile device sales reps, I asked the question:

"How many of you notice people using mobile phones in public?"

All the hands went up.

"How many of you notice people using outdated phones or phones with cracked and damaged screens?"

All the hands went up.

"How many of you think that most of these people would like an upgrade to the newest equipment or a phone screen that doesn't look like a kaleidoscope and cut their fingertips?"

Most hands went up.

"How many of you hand those people your business card and let them know that you can get them a new phone for little or no cost?"

Not a single hand went up.

Final point: Awareness without action is useless. Be fanatical. Put on the sales brake, walk up to people, ask questions, and hand them your business card. Sure, some people might get irritated, but most people will help you, talk to you, and give you a chance.

19 | E-Mail Prospecting

Your e-mail inbox is a bit like a Las Vegas roulette machine. You know, you just check it and check it, and every once in a while there's some juicy little tidbit of reward, like the three quarters that pop down on a one-armed bandit. And that keeps you coming back for more.
—Douglas Rushkoff

E-mail is a powerful part of a balanced prospecting approach, and when leveraged intelligently it opens doors, gets results, and generates far more engagement and response than social prospecting. When I say far more, I mean 10 to 20 times more.

It also has the added benefit of extending your prospecting window, which makes you more efficient. With the many e-mail communication tools that are available, including Yesware, Signals, Tout, Tellwise, and your own CRM, you can create e-mails outside of the Golden Hours and schedule them to go out during prime selling time while you are on the phone or face to face with prospects and customers.

The data these tools provide also make your e-mail prospecting efforts more effective because you can test and measure response rates. This helps you hone and perfect your message. Once you have a message that you know works for a particular market vertical or group of similar prospects, you can send it out with minimal effort.

It's also easier than ever to build a database of e-mail addresses. Besides just asking for them, you can grab e-mail address through Google searches, social media, scraping programs line eGrabber's E-Mail Prospector, various apps and browser plugins, and tools like Toofr and Prospect Ace that help you make educated guesses on e-mail addresses for prospects when you don't have them.

E-mail has also moved beyond the traditional inbox and into the social channel. The LinkedIn inbox, Facebook Messenger, and direct messaging on Twitter are often used as proxies, supplements, or complete replacements for traditional e-mail. The benefits of the social channel include skipping past gatekeepers, the spam box, and the ability to send mail to prospects even if you don't know their e-mail address.

The downside of e-mail in all forms is if you irritate your prospect by sending them spam-laden crap, they'll block or unfriend you in a heartbeat. The rules and techniques in this chapter apply to both traditional and social e-mail prospecting. E-mail done wrong wastes your time, makes you look like a chump, and exasperates your prospects.

My goal with this chapter is to give you a set of tools, techniques, and formulas that will instantly make your prospecting e-mails more impactful and generate better results. These techniques are just a snapshot of the available information on e-mail prospecting.

There is simply no way to include everything in this short chapter. However, you'll find a comprehensive list of tutorials, e-books, podcasts, videos, resources, tools, and articles on e-mail prospecting techniques at FanaticalProspecting.com.

The Three Cardinal Rules of E-Mail Prospecting

Effective e-mail prospecting requires thoughtfulness and effort to get the message right. E-mail done right is an extremely powerful prospecting methodology that will reward you with a consistent stream of qualified prospects that keeps your pipe full.

Effective begins with adhering to the Three Cardinal Rules of E-Mail Prospecting.

Rule #1: Your E-Mail Must Get Delivered

This means that your e-mail must make it into your prospect's main e-mail inbox. Most companies and individuals today have filters set to either block or move "spam" e-mails to a junk folder. In some cases, entire IP addresses may be blacklisted when too much e-mail that is considered spam emanates from that server or address.

There is no perfect science to staying completely clear of spam filters. However, there are things you can do to increase the probability that your e-mail will get delivered. This is not a comprehensive list—rather, it's a list of the most obvious and important tactics.

- *Don't send bulk e-mail.* Prospecting e-mail is one to one. It is one e-mail from your address sent to one individual, one e-mail at a

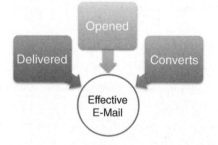

Figure 19.1   Three Cardinal Rules of E-Mail Prospecting

time. This alone should help you clear 90 percent of spam hurdles. Sending bulk e-mail (to multiple people) from your personal e-mail address is the easiest, fastest way to get black-listed, get blocked, and look like a total imbecile.

- *Avoid attaching images.* Because hackers and spammers embed malware in images, many e-mail programs mark e-mails with images as spam or block images until permission is given to download. Your best bet on prospecting e-mails is to avoid sending images.

- *Avoid hyperlinks.* The primary tool of hackers is the hyperlink. You click on it and the hacker inserts malware on your computer and steals your information. Because of this, people are super suspicious of hyperlinks embedded in e-mails. Your best bet is to avoid hyperlinks altogether in prospecting e-mails because they also trigger spam filters. If you do include a link:
  - Avoid embedding the URL in text.
  - Include the entire URL for complete transparency.
  - Avoid shortened URLs that obscure the website address.
  - Limit the total number of URLs to one—including any links in your e-mail signature.

- *Avoid attachments.* Hackers have become adept at using attachments to infect computers with malware, hack websites, and infiltrate networks. Because of this danger, spam filters may grab your e-mail if it contains attachments. Your best bet is to avoid sending attachments in prospecting e-mails.

- *Skip spammy words and phrases.* What you say and how you say it can trigger spam filters. For example, using ALL CAPS in a subject line, adding lots of exclamation points, or using words like *free* or "special buy now!" can light up spam filters like a Christmas tree.

  Kevin Gao, CEO and founder of Comm100, lists 200 words and phrases that he says trigger spam filters when placed in e-mail subject lines, including *amazing, free access, cash, don't delete, do it today, increase sales, 100 percent guaranteed,* and *save $.*[1] The point is, you must be careful and thoughtful about the words and symbols you use and how you phrase those words—especially in your e-mail subject line. The best thing to do is step into the spammer's shoes—look at the annoying spam you get and then do the opposite.

- *Don't send to many people in the same company at one time.* Spam filters look to see how many messages you're sending at a time. This is primarily designed to catch bulk e-mailers who are sending to large lists. However, if you are sending e-mail to multiple prospects in the same company, it pays to drip these e-mails in at different times of the day rather than sending them all at once.
- *Don't send too many e-mails to the same person.* This may seem counterintuitive, but with e-mail, too much persistence can hurt you. If you become annoying, the recipient of your e-mail can mark it as spam. That may impact more than just their individual inbox; with some systems, this may get you black-listed across the entire enterprise.
- *Scrub bounces.* Many e-mail filters will catch you if you send multiple e-mails to an e-mail address that doesn't exist. This usually happens when the person you are trying to contact no longer works at the company or you have a bad e-mail address. When you get a bounce, view it as an opportunity to gather better information.

    First, update the contact in your CRM and remove the e-mail address so you won't mistakenly send to that address again. Next, check LinkedIn or do a Google search to find out if that contact is still at the company. If not, remove the contact from your CRM or update their record to reflect their new company. If yes, get to work by phone or online finding an accurate e-mail address.
- *Be careful with sensitive industries.* Use extra caution when contacting sensitive industries like financial institutions, defense contractors, and health care. Hackers are relentlessly trying to get into these organizations to steal data, and as a result, there are strict firewalls in place. I recommend using text only with no links, attachments, or images.

Rule #2: Your E-Mail Must Get Opened

Here's a fact of life: According to the *Harvard Business Review*, the average business executive gets 200-plus e-mails a day.[2] Add to that the mail they get in their social media inboxes, instant messages, and the chatter on crowdsourcing tools deployed by many companies, and there is simply no way they can possibly get to it all.

So your prospects cope with being crazy busy and overwhelmed by an inbox that is set to "infinite refill" the same way you do: scan and triage.

They, like you, must make instant, split-second decisions to open, delete, or save for later.

In this paradigm, to get opened, your prospecting e-mail must stand out from all of the noise and be compelling enough to entice a click.

Familiarity Gets Your E-Mail Opened

One way to stand out is familiarity.

Imagine that you are scanning your inbox. An e-mail from a person you recognize catches your eye. What is the your most probable next action?

The Law of Familiarity is always in play with e-mail prospecting. The more familiar your prospect is with your name, brand, or company, the more likely they are to open your e-mail. This is why leveraging the phone and social channels prior to sending an e-mail can increase the chances of getting your e-mails opened. For example, you might call and leave a voice mail, ping them on LinkedIn, and follow that up with an e-mail (or vice versa). This "triple threat" increases familiarity and leverages your persistence across multiple channels.

The layering of channels to build familiarity is extremely powerful. If you leave an effective voice mail and they hear your name and company name, then when they see your name and e-mail address in their inbox you will be more familiar.

If you connect with them on a social channel and like, share, or positively comment on something that they have posted, this

increases the probability that your e-mail will get more than a
cursory glance when it hits your prospect's inbox.

If you meet them in person at a trade show or networking
event and leave a positive impression, then connect with them on
LinkedIn, follow that up with a voice mail, and then send an
e-mail, the probability that your e-mail will get opened improves
exponentially.

Layering prospecting channels to open doors should be focused,
targeted, intentional, and strategic. You need to plan your touches
across the various decision makers and influencers to improve e-mail
open rates without becoming annoying.

Your Subject Line Must Scream "Open Me"

The subject line, however, depending on the level of familiarity
your prospect has with you, can be the most important key to
getting your e-mail opened. Sadly, though, most prospecting e-mail
subject lines neither stand out nor are compelling. Most, in fact,
scream "Delete me!"

The three most common subject line mistakes:

- *They're too long.* Data from many sources across the sales
  ecosystem prove that shorter subject lines outperform longer
  subject lines by wide margins. Frankly, it's intuitive. A long
  subject line requires your prospect's brain to work harder. That
  extra effort in the context of split-second decisions about the
  value of an e-mail gets you deleted.

    Neither do long subject lines play well on mobile. It's
  estimated that 50 percent or more of e-mails get opened on a
  mobile device. With the limited screen size, you get but a
  glimpse of the e-mail subject line. If you think about your own
  behavior on your mobile phone, you are even quicker to delete
  a message there. More than 50 characters in your subject line
  and the open rate goes down exponentially.

Solution: Keep e-mail prospecting subject lines super short—three to six words or 40 to 50 characters including spaces. Remember—less is more.

■ *They include questions.* E-mail prospecting subject lines in the form of questions are delete bait. Virtually every major study conducted on the efficacy of different types of e-mail subject lines conclude that subject lines in the form of a question quickly doom your e-mail to the delete-button death-roll. Though there may be a time and place for using a question in your e-mail subject line, in most cases you should step away from the question mark.

Solution: Use action words and directive statements instead of questions. List-based subject lines that include a testimonial like "3 Reasons Why ABC Chose Us" are especially powerful, as are referral subject lines like "Jeb Blount Said We Should Talk" and statement-based subject lines like "Biggest Fail in Industrial Pumps."

■ *They're impersonal or boring.* Generic, impersonal subject lines are boring. When you are attempting to engage hard-to-reach executives, a failure to connect will send you straight to the trash. Think about it. Every salesperson in your industry is trying to connect with the highest-value prospects in your market. These executives are inundated with requests for appointments. You will never break through this noise and get their attention with cheesy, impersonal subject lines. Instead of standing out, you'll look like all of the other schmucks junking up your prospect's inbox and wasting their time.

Solution: Connect your subject line to an issue your prospect is facing—especially if it is emotional or stressful— or compliment them on a recent accomplishment or something that you know makes them feel proud. For example, the easiest, fastest way to get me to open your e-mail is a subject line that reads: "Loved Your Book!"

You can also use relevant humor or tongue-in-cheek phrases to catch your prospect's attention when appropriate. One of the participants in a recent e-mail prospecting workshop created the subject line "Keep Those Kegs Rolling" for an e-mail he crafted to send to a beer distributor. It was relevant, connected with his message, and was sure to catch the eye of his recipient.

We are all self-centered and almost always focused on our own problems, issues, accomplishments, and ego. The fact is, 95 percent of the time we are thinking about ourselves and the 5 percent of time that we are not thinking about ourselves, something—maybe a mouthy salesperson—has gotten in the way of us thinking about ourselves.

So, play the odds, and make your subject line about your prospect. It's really easy to do if you take a little extra time to research the recipient of your prospecting e-mail through an Internet search, company website, and social media sites.

No One-Size-Fits-All Solution

The brutal reality, though, is there is no secret formula for creating the perfect e-mail subject line every time. What works in one situation may not work in another. Advice that works in one industry vertical may not be applicable within your industry or prospect base. This is why experimentation and testing are the real secrets to success with subject lines.

Testing helps you zero in on which subject lines get the most opens. With this data in hand, you'll often find patterns that lead to subject lines that work phenomenally well with certain prospect groups, job titles, geographic areas, and business problems.

Yet most salespeople don't test. Instead, they create subject lines on the fly and then send their e-mails into a black hole, hoping that they'll get a response. It's an incredibly frustrating way to prospect because it's like throwing darts at a target while blindfolded and hoping you hit a bull's-eye, without any feedback to let you know if your aim is true.

There are fantastic tools available today that make testing e-mail response rates unbelievably easy and affordable. Sales e-mail prospecting, automation, and intelligence services like Yesware, Tellwise, Tout, and Signals give you instant insight into what happens with your prospecting e-mail after you push "send."

With this information, you'll be able to narrow down and home in on the words and phrases that get the best response, and your e-mails will stand out and get opened while those your competitor sends are relegated to the "delete" folder.

Rule #3: Your E-Mail Must Convert

Unless you are sending pure spam—generic e-mail templates that are copied and pasted, then sent randomly to a large swath of prospects regardless of relevance and with no research—developing and crafting prospecting e-mails takes a significant investment of time.

With conquest prospects, C-level contacts, and strategic campaigns, you will need to personalize each e-mail message. Thought and effort will be required to craft a relevant e-mail that connects with the recipient emotionally and moves them to take action.

This doesn't mean that every e-mail you send must be built from scratch. Certainly within specific industry verticals, markets, and decision-maker roles, there will be enough common ground and patterns that you'll be able to develop templates that can be mass customized. These customizable templates allow you to deliver more prospecting e-mail touches in a shorter period of time.

Even with a customizable template, though, to be effective, you must do research so the e-mail looks and feels unique to the recipient. It will fall on deaf ears if the recipient doesn't feel that the message was crafted specifically for them.

This investment of your precious and limited time is why it is imperative that your prospecting e-mails convert. In other words, generate a response that leads to your desired outcome:

- An appointment
- Qualifying information

- An introduction to a decision maker
- A forward to other influencers
- Download of documents, a video view, or a webinar registration
- A sales conversation

If your e-mail doesn't compel the recipient to take action, your time and effort were wasted. This is why investing the time to get your message right is critical.

A Good Prospecting E-Mail Begins with a Great Plan

A plan helps you define who will be getting your e-mail, the method or technique you will use to get their attention, the message

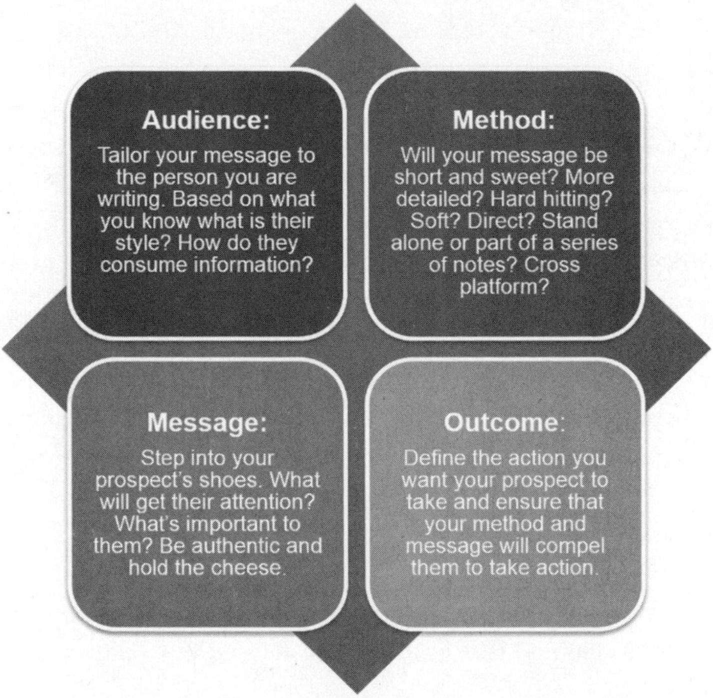

Audience:
Tailor your message to the person you are writing. Based on what you know what is their style? How do they consume information?

Method:
Will your message be short and sweet? More detailed? Hard hitting? Soft? Direct? Stand alone or part of a series of notes? Cross platform?

Message:
Step into your prospect's shoes. What will get their attention? What's important to them? Be authentic and hold the cheese.

Outcome:
Define the action you want your prospect to take and ensure that your method and message will compel them to take action.

Figure 19.2   Audience Method Message Outcome

you will craft to connect with them and compel them to take action, and finally, the action you want the recipient to take. With e-mail prospecting, this is your AMMO.

You don't have to look far to see that planning is rare when it comes to prospecting e-mails. The vast majority of prospecting e-mails are awful. We've cataloged enough examples to last a lifetime in the "E-mail Hall of Shame" at FanaticalProspecting .com.

Because I am a business owner and decision maker, I get blasted by prospecting e-mails from every direction—on my work e-mail, LinkedIn, Twitter, and Facebook. I receive dozens each week that are laughable and an embarrassment to the person who sent it and the company that allowed the e-mail to hit my inbox.

I'm baffled at how often the salespeople who took the time to send an e-mail to me did no research. I received an InMail last week on LinkedIn from a rep at a large sales training company pitching me on sales training. Seriously, a 20-second review of my LinkedIn profile would have saved this rep the bother. But what does that say about the brand he is selling for? This guy is pitching me on the awesome sales training his firm delivers and demonstrating the worst of sales behaviors.

Bad e-mails destroy your brand equity, credibility, and image. It stuns me that so many companies allow their salespeople to disseminate this crap. Worse, the majority of sales organizations spend no time teaching their salespeople how to write effective prospecting e-mails.

The worst e-mails are:

- Long, important-sounding pitches using incomprehensible jargon—a lot of words with no meaning
- Feature-focused product dumps
- Cheerleaders who blab on and on about their "amazing" company, product, or service
- The ones that get my name wrong—seriously, it is Jeb: three letters

- The long ones that cause eyes to glaze over. WTF, we live in the age of Twitter, text messaging, infographics, OMGs, and LOLs. Prospects have the attention span of mosquitos.

I delete 99.9 percent of them.

Every once in a while, though, I'll get a brilliant e-mail that makes me stop in my tracks. This golden e-mail connects with me, makes sense, is relevant, and compels me to respond. The sender took time to research and plan.

Consider your audience. Prospects are people—not robots—so your prospecting e-mail should be authentic and personal. It should connect emotionally. Consider who you are writing to:
- What is their role?
- What do you know about their style?
- How do they consume information?
- When do they consume information?
- How familiar are they with you?

These questions help you match the tone, structure, and formality to the person to whom you are writing so that it connects. The emotional connection is vital because your e-mail will only be effective if it causes your prospect to take an intended action.

Determine your method. E-mail prospecting methods cross the spectrum from a single, standalone e-mail to a multi–e-mail, multi-message strategic prospecting campaign. The method you choose will impact your message and should be driven by your intended audience and defined outcome. Will your message be:
- Short and sweet?
- More detailed?
- Hard hitting?
- Soft?
- Direct?
- Standalone?
- Part of an SPC campaign?
- Nurturing or action oriented?
- Cross-platform?

This is where planning and strategy are crucial—especially with conquest prospects. You want to avoid being random with your most important opportunities.

Tailor the message to your audience. The message you craft must be strong enough to compel your prospect to take action. Your prospect wants to know that you get them and their problems, so your message must be relevant to their situation. The most effective way to tailor your message to the person you are writing is to step into their shoes and ask some basic questions:

- What will get their attention?
- What's important to them?
- What will cause them to give you what you are asking for?

The key here is taking time to do some basic research to get to know your prospect and using that information as the foundation on which you construct your message.

Define your desired outcome. If you don't know what you want, you won't get what you want. If you fail to clearly define what you are asking your prospect to do or provide, they will be confused and your e-mail won't convert.

The Four Elements of an Effective Prospecting E-Mail

The AMMO framework assists you in planning and developing your strategy. Once you have your plan in place, you'll use a four-step framework to craft your e-mail:

1. *Hook:* Get their attention with a compelling subject line and opening sentence/statement.
2. *Relate:* Demonstrate that you get them and their problem. Show empathy and authenticity.
3. *Bridge:* Connect the dots between their problem and how you can help them. Explain the WIIFM.
4. *Ask:* Be clear and straightforward about the action you want them to take, and make it easy for them to do so.

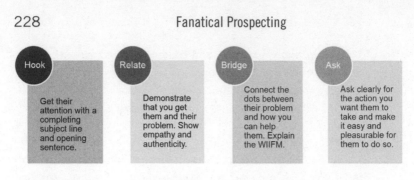

Figure 19.3   Four Elements of an Effective E-mail

Here is an example of an e-mail to a COO of a bank. It leverages the four-step framework:

Subject: COO—The Toughest Job in the Bank

Lawrence,

Ernst & Young recently reported that the COO has the toughest role in the C-suite. The COOs I work with tell me that the increasing complexity of the banking environment has made their job harder and more stressful than ever.

My team and I help COOs like you reduce complexity and stress with strategies to optimize growth and profit, mitigate credit risk, allocate resources effectively, and minimize regulatory surprises.

While I don't know if we are a good fit for your bank, why don't we schedule a short call to help me learn more about your unique challenges? From there we can decide if it makes sense to set up a deeper conversation.

How about next Thursday at 3:00 PM?

Dave Adair
Senior Account Executive
JunoSystems

Let's break this down into each of the four parts.

Hook

You have about three seconds to grab your prospect's attention—hook them. In that three seconds, your subject line must compel them to open the e-mail and the first sentence must entice them to keep reading. Kendra Lee, author of *The Sales Magnet*, calls this the "glimpse factor."

Prospects choose to read your e-mail for their reasons, not yours—their unique situation and interests. Therefore, the best way to hook them is to make your subject line relevant and the opening sentence about them.

Here is an example of a subject line and opening sentence that bombed—real e-mail sent to me from a guy named Brandon:

Subject: Cloud Based Software

Hi Jeb,
   I was browsing Linked-in and wanted to reach out to you.

First, the subject line is all about him, not about me. Also, never use "Hi" or "Hello" or "Dear" or any other salutation in front of your prospect's name. No one in business does that except salespeople. "Hi __" is a complete turnoff for prospects.

Next, how does the fact that you were "browsing LinkedIn" in the least bit interest me?

Finally, you "wanted" to reach out? That is past tense and all about you and nothing about me.

Let's take a look at our model e-mail:

Subject: COO—The Toughest Job in the Bank

Lawrence,
   Ernst & Young recently reported that the COO has the toughest role in the C-suite.

This e-mail is being sent to a bank COO. The subject line uses the acronym *COO* and the word *bank*. It implies that the COO has the toughest job in the bank. That is compelling because it plays on emotions. We all believe we have the toughest job in our company.

Next, we address our prospect professionally, as if he were a colleague.

Finally, the opening sentence is a great hook. Using a credible source, Ernst & Young, we hook the COO by stepping into his shoes and demonstrating that we *get* him (the toughest role in the C-suite).

Relate

Effective e-mails connect with prospects on an emotional level. The reason is simple: People make decisions based on emotion. The easiest way to connect with your prospect emotionally is to demonstrate that you get them and their problems—that you can relate to their struggles and issues.

Here's Brandon's attempt to relate:

> We build custom software solutions; web, cloud, mobile, desktop. Whether you have need to modernize outdated software, build something new from scratch, or augment your team to meet a critical deadline, I'm confident we can help.

How does this relate to me or any of my problems? Notice that this paragraph is all about him. Just a features dump. My reaction: So what?

Conversely, in our model e-mail, Dave makes the effort to relate. Of course, since he is not himself a COO, nor has ever been a COO, it would be disingenuous to say that he understands Lawrence's situation. So instead, he uses his relationships with other COOs to demonstrate that he can relate.

> The COOs I work with tell me that the increasing complexity of the banking environment has made their job harder and more stressful than ever.

Bridge

Since people do things for their reasons, not yours, you must answer their most pressing question: "If I give you what you want—my time—what's in it for me?" If you are unable to answer WIIFM with value that exceeds the cost of your prospect giving up their time, your e-mail will not convert.

This is where your research pays off. When you know a specific issue that your prospect is facing in their business, you should bridge directly to that issue and how you might be able to solve it. When you are unsure of a specific issue, bridge to issues that are common to your prospect's role, situation, or industry.

Here is our buddy Brandon's attempt at bridging to WIIFM:

> We've been able to figure out how to maintain high quality and keep our rates competitive. It's a model that has led us to three straight years on the INC 5000.

Again, so what? Everybody brags. How is this important to me? How does this add value to my unique situation? How is it relevant to me? He toots his horn but gives me no reason to waste my time with him.

Dave, on the other hand, ties his subject line, opening sentence, and relate statement together with a bridge that connects the dots between Lawrence's perceived issue—stress—and solutions that reduce stress. He answers Lawrence's WIIFM question.

Most importantly, he speaks Lawrence's language—the language of COOs: *growth, profit, risk, allocate resources, minimize surprises.* By speaking Lawrence's language, he continues to relate and demonstrate that he gets him and his problems.

> My team and I help COOs like you reduce complexity and stress with strategies to optimize growth and profit, mitigate credit risk, allocate resources effectively, and minimize regulatory surprises.

Ask

To get what you want, ask for what you want, and make it easy for your prospect to act.

Our buddy Brandon:

I'd love to schedule a time to connect and outline how we're
able to do this while discussing any projects or plans you
might have. Just let me know a time that works with your
schedule for a free consultation & quote.

Brandon does the expected. He says what he would love to do.
"I'd love to schedule a time to connect and outline how we're able
to do this [I assume deliver high-quality at low prices]." Here is what
I hear Brandon saying: "I would love to hear the sound of my own
voice as I pitch you on all of our wonderful features and tell you how
great we are. Oh, and good news for you, it's free!" Uh, no thanks.

Then he puts the burden on me to find time on my schedule
and get back to him. How does making it hard on me make sense?
Even if I wanted to meet with him, I'd probably save this until later
(see never) because I would not have time at that moment to go
through my calendar and find time for some sales guy.

Here's how Dave asks:

While I don't know if we are a good fit for your bank, why don't
we schedule a short call to help me learn more about your
unique challenges? From there we can decide if it makes
sense to set up a deeper conversation.
How about next Thursday at 3:00 PM?

Dave disrupts expectations. He tells Lawrence up front that he
might not be a good fit for his bank. That is exactly the opposite of
what Lawrence would expect of a salesperson. Unlike pitching that
pushes prospects away, disrupting expectations pulls prospects
towards you.

Then Dave continues and sends a subtle but powerful message.
He says he wants to "learn" (see *listen*). This pulls Lawrence in deeper
because everyone wants to be heard. We love to tell our story to
people who are willing to listen.

Dave caps things off with the phrase "your unique challenges." This makes Lawrence feel important because everyone believes that their situation is unique. Finally, Dave takes away the pressure by implying that the call will be short and lowers risk by saying if it doesn't make sense, "I'm not going to push things."

Then he assumptively ("How about") asks for a meeting and offers a day and time, which takes the burden off of Lawrence to make that decision.

Practice, Practice, Practice

The truth is, writing effective prospecting e-mail messages is not easy. The most difficult step is training yourself to stop thinking about your product or service and alternatively step into your prospect's shoes, relate to their situation, and learn to speak their language. Develop the habit of researching prospects and becoming aware of trigger events that are impacting them and opening up buying windows.

You will struggle at first. Everybody does. The key is practicing until effective, authentic e-mails roll off of your fingertips. The more you practice, the faster and more proficient you will become at writing prospecting e-mails that convert.

The Best Time to Send E-Mails

The million-dollar question with prospecting e-mails is, "When is the best time to send them?" Like telephone prospecting, the verdict on this is all over the board. Some experts say in the morning, some say at night, others say on Tuesday afternoons at 3:12 PM on leap years. It's mostly noise.

The best time to send a sales prospecting e-mail is when your prospect is most likely to open it and take action (convert).

For most B2B salespeople, this will be first thing in the morning to midmorning because that is when your prospects are fresh and usually handling e-mail. For B2C sales, you may need to adjust your timing to capture your prospect's attention when they are most likely to take immediate action on your request.

It is easy to test timing with e-mail intelligence tools, and the good news is you can write e-mails anytime (preferably outside of the Golden Hours) and schedule them to be sent at a time of your choosing.

Pause Before You Press "Send"

I am the typo king. I'm quite sure you may have found a few of my mistakes while reading this book. So I end this chapter with humble advice from a man who has made the terrible mistake of not pausing before pushing "send" and launching a typo-, spelling-, and grammatical-error-laden e-mail to a prospect. It is a lesson you want to avoid learning the hard way.

Proof your prospecting e-mail before you send it. Read it once. Read it twice. Step away from it for 10 minutes and read it again (you'll be amazed at what you catch using this process). Print the really important e-mails and proof the hard copy.

Your e-mail is a reflection of you, your professionalism, and your personal brand. Pause before you push "send" to ensure that the impression you make is positive.

20 | Text Messaging

Sometimes I text the "wrong" person . . . on purpose. Just to start a conversation.

—Frank Warren

Here's a fun game to play at your next gathering of friends and family. Ask them how they feel about salespeople using text messages for prospecting. Then sit back and watch the fireworks. You'll likely start a heated, expletive-laden argument. My wife, for example, upon learning that I was writing a chapter on text message prospecting, said (in a holier-than-thou tone), "I can't believe you are teaching salespeople to do that—you are pure evil!"

That sentiment correlates to the reception I get when opening up discussions on texting as a prospecting tool. It's the third rail of sales prospecting and a concept that I approach lightly. The mere mentioning of text as a prospecting tool causes negative reactions, from "I don't think that will work for our prospect base" to pure revulsion.

I get it, because it makes sense. We can all relate. We don't want our text message inbox to be filled with texts from salespeople, either.

This is due to a weird irony. Text messaging as a communication channel is impersonal because it lacks the emotional connectivity of face-to-face and verbal communication, yet it feels extremely personal. Text has become the go-to medium for communication with family, friends, and coworkers and a haven on our phones that is typically not touched by spam or outside influence. The people we text with are most often people we know—even when it is business.

This is one of the key reasons that a study commissioned by Lead360 concluded "for the same reasons that text messages can be a more effective way to communicate with sales prospects, they also have the potential to be interpreted as intrusive or in violation of one's personal domain when used for business purposes."

The fact that texting is so personal makes it an extremely powerful channel for getting the attention of prospects. Because it is so personal, though, timing and technique become more important than any other prospecting channel.

Texting as a Business Tool Is Accelerating

What makes text messaging an increasingly valuable prospecting channel is the inevitable and total integration of mobile phones as the primary communication device in our lives.

My entire staff at Sales Gravy's offices is connected to a Voice over Internet Protocol (VoIP) hub that distributes our calls to our mobile devices no matter where we are in the world. There are no traditional handsets at our desks. That VOIP system also integrates with our CRM and allows us to easily send and receive text messages to and from our prospects via desktop and mobile apps.

We are not alone. Small and midsized businesses across the globe are adopting these systems because they are inexpensive and make it easy to integrate all forms of communication in one cloud-based communications center.

Large companies are also jumping onto the bandwagon, moving toward desktop and app-based phone systems that make it easier to use text as an integrated part of a complete communication system. Bring-your-own-device programs also allow employees to use their own phones for business calls, e-mail, and text messages.

Familiarity Is Everything with Text

We talk to strangers on the phone, e-mail strangers, and meet strangers in person, but we rarely text strangers. This is why, more than with any other prospecting channel, familiarity is critical for prospecting via text. The probability of your text message converting—compelling your prospect to take action—increases exponentially if your text comes after contact through another channel.

This is not to say that you shouldn't take a gambit on a text message to a hard-to-reach prospect when all other means have been exhausted and the buying window is rapidly closing. When you have nothing to lose, the chance of causing offense is worth the risk. However, using text messaging in these circumstances or when the person does not know you is a low-probability play.

One of the key reasons why text messages work is that most people feel compelled to read and/or respond to them immediately. This is why familiarity plays an important role in getting prospects to respond to your text messages (and not report you as spam).

Text messaging works best as an integrated part of a larger prospecting system and strategy rather than a standalone channel. According to the Lead360 study[1] that covered 3.5 million lead records from more than 400 companies, a text message sent alone converts at 4.8 percent. That same message, sent after a phone contact, increases conversion by 112.6 percent. Why? The Law of Familiarity.

You can amplify that impact even further when your text message follows an e-mail contact or social media interaction. And you gain even more traction when you text following a positive in-person networking interaction. The better the prospect knows you, the more effective your prospecting text message will be. The less they know you, the more likely you will be seen as annoying spam. People are averse to getting random text messages from people they don't know—especially salespeople.

Use Text to Anchor Conversations at Networking Events

Text messages are excellent vehicles for setting appointments following face-to-face interactions at networking events, trade shows, conferences, and other situations where you've had a positive encounter with a potential customer. Many of those encounters end with a vague promise to get together sometime in the future. Yet, most of those promises are never fulfilled because you get busy and fail to send an e-mail or make a phone call; or, your prospect gets busy and ignores your e-mails and phone calls or your e-mails get missed among the clutter in their inbox.

Text messaging is a much easier, faster way to get through the noise, get their attention, and set a meeting. Since almost everyone includes a mobile phone number on business cards these days, it's easier than ever to text a quick follow up thank-you message and ask for the next step. Here's what you do:

1. *During your conversation, when the vague agreement is made to meet sometime in the future, casually say, "Sounds good. I'll text you and we can get together."* (It is highly unlikely they'll protest if your conversation has been positive.)

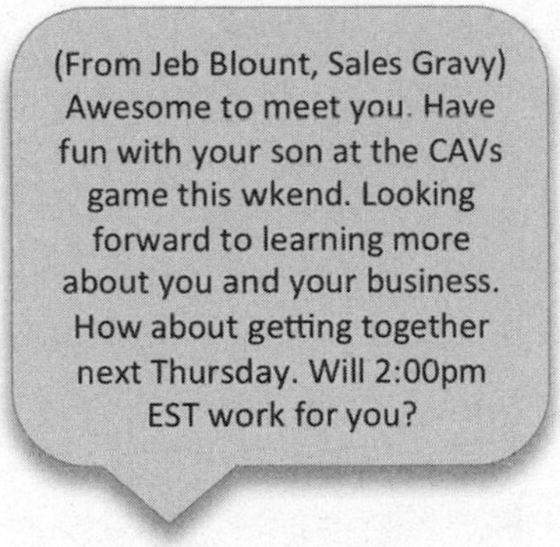

(From Jeb Blount, Sales Gravy) Awesome to meet you. Have fun with your son at the CAVs game this wkend. Looking forward to learning more about you and your business. How about getting together next Thursday. Will 2:00pm EST work for you?

Figure 20.1   Text Message After a Networking Event

2. *As soon as you walk away from the conversation, send a personalized connection request on LinkedIn (use the LinkedIn app on your phone).* This further anchors your name so they'll remember you.
3. *Within 24 hours of the event (give it two days if travel is involved), send a text message thanking them for the conversation and request a meeting.* Personalize it with information you gleaned in your conversation.
4. *If you don't get a response, try sending your text again a day later.* In many cases, they will not recognize your phone number and will ignore your initial attempt. They may also be busy or traveling and don't get to it.
5. *If your second attempt fails, shift to the phone and e-mail to make contact.* It serves no purpose to potentially create ill will by continuing to text.

    Bonus step: Always send a handwritten note within a week of the event via snail mail—this will really make you stand out from the crowd.

Use Text Following Trigger Events

A trigger event is a disruption in the status quo that may compel your prospect to act. For example, a move by your prospect's competitor that threatens their competitive edge might compel them to accelerate their investment in marketing automation. When you become aware of a trigger event, it creates an opportunity to reach out to your prospect via text messaging.

Text messaging works with trigger events because trigger events create urgency to act and text messages are perceived as more urgent. Be warned, though, the Law of Familiarity is at play in a big way with trigger-event text messages. Make sure the prospect knows who you are before sending this type of message.

I've found a soft approach with trigger events works best. It requires a bit of patience and creativity. The key is becoming a resource by adding value and leveraging that into a deeper conversation.

When I have a relationship with the prospect or at least a level of familiarity, I'll simply text over a link to an article or resource relevant to their situation. That usually turns into a phone call where I can engage them in a conversation.

If I know them well and I can't find anything relevant to send them, I'll just send a text message that references the trigger event and asks how things are going. A response creates a path to a deeper conversation.

> (From Jeb Blount, Sales Gravy)
> Patricia – saw the announcement that Halcon is merging with Remco. Sure things are buzzing over there. Here's an article I thought you might find helpful. http://www.salesgravy.com/leading-change Let's catch up when you get a moment.

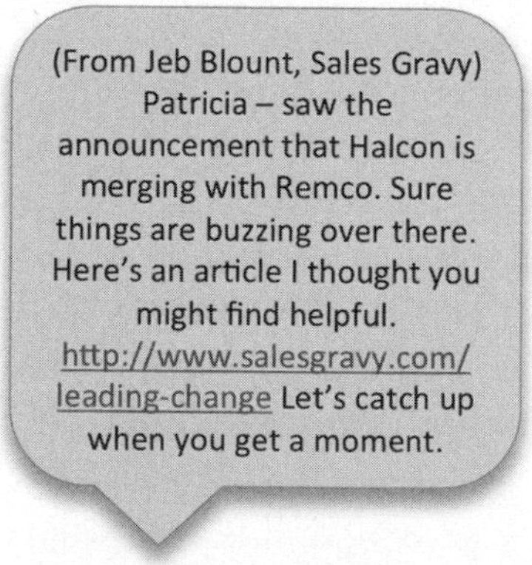

Figure 20.2   Text Message Following a Trigger Event

Use Text to Nurture Prospects

Text messaging can play an integral role in nurturing prospects with whom you have a relationship but are not yet in the buying window. A quick, value-added text message is an easy way to remain top of mind without seeming too intrusive. For example, Matt, who sells a cloud-based business intelligence program, has done an outstanding job of using text messaging to nurture his relationship with me.

Matt first contacted me nine months ago. We spoke for a few minutes. He believed his program could help my company optimize our marketing channels and improve the ROI on our advertising spend. He did a really nice job of connecting with me on that initial call, so I agreed to a demo.

The demo was impressive, and I liked the system Matt and his team showed me, but two factors stopped me from buying.

First, to integrate his platform with our marketing automation system would take a hundred or so man-hours and a ton of work to calibrate. I've been around the block enough times to know that, despite the promises of seamless integration from Matt's team, nothing ever goes smoothly. We were already knee-deep in a major upgrade of our job board technology and I could not fathom taking on another project.

Second was the cost. Moving to Matt's system required a significant up-front investment that would have to be recouped over time through savings from the automation and additional lead gen. That promise of ROI sometime in the future was difficult to wrap my head around because of the investment we were already making in the job board upgrade.

Honestly, I was completely overwhelmed (and like so many of your prospects, the status quo was a more comfortable place than change). So I told Matt that although I thought his software was fantastic, I would not be buying his system. This didn't mean that I would never be a buyer—just not now.

Matt was smart enough to realize that I was a qualified prospect because I had a need for his software and the means to purchase it. However, I had no urgency to pull the trigger. So he began systematically nurturing the relationship using four prospecting channels—phone, e-mail, social, and text.

He calls me once a quarter to find out where I am with other projects and to test my engagement. He supplements those calls with monthly e-mails and text messages with links to studies, white papers, and news about the upgrades to his systems he feels are relevant to me. He also follows me on Twitter and retweets or favorites my posts.

Matt's text message strategy has been brilliant. He reserves his best value-added information for text messages. Because he is familiar with my interests and my company, he often texts links to relevant articles that he knows I will want to read. Most of these have nothing to do with his product, but they add value to me. When I get these text messages, I always text back a thank you. That usually creates a short dialogue on some area of interest (usually sports), which, in turn, keeps us connected. Every once in a while he'll send a text to tell me that he enjoyed reading one of my articles or listening to a podcast.

Matt's strategy keeps me engaged and nurtures our relationship. His text messages are appreciated and nonintrusive because they are valuable to me and personal. Because of this, Matt and his company stay on my mind (as evidenced by this story), and when I do make a buying decision on BI software, I'll be doing so with him.

Use Text to Create Opportunities for Engagement

Text messages are also well received when they make your prospect feel important. Short text messages to congratulate them on a promotion, a mention in the news, an award or recognition, or to say something nice about an article they wrote, video they produced, or something they posted on social media that caught your eye—get your prospect's attention. This can be especially powerful if you like, comment on, or share the post as well.

Engagement text messages usually get a positive response as long as they are sincere, personalized, and free of direct solicitations for anything. The goal is simple: Give your prospect a reason to engage you in a conversation. You increase this possibility by making them feel important.

Seven Rules for Structuring Effective Text Prospecting Messages

For your text message to be effective, you need to engage your prospect and get them to take action in a blink of an eye. Packing your message into a small space requires you to be thoughtful, creative, and focused. It is difficult to make an impact in 250 characters or less.

There are seven rules for effective text messages:

1. *Identify yourself.* Never take for granted that your prospect has your information saved on their phone. In most cases they don't, and when you send a text message they won't know who you are. As a best practice, include your name and company at the top of the message.
2. *Message matters.* What you say and how you say it carries impact. Be very careful that your tone is not misinterpreted in a negative way. Use complete sentences to avoid sounding abrupt, harsh, sarcastic, or flippant.
3. *Be direct—be brief.* Say exactly what you mean in clear, precise, well-written sentences using good grammar and spelling. Remember that this is a professional message. Keep the text to one to four short sentences or less than 250 characters when possible. Avoid rambling, run-on sentences. Do not use emoticons (little smiley faces)—be professional.

4. *Avoid abbreviations.* Avoid using abbreviations on text messages
   to prospects. Abbreviations like LOL, OMG, WTF, and others
   don't come off as professional, and the person on the other end
   might not understand what you mean. Likewise, you should
   avoid acronyms and slang.

5. *Use transparent links.* People are extremely suspicious of shortened hyperlinks. Just like with e-mail, when you send URLs to
   prospects that link to articles or other resources, send the entire
   URL so they know where they are clicking.

6. *Before clicking "send"—pause and read it again.* Make this your rule
   when it comes to text messages (and, frankly, all written
   communication).

7. *Know your numbers.* Finally, as with all prospecting channels,
   know your numbers. Track the number of texts you send each
   day, response rates, and conversions into appointments and,
   ultimately, sales.

DO NOT TEXT WHILE DRIVING—PUT THE SMARTPHONE DOWN!

21

Developing Mental Toughness

When the going gets tough, the mentally tough keep going.

This is the brutal, undeniable truth. Sales is a tough, grueling, and sometimes heartbreaking profession. The pressure to deliver and the demand to perform in sales is unrelenting. You must deliver results or you will be fired. In the sales profession, it's not about what you have sold, it is about what you sell today.

Fanatical prospectors receive more rejection before 9:00 AM than the average person gets in an entire year. The fact is, most people wouldn't last a minute in sales. They are so afraid of rejection that they'd rather starve to death than make a single prospecting call.

This is why salespeople are the elite athletes of the business world. The employees of your company (even if they don't act like they understand this) count on you for their jobs and paychecks.

The owners and executives need you to deliver on your numbers to keep the shareholders happy.

Simply put, no salespeople (elite athletes), no customers, no profit, no growth, no company, no team. If your company were a professional sports team, the salespeople would be on the field playing the game and everyone else would be on the sidelines supporting the you.

I want you to stop for a moment and look at yourself in the mirror. See yourself for who you really are, an elite athlete. Just as a professional sports team counts on its players to deliver in the game, your company counts on its elite athletes (you) to deliver in the marketplace. When the whistle blows each morning, you've got to be ready to rock it.

Like top athletes, you must train hard to deliver peak performance. What research[1] tells us, though, is it takes more than training and conditioning to deliver peak performance day in and day out. All elite athletes—in sport and business—train hard and work hard. That is a given. Champions, however, gain their competitive edge from mental toughness.

Data from multiple research studies tells us that mental toughness is more important than talent, experience, education, skills, or technique. Mental toughness is why some athletes thrive under pressure while others disintegrate. It is so important that at Sales Gravy we help our clients hire better salespeople with our Sales Drive® assessment that tests exclusively for mental toughness.

Mental toughness, sometimes called grit,[2] is the real reason some salespeople are perennial superstars while others, with the same level of talent, fold up like a cheap lawn chair as soon as things get difficult.

James Loehr was one of the first experts to identify the "psychology of winning." He described seven core dimensions of mental toughness:[3]

1. Self-confidence
2. Attention control

3. Minimizing negative energy
4. Increasing positive energy
5. Maintaining motivation levels
6. Attitude control
7. Visual and imagery control

More recently, groundbreaking studies like Angela Duckworth's study "Grit: Perseverance and Passion for Long-term Goals" are helping us understand just how much mental toughness matters in achievement.

This is why, to reach the top of your game, you must develop grit. The good news is, unlike talent and intelligence that are baked into your DNA, mental toughness can be learned and developed. The formula is simple: Change your mindset. Change your game.

It Takes Grit—You Have to Grind to Shine

In sales you can only control three things: your actions, your reactions, and your mindset.

Losing is a choice. Mediocrity is a choice.

Yes, I've heard the argument—salespeople are born, not made. I certainly believe that some people are born with the talent to be accountants, NFL quarterbacks, leaders, and sales professionals. However, thousands upon thousands of salespeople wash out because they make the choice—yes, the choice—to lose.

When you choose mediocre behaviors, you get mediocre results, and once you allow mediocrity into your sales day, you become a bad-luck magnet.

This choice is one of the key reasons so many salespeople find themselves job hopping. Despite the training each new company provides, despite the coaching, despite the mentoring, despite the tools, eventually these salespeople wash out. They have everything they need to succeed except mental toughness.

Last year we hired a sales rep to sell advertising for Sales Gravy. We gave her training, guidance, support, and leads. When she started, I had a heart-to-heart conversation with her. I explained that the first 60 days would the hardest she would face. She would have to work hard to build her pipeline. Along the way she'd get lots of rejection, make mistakes, and become embarrassed from time to time as she learned to present a new, unfamiliar product.

Our new rep worked hard for exactly 29 days. Then I got the call. She was quitting. There were lots of excuses: The job was overwhelming, she didn't feel like she was having success, maybe advertising sales wasn't the best fit. I explained again that these feelings were to be expected with something new, and if she just stuck with it for a little while longer, her efforts would pay off. But her mind was already made up. She quit.

We jumped on the phone and followed up with all of the prospects she'd put into her pipeline. She did a great job in her first 29 days of getting qualified prospects into the pipe. So good, in fact, that we closed almost all of the opportunities she had developed. Her commission on these sales would have been $7,000. Instead she received zero.

Quitting is a choice. Most people when faced with challenges quit too soon—often right as they are on the cusp of success. This is especially true with salespeople in new sales jobs. Starting a new sales job and taking on new challenges is frustratingly hard. There are many dark days when you feel like all you do is fail and there is no hope. As you get closer to breaking through, things actually seem bleaker. You are tired, beat-up, and worn-down. It is at this point that mental toughness in the form of faith and persistence takes you the last mile.

Winston Churchill said that "when you are going through hell, keep going." Faith is crucial. Faith that by doing the right things every day, the cumulative impact of these actions will pay off. Faith keeps you focused on your goal when no tangible evidence exists that the hard work you are doing will get you there.

Persistence is the fuel of winners. It is the tenacity and determination to keep going in spite of self-doubt, roadblocks, failure, embarrassment, and setbacks. Persistence picks you up off the ground, dusts you off, and sends you back into the game. Persistence gives you that last, final push across the finish line.

The fact is, sales is a grind. Prospecting is a grind. But you've got to grind to shine.

Everybody wants the glory of the close, but most people are unwilling to grind—to pay the price for success. In any endeavor, success is paid for in advance with hard work. In sales, success is paid for in advance with prospecting. You will never excel at anything if you don't put the hard work in first.

Mental toughness is the one trait that defines all top performers. Mental toughness is the ability to get back up when you've been knocked down and be resilient in the face of rejection, adversity, and failure. It is the ability to accept pain and sacrifice today for a win in the future. It's the ability to block out negative self-talk, manage disruptive emotions, ignore people who tell you what you can't do, and put singular focus on a desired goal.

This grit is the foundation of faith, persistence, tenacity, resilience, hustle, and a winning mindset. The top people in business, sports, sales, and every other walk of life hit the same walls and face the same mental and physical suffering as everyone else. What makes them different is their ability to lean into their challenges and disrupt the desire to quit.

Mental toughness cuts through any delusion that things will be easy. It embraces the "suck"—and in our case, what sucks is prospecting—and keeps grinding.

In their book *Never Hire a Bad Salesperson* again, Dr. Chris Croner and Richard Abraham describe mental toughness in salespeople using three dimensions.[4]

- *Optimism:* When you get knocked down, optimism tells you that if you can look up, you can get up. Optimism is the mother of perseverance. It powers a positive belief system and attracts positive energy.

- *Competitiveness:* Do you hate to lose or love to win? The drive to avoid losing is what keeps superstars working longer, harder, and doing whatever it takes to win. Competitiveness is the mother of persistence.
- *Need for achievement:* Psychologist and researcher Henry Murray defined the need for achievement as "intense, prolonged and repeated efforts to accomplish something difficult. To work with singleness of purpose towards a high and distant goal. To have the determination to win."[5] The need for achievement is the mother of self-motivation.

Four Pillars of Mental Toughness in Sales

What does it take to develop and maintain mental toughness in sales? How do you incubate optimism, competitiveness, and need for achievement? What steps can you take, starting today, to reach peak performance and become an elite sales athlete?

Over the course of my career, while working with thousands of superstar sales professionals, I've discovered that there are four pillars that make up the foundation of mental toughness in sales.

Desire

The great Napoleon Hill said that "Desire is the starting point of all achievement, not a hope, not a wish, but a keen pulsating desire which transcends everything." Likewise, my good friend Brian Stanton says, "Desire is the mother of sales activity."

Desire is the singularity of achievement. Anything truly worth achieving must begin with desire. Otherwise you'll fail. It's the key to tapping into the motivation you need to get past real and self-inflicted performance roadblocks. It's just easier to develop mental toughness and self-discipline when you have a goal.

For example, if you desire more than anything to buy a house but you need a down payment, then you'll do what it takes to earn bigger commission checks. If you desire to go on your company's elite sales trip, you will find the will to wake up early every morning and hit the phones. If you desire to be promoted to sales manager, you'll find a way to excel as a sales rep so that you stand out.

Desire, though, is just the beginning. It's a spark. To ignite, you need a clear definition of what you want and where you are going. This requires you to answer three questions:

1. What do you want?
2. How do you plan to get what you want?
3. How bad do you want it?

That's it. Begin with defining what you want, building a plan, and writing it down. Not empty promises. Not fleeting wishes and or vague hopes. Real goals that mean something for your career and life.

Here is the brutal reality. If you don't have a plan, you will become a part of someone else's plan. You can either take control of your life or someone else will use you to enhance theirs. It's your choice.

So start here: Define what you want and write it down. This means gathering up the discipline to stop what you are doing, sit down, and actually think about your future.

Writing down your goals and plan makes you unstoppable. When you write down your goals, ink on paper, you tap into a powerful motivational force. A written plan forces action. Something inside of you begins to drive you forward, pushing you toward your destination. It is there, written in stone, and it cannot be ignored until it has been accomplished.

Prospecting creates adversity. There will be hurdles, roadblocks, disappointment, and loads of rejection. There will always be a mountain you'll have to climb and an uphill battle you'll have to fight. There will always be a temptation to slack off. There will always be an excuse for why you can't do something. There will always be something more pleasurable in the short-term than sacrificing in the long-term for what you really want.

This is why tapping into desire is so powerful. A set of written goals with clear steps to success leads to action. Action creates forward momentum. As momentum shifts into overdrive, you'll hurtle past and skip over the quicksand of procrastination, perfectionism, and paralysis.

To help you design your goals, I've developed a Goal Planning Workbook that can be downloaded free at FreeGoalSheet.com.

Mental Resilience

A few years ago during a storm, a large tree fell down in my back yard. It left a huge mess, but I was thrilled because this was my chance! I'd wanted to purchase a chainsaw for years—probably some man/machine thing in my DNA. Thing is, I've never had much to cut up. At the time I lived in the city and my fireplaces were all natural gas.

With my entire backyard covered in fallen tree, somebody had to take care of the problem. I ignored the rational pleas from my wife to just hire someone to remove it and marched right down to the hardware store and purchased a new chainsaw and all of the accessories. Urban warrior personified.

- Gloves? Check.
- Safety glasses? Check.
- Chain oil? Check.
- Fuel? Check
- Brand new leather tool belt just so I'd look bad ass? Check.
- Fourteen-year-old son to haul the branches I cut to the curb? Check.

I pulled the cord several times to crank the machine and finally it fired up. The engine rumbled. It felt awesome in my hands. Power!

I hit the throttle several more times, just to let the tree know who was boss, and then got down to work. The smell of burning fuel filled the air, sawdust was flying, and defeated branches crashed to the ground. I worked through the tangle of limbs, taking the small branches off first. The new saw cut through the wood like a hot knife through butter. Man versus tree and man was winning.

An hour later, the tree was getting the best of me. Drenched in sweat, I struggled for what seemed like hours just to make a single cut through the trunk. Looking at what remained of the tree, and doing the math in my head, at the pace I was going it would take days to finish the job.

Exhausted and frustrated, I turned the saw off and sat down on the back steps to rest, ignoring the "I told you so" look I got from my wife as she handed me a glass of iced tea.

My son, who had been doing the same calculation and realizing that at this pace he would never get back to his video games said, "Daddy, maybe you need to sharpen the saw."

I shook my head no and explained to him, "It's brand new; it should be plenty sharp. I think the wood in the trunk is just harder than in the limbs." I didn't say it out loud, but I really didn't want to go through the hassle of driving to the hardware store to get a saw sharpener.

An hour later, again exhausted and getting nowhere, I reluctantly took his advice and took the 10-minute trip to the hardware store to get a rasp to sharpen the chain.

After 15 minutes of sharpening, the saw was once again going through the wood like it was butter. I shook my head in disbelief. If I had taken the time to just sharpen the saw when it started bogging down, I would already be finished with the job.

This got me thinking about other areas of my life where I was bogging down and getting nowhere. Honestly, there were dozens of opportunities to sharpen up. I realized that with all of my focus on building my business, I'd ignored investing in myself.

With my chainsaw lesson firmly in mind I registered for a seminar, ordered a book, and subscribed to several blogs focused on the areas in my life that needed some sharpening. The techniques I learned made an immediate impact on my mindset.

I felt more energized and focused, and my drive increased exponentially. Over the next few months, my already successful business doubled in size. We had to open a new office to make room for our growing team. It was a direct result in an investment in me.

So how about you? Where are you bogging down or expending lots of effort but getting nowhere? When was the last time you sharpened your own saw? When was the last time you slowed down and invested in yourself?

The most successful people are constantly investing in them-selves to increase their knowledge, gain insight, and sharpen their skills. They understand a principle that was true with my chainsaw and true in life. Sometimes you need to slow down to speed up. It is not always about trying harder. Sometimes it is doing or thinking differently.

And though in the heat of the moment, you may feel that you don't have time to read a book or attend a seminar (or run to the hardware store to purchase a sharpener), more often than not, slowing down and sharpening your saw will actually help you move faster, with less effort, and generate far better results.

Outlearn = Outearn

Cicero said, "The cultivation of the mind is as necessary as food to the body." Gandhi said, "We should live as if we will die tomorrow and learn as if we will live forever." In sales, and in life, when you outlearn your competitors (and peers), you'll outearn them. People who invest in learning are more motivated, develop a stronger belief system, and are invariably more successful than their peers.

Want to become an elite sales athlete? One of the keys is to have more knowledge about the sales profession, your industry, and your products and services than any of your competitors.

Learners invest their own money in books, seminars, and workshops to keep their skills updated and sharp. They subscribe to newsletters, trade magazines, industry publications, blogs, and sales publications to stay current on their own industry and the sales profession. They follow top experts on Twitter, LinkedIn, and Google+. They listen to podcasts, show up for webinars, and watch educational videos online.

They read books.

Everything you ever need to know about anything is contained in a book. Everything! If you want to learn something or become an expert at anything, all you need to do is read. Yet, I am saddened at how many people tell me that they don't like to or just plain won't read.

I've got limited patience for salespeople who don't read. There is absolutely no excuse for it. When you decide not to read, you are making the conscious choice to limit your growth and income, and I have zero sympathy for you.

Reading helps you think more thoroughly. It helps you see the world differently. It makes you a better resource to your customers and company. It helps you become a better conversationalist. Reading gives you insight. Improves your writing skills and vocabulary. And because so few people read, reading can help you become an expert whom people—including prospects—who don't read seek out for advice. Reading programs the subconscious mind to find answers when you need them.

There has never been a time in human experience where books were more accessible or affordable. With mobile devices, you can read anywhere. I'm a fan of Kindle and Audible, but you'll find dozens of outlets, including iBooks, Barnes & Noble, Amazon, and Oyster to buy books. I buy hardcover, digital, and audio books. With just a click on my smartphone, I have access to millions of books in an instant. With Audible, I am able to plug my phone or tablet into my car and listen to books while I drive or while I walk my dog or work out at the gym.

The real secret is breaking reading up into small chunks of just 15 minutes each day. Fifteen minutes a day of professional reading adds up fast. Most people are shocked at how many books they go through.

Here's how it works:

- There are 52 weeks in a year.
- Let's assume that you get in professional reading (nonfiction) only on weekdays and that you take 2 weeks off for vacation.
- You are left with 250 days for professional reading.
- That 250 days multiplied by 15 minutes gives you 3,750 minutes, or roughly 62.5 hours of professional reading in a year.
- The average business, sales, or personal development book requires between 2 and 3 hours to read, depending on your speed. That's around 250 pages or 50,000 words, with the average adult reading between 300 and 500 words per minute.
- Do the math: 62.5 hours divided by 3 hours per book, and over the course of a year, reading just 15 minutes a day, you will read approximately 21 professional books.

This is an astounding number of books. Reading just 15 minutes a day will change your life and your income. On your lunch break, when you are waiting for a customer, on the train or plane, or when you have a moment to spare, pull up your reading app on your phone and knock a few pages out.

Use drive time wisely. The average inside salesperson has a commute of one to two hours a day. The average outside sales rep spends between four and five hours a day in a car. Why not spend it learning rather than listening to music or talk radio? The late Zig Ziglar called this "Automobile University."

Listening to educational and personal development audio programs in your car can give you the equivalent of a university education many times over. It's easy. Add the Audible app on your phone and download audio books. Add the Podcasts app (Apple) or Stitcher app (Android) on your phone and listen to podcasts.

I am a huge fan of podcasts because they are F-R-E-E. Many of the world's preeminent thought leaders and authors produce incredible podcasts that help you grow and develop. Be sure to subscribe to my podcast (the most downloaded sales podcast in iTunes history) while you are out there.

For salespeople, the key to building mental resilience is using every spare moment to invest in yourself.

Physical Resilience

In sales, the mental discipline to put yourself out there and be vulnerable to rejection requires a tremendous amount of mental energy. Your mental energy will always be limited by your physical resilience. You won't win consistently if you lack the endurance to outwork and outhustle your competitors.

Keeping yourself in great physical condition improves creative thinking, mental clarity, and optimism. It makes you more nimble and adaptive, and helps you gain the discipline to maintain emotional self-control in the face of endless rejection. It also boosts your confidence and enthusiasm—the two most important emotions in sales.

Physical resilience is built on three foundational pillars.

Regular Exercise

Sales professionals spend an inordinate amount of time sitting and staring at screens. With the increase in inside sales roles and the advancement of technology like video calls, e-mail, and social media, salespeople spend less time on their feet than ever before.

There is mounting evidence that sitting all day is extremely hazardous to your health[6] and impacts your mental capacity. Turns out when you sit too long staring at a computer screen, "everything slows, including brain function."[7]

Reams of research[8] indicates that 30 minutes to an hour a day of exercise keeps you healthy, reduces the chance of disease, and develops physical resilience. Most people can find 30 minutes a day to exercise. You've just got to commit and sometimes get creative. Maybe you don't have time for 30 minutes all at one time. That's okay. Studies[9] indicate that 10 minutes here and 10 minutes there can be just as or even more effective than a single long session.

You can go to the gym, take a walk at lunch, or ride your bike when you get home at night. Supplement this with 50 sit-ups and 50 push-ups. On the weekends, play sports or go for a hike. Carry your bag on the golf course instead of riding in a cart. Park at the back of the parking lot, walk the stairs, walk to the next terminal at the airport rather than taking the train. Work in your garden.

Stand up while you are making prospecting calls and walk on your breaks or between meetings rather than sitting in the break room or in a conference room gossiping.

There are literally hundreds of ways to build a 30-minute-a-day workout routine into your busy life. It doesn't matter what you do; it just matters that you do something that makes you sweat, for at least 30 minutes every day.

Sleep

Nothing impacts your health and mental well-being more than sleep. When you get plenty of sleep, your physical and mental energy is at a peak state. You are more creative, more disciplined, and agile. You are more confident, can think on your feet, are more apt to push past adversity, and frankly, look and feel better.

Humans need between seven and nine hours of sleep every night for optimal performance. In today's society, though, it has become a badge of honor to live on little sleep.

All sorts of ugly things happen to you when you are not getting enough sleep.[10] Over the long term, you become more susceptible to immune deficiencies, obesity, heart disease, and mood disorders, and it reduces your life expectancy.

In the short term, sleep deprivation has a profound impact on your cognitive ability. You're grumpy, mentally unfocused, and stressed out; your memory fails you; and you become susceptible to breaks in discipline. It is very, very difficult to maintain the mental toughness required for prospecting when you are not getting enough sleep.

Eat Healthy

In the hectic, fast-paced world of sales, it can be difficult to eat well. Field salespeople swing into fast-food joints to fuel up and inside salespeople reach for the bag of chips or candy bar hidden in their desk drawer and wash it all down with sugar-laden sodas and energy drinks.

Eating poorly is like putting low-grade gasoline in a high-performance race car. To gain the mental toughness and resiliency to work at your peak throughout the sales day, you need to fill up with high-test rocket fuel.

Healthy eating is a conscious choice. It is a commitment that is easy to break when you are not getting enough sleep or exercise. The good news is that these days, even fast-food restaurants have healthy choices. With just a little discipline and planning, you can easily find nutritious food on the road, and you can certainly prepare healthy meals at home.

There is one cardinal rule for salespeople and food. No matter what, eat breakfast. Breakfast is the most important meal of the sales day. It kick-starts your metabolism, energizes your attitude, and helps you muster the discipline to start your day with a high energy prospecting block.

Feed Your Attitude

You are what you believe. Your beliefs either attract success or push it away. Your beliefs drive your attitude. When it comes to prospecting and sales—attitude is everything. When you feed your attitude the fear and reluctance associated with prospecting starve to death.

Therefore, an investment in a strong belief system is foundational to mental toughness. In my travels around the world, I've discovered that people with a positive attitude share two common beliefs:

1. They expect to win.
2. They believe that everything happens for a reason.

When you internalize an expectation that you are going to win and are supposed to win, you'll win far more often than the person who expects to lose. You'll ask confidently for what you want, achieve your prospecting objectives more often, and close more deals.

When you believe that everything happens for a reason, your perspective on potentially negative events will be optimistic. Instead of complaining, "Why me?" when you face a setback, you ask, "How can I learn from this?"

In other words, when you choose to believe that you are in control of your own destiny, you no longer fear failure and rejection because you believe that failure is the path to learning, growth, and improved performance.

Because you are human, your beliefs will tend to wax and wane. Sometimes you'll get caught up in "stinking thinking" without even realizing it. Some days other people see it in you. They may even tell you that you need an "attitude adjustment." The most obvious place a deteriorating mindset shows up is in your sales performance. When your attitude loses altitude—you lose your winning edge.

The key to keeping your attitude tuned in to the right channel is self-awareness. When you start to feel uncentered, your language turns negative, or other people start pointing out that your attitude sucks, it's time to take action.

> *Change the company you keep.* Misery loves company, and it wants you on its team. Hang out with people who have poor attitudes and they'll destroy yours. Make sure the people you are hanging out with build your attitude up rather than tear it down.
>
> *Change your self-talk.* There is a little voice inside of you and it jabbers away 24/7. Self-talk, what you say to yourself internally, manifests itself in your outward attitude and actions. Stop and listen to what you are telling yourself. If you are drowning in self-pity, blaming the world for your problems, and telling yourself what you can't do, then it is time to change your language. You cannot afford the luxury of a negative thought.
>
> *Change your input.* What you put into your brain is what will come out. If you are reading, watching, or listening to negative things, it will impact your attitude. Take a break from the news. Turn off talk radio. Start feeding positive messages to your brain and your attitude will gain altitude.
>
> *Change your focus.* Yes, you lost. You had a setback. You failed. When confronted with failure, some people waste all of their energy dwelling on it. They play the tape over and over again in their head. Change your view. Embrace the gift of failure. Leverage that hurt to become stronger and more agile. Harness the energy you are wasting playing the defeat tape and use it to drive you toward your next goal.
>
> You are not defined by what happens to you but rather by how you deal with what happens to you. Each time you face adversity or when things don't go your way, you have a choice. You can either choose to whine and complain, or choose to learn and grow.

Be grateful. Gratitude is the cornerstone of a positive attitude, the spark that ignites self-motivation, and one of the true keys to happiness. It is an appreciation for what you have, what you have been given, your opportunities, lessons learned through failure and adversity, and the help others have given you along the way.

Elite salespeople are thankful to have a career that allows them to outearn almost everyone around them. Grateful for the roadblocks and challenges that help them learn and make them stronger. Grateful for the customers and prospects that generate their incomes. Grateful for the companies that pay their commission checks. Grateful for the bad bosses who help them learn what not to do and the great bosses who inspire them to stretch and become more.

The good news is you can deliberately cultivate gratitude and the positive attitude that comes from it by reminding yourself to be thankful.

When You Are on Top, Attack Yourself

Maybe you've crossed the finish line first, raised your hands in the air, pumped your fists, and celebrated. Maybe you've just come off of a big year, quarter, or month. You've been given accolades, a trophy, a President's Club trip, the admiration of your peers, or a huge commission check.

You may wonder, "How much better can I get?"

While you are cashing that big commission check, relaxing on the beach, or walking onstage at your national sales meeting to pick up your trophy, remember that just because you are a winner today does not guarantee that you will be a winner tomorrow.

When you have worked this hard, singularly focused on one thing, it is natural to believe that you have reached an apex, a peak, or a mountaintop. Now that you are sitting at the top on that mountain, you feel you can rest, take in the view, and be content. You can breathe a sigh of relief and allow yourself to believe, for the first time in a long time, that it is all downhill from here.

Take a moment, celebrate, congratulate yourself, bask in the spotlight, but do not slip into the false comfort of contentment or the delusion that it is all downhill from here.

Here is my advice: When you're in second place, attack the leader. When you're in first place, attack yourself.

There is no time for complacency. You cannot afford the luxury of comparing yourself to those behind you. Achieving by dumbing down your expectations is just plain stupid.

Create new goals for yourself and new challenges. Raise the bar so that you keep reaching higher. There is no time to rest—the 30-Day Rule will get you.

It is easy to look back at poor performance or a failure with 20/20 vision and find all of the areas where improvement can be made. But it takes loads of self-discipline and the heart of a winner to break down a brilliant performance and then take action to make small adjustments and improvements that keep you ahead of the pack.

The great NFL quarterback Steve Young said that "the principle is competing against yourself. It's about self-improvement, about being better than the day before."

This is what all elite athletes and elite sales professionals do. Real winners constantly attack themselves. They pick apart each performance and seek ways to improve. They view each victory as a small step toward new goals. It is this unwavering focus on constant improvement that separates the good from the great and makes today's winners tomorrow's champions.

22 | Eleven Words That Changed My Life

Do more than is required. What is the distance between someone who achieves their goals consistently and those who spend their lives and careers merely following? The extra mile.

—Gary Ryan Blair

I don't remember where I found the eleven words that changed my sales career. What I do remember is the words resonated with me instantly:

When it is time to go home, make one more call.

I wrote the sentence on an index card and taped it over my desk. It was always the last thing I looked at before I hit the streets to go on my sales calls.

Those words became my mantra. On days when I was dragging my ass because I'd had it handed to me by prospects I couldn't close; when it was hot, cold, raining, or snowing; when I was tired, worn out, burned out; or when I was coming up with really "good" justifications to knock off early for the day, this mantra, "When it is time to go home, make one more call," kept me going for one more call (and sometimes two, three, or four).

The impact of those extra calls was mind blowing. So many of my "one more calls" turned into sales. It was as if the universe was rewarding me for sticking to it. That final push paid off and kept paying off in my performance and my paycheck. Income I would never have generated if I had not developed the discipline to make one more call.

Over the years I've shared this mantra with the sales professionals who've worked for me, and I continue to share it with the new generation of sales professionals I train. I get dozens of calls, text messages, and e-mails on Friday afternoons or near dark from sales-people who say things like:

"Hey, Jeb, you are not going to believe this. I was about to give up but decided to make one last call, and the guy bought from me right on the spot—can you believe that???"

This kind of sales serendipity happens every day across the globe to the sales pros who are fanatical about making one more call.

Fanatical prospectors have the self-discipline to do the hard things in sales. Do these top performers get tired, hungry, feel their resolve wavering and want to give up and go home? Of course they do. Do these top performers love prospecting or the other activities required for success in sales? Of course not! They don't enjoy these activities any more than the salespeople who are failing.

What top performers understand is that to succeed at the highest level, they've got to pay for their success in advance with hard work, sacrifice, doing things they hate, and making one more call.

23 | The Only Question That Really Matters

My son plays wide receiver for a small-town high school football team in the heart of the South where football is more than a game—it's a religion. Friday nights under the lights are sacred, and in this cathedral of sport, few things are worse than going into a game knowing that your chances of winning are slim to none.

But that was how the stage was set for what we call the Backyard Brawl: the traditional first game of the season between our school and a rival just across the county line.

Years ago when this rivalry was first conceived, the game was an even match. But over time, economic expansion in the county next door helped our rival school grow in size. With that growth, they gained more resources, funding, and players. Their facilities are beautiful and their crowd of fans large. This inequity had been a major contributor to our six straight Backyard Brawl losses.

As our small contingent of parents entered their stadium on Friday night and walked across the manicured field and past our rival's huge crowd, there was little hope to lift us up. We knew and they knew what the outcome of this game would be. So we settled in for our traditional beating and prepared for the after-game clichés and platitudes we'd use to lift the spirits of our sons.

At midfield the opposing team towered above our boys. Taller, bigger, faster, stronger, and there were many more of them compared to our limited bench. It was intimidating. A casual observer comparing the two teams would quickly conclude that our team had no chance of winning.

The whistle blew and on the first series of downs they stopped us dead in our tracks. The parents sighed and the team punted. On the next set of downs, the other team began systematically advancing toward our end zone. That's when our coach started screaming from the sideline: "How bad do you want it, boys? How bad do you want it?"

Then we slowed them down, then we stopped them, then we forced a punt. It was a stunning, unexpected moment for both teams and a payoff for three solid months of planning, practice, and focus directed at this one moment of truth. The turning point when our young men truly believed that they could play head to head against their much larger rivals and not get pushed around.

Our players and coaches had invested endless hours viewing film. They worked harder and pushed harder than ever before in brutal practices. Coach Bo, our head coach, took them to watch the other team play in the preseason and showed them where they were weak. And, there were the infamous sled drills. Coach Bo prepared his players to win mentally by making them push a heavy sled, laden with the extra weight of the entire coaching staff, six times a day. Six times for each of the six previous losses! Pushing the sled was awful and grueling and designed to harden them mentally. Coach Bo knew that when the team reached their breaking point, nothing they faced would be worse than pushing that sled, and, of course, the thought of adding a seventh rep if they lost was unbearable.

Our underdogs turned it on and battled their Goliath adversaries as equals. Time and time again we stopped them. Tackles behind the line, balls batted down on passes that would have been touchdowns, sacks that made the pocket a dangerous place, and punts that pinned them back to their end zone. With each stop the refrain, "How bad do you want it?" gained more meaning.

Everything the other team poured at us we somehow, some way, improbably stopped. Then we scored. Our running back scrambled, broke tackles, and managed to stay on his feet. Out in front of him, our blockers threw themselves at the defenders. As he dove across the goal line, a roar erupted from our stands. We'd drawn first blood.

The other team was stunned. It was not supposed to happen this way. Beating our team had become so routine that they'd checked the win column on their schedule before the game even started. Their fans fell silent as their players, heads hung low, limped off the field to the locker room at the half.

Our boys, who were playing both sides of the ball, sprinted off the field. Their bodies were exhausted and the steaming South Georgia heat had taken its toll, but mentally they were on fire. They wanted it.

On the opening play of the second half, the other team caught a break on a missed tackle and took the ball all the way down to our five-yard line. It appeared that they'd regrouped and reenergized at half-time. But our boys held them in the red zone and we got the ball back on downs. It was unbelievable!

For the next 30 minutes it was a bare-knuckle brawl—back and forth and back and forth. They threw everything at us, including the kitchen sink. Each time we held the line and pushed them back.

But with just two minutes left on the clock, we turned the ball over. In a gut-wrenching final push, the other team somehow got a second wind and marched down the field, completing pass after pass. Our boys were past the point of exhaustion. Coach Bo was screaming from the sidelines. "One more play, one more down! How bad do you want it?"

We finally stopped them on third down, but the clock refused to die. There was still time for one more play. Fourth down and five seconds left on the clock—the final play of the game with everything on the line.

The suspense was almost unbearable. It was a heart-stopper. Five seconds on the clock. One shot to get into the end zone. "How bad do you want it, boys? How bad do you want it?"

From our 15-yard line the ball was snapped and that's when everything shifted into slow motion. Their quarterback stepped back into the pocket, searching desperately for an open receiver. Then he cocked his arm and hurled the ball into the air toward the corner of the end zone. The ball seemed to float for an eternity. Their star receiver leaped high, his fingertips reaching and grasping for the perfectly thrown pass. Our outgunned defender scrambled, frantically trying to knock it loose.

For one still second there was silence in the stands. Everything stopped. It looked as if their receiver would come down with the ball. I could hear Coach Bo's words echoing in my head. "How bad do you want it, boys? How bad do you want it?"

Our defender reached for the ball, stretching himself to the very limit. With one final push he connected and tipped the ball out of the receiver's hands. It dropped uncaught onto grass in the back of the end zone and as it rolled to a stop, there was a sudden, deafening realization that we had won! Then there was bedlam. We screamed and danced and hugged and congratulated. Our boys had done the impossible. They had won the Backyard Brawl.

In sales and life there will always be somebody or something intimidating, a competitor, or some problem that is bigger, faster, stronger, or smarter than you. There will always be a mountain you'll have to climb and an uphill battle you'll have to fight to reach your goal.

The Briarwood Buccaneers proved, once again, what great teams and great people have always known:

When you are faced with a challenge or when the game is on the line, it is not about how big you are, how strong, how much

training, resources, experience, background, degrees, talent, intelligence, money, that BS story you keep telling yourself about why
you can't, or any of the other things that far too often become
excuses that hold you back.

When you face your Goliath, when you set your goals, when
you face fear, rejection, and adversity; when you're tired, worn out,
and have the choice to go home or make one more call—the only
question that really matters is:

How bad do you want it?

Notes

Chapter 7

1. Carolyn Gregoire, "Fourteen Signs Your Perfectionism Has Gotten Out of Control," *Huffington Post*, www.huffingtonpost.com/2013/11/06/why-perfectionism-is-ruin_n_4212069.html.

Chapter 8

1. Ryan Fuller, "3 Behaviors that Drive Successful Salespeople," *Harvard Business Review*, http://www.hbr.org/2014/08/3-behaviors-that-drive-successful-sales-people.
2. Anthony Iannarino, "Prospecting Rule One: Don't Check Email in the Morning," *The Sales Blog*, http://thesalesblog.com/blog/2011/06/24/prospecting-rule-one.

Chapter 13

1. "New Research Study Breaks Down 'The Perfect Profile Photo,'" https://www.photofeeler.com/blog/perfect-photo.php.

Chapter 14

1. www.merriam-webster.com/dictionary/confidence.
2. www.merriam-webster.com/dictionary/enthusiasm.

3. http://jamesclear.com/body-language-how-to-be-confident.
4. http://lifehacker.com/the-science-behind-posture-and-how-it-affects-your-brai-1463291618.
5. https://youtu.be/Ks-_Mh1QhMc.
6. www.jillkonrath.com/sales-blog/value-proposition-components.
7. Jill Konrath, *Irresistible Value Propositions* (e-book), 2012.
8. Ellen J. Langer, Arthur Blank, and Benzion Chanowitz, "The Mindlessness of Ostensibly Thoughtful Action: The Role of 'Placebic' Information in Interpersonal Interaction," *Journal of Personality and Social Psychology* 36, no. 6 (June 1978): 635–642.
9. Jeffrey Gitomer, http://www.gitomer.com/articles/View.html?id=15068

Chapter 15

1. Insight Squared, "Best Time to Make Cold Calls," www.insightsquared.com/wp-content/uploads/2015/02/Cold-Call-Timing-v8.pdf.
2. Brian Tracy, *Eat That Frog!: 21 Great Ways to Stop Procrastinating and Get More Done in Less Time*, 2nd ed. (San Francisco, CA: Berrett-Koehler, 2007), 2.

Chapter 16

1. Godin, Seth. "Why Lie," http://sethgodin.typepad.com/seths_blog/2012/03/why-lie.html.
2. http://dictionary.reference.com/browse/overcome.

Chapter 18

1. Robertson, Kelly. "How to Lose a Prospect's Attention in 5 Seconds or Less" http://fearless-selling.ca/how-to-lose-a-prospects-attention-in-5-seconds-or-less/.

Chapter 19

1. Kevin Gao, "A List of Common Spam Words," http://emailmarketing. comm100.com/email-marketing-ebook/spam-words.aspx.
2. Michael C. Mankins, Chris Brahm, and Gregory Caimi, "Your Scarcest Resource," *Harvard Business Review*, May 2014, https://hbr .org/2014/05/your-scarcest-resource.

Chapter 20

1. Lead360, www.marketingprofs.com/charts/2013/10210/texting-prospects-at-the-right-time-boosts-conversion.

Chapter 21

1. "Mental Toughness Profiles and Their Relations with Achievement Goals and Sport Motivation in Adolescent Australian Footballers," www.ncbi.nlm.nih.gov/pubmed/20391082.
2. A. L. Duckworth, C. Peterson, M. D. Matthews, & D. R. Kelly, "Grit: Perseverance and Passion for Long-Term Goals," *Journal of Personality and Social Psychology* 92, no. 6 (2007): 1087–1101.
3. James E. Loehr, "Mental Toughness Training for Sports: Achieving Athletic Excellence," *Plume*, September 1, 1991.
4. Chris Croner PhD and Richard Abraham, *Never Hire a Bad Salesperson Again* (The Richard Abraham Company, LLC; 1st edition, 2006)
5. H. A. Murray, *Explorations in Personality* (New York: Oxford University Press, 1938).
6. Aviroop Biswas, Paul I. Oh, Guy E. Faulkner, Ravi R. Bajaj, Michael A. Silver, Marc S. Mitchell, and David A. Alter, "Sedentary Time and Its Association with Risk for Disease Incidence, Mortality, and Hospitalization in Adults: A Systematic Review and Meta-analysis," http://annals.org/article.aspx?articleid=2091327.

7. Bonnie Berkowitz and Patterson Clark, "The Health Hazards of Sitting," *Washington Post*, January 20, 2014, www .washingtonpost.com/wp-srv/special/health/sitting/Sitting.pdf.
8. "Physical Activity Guidelines," U.S. Health and Human Services, www.health.gov/paguidelines/.
9. Louise Chang, Review of *How Much Exercise Do You Really Need?* by Colette Bouchez, June 24, 2010, www.webmd .com/fitness-exercise/getting-enough-exercise.
10. Harvard Medical School, "Consequences of Insufficient Sleep," http://healthysleep.med.harvard.edu/healthy/matters/ consequences.

Acknowledgments

Over the past 10 years I've made several stabs at writing this book. Yet each time I attempted to write down the things that I do, teach, and coach so freely, I couldn't seem to find the words. So I wrote other books instead—six of them.

I think part of the reason I had such a hard time getting this book out of my head and onto paper is that *Fanatical Prospecting* is such a part of me. Rather than an abstract idea, it is who I am. The air that I breathe. Finding the words to express the very essence of what drives me as a sales professional and entrepreneur was difficult.

On the other hand, maybe the timing wasn't right until now. All of the stars finally aligned for *Fanatical Prospecting*—the right people to inspire me, the right editor, the right publisher, the right clients, and the right business climate. I am so grateful for all of the people who played a role in making this book a reality—my family, friends, employees, clients, mentors, and the team at John Wiley & Sons.

First, to my amazing editor Lia Ottaviano, your enthusiasm for this project was so motivating. When I was tired, frustrated, and worn out from writing, your words picked me up and pushed me to work harder. Thank you so much for being in my corner. I can't wait to start the next project with you.

If you are married to an author, you know just how tedious and boring it can be to listen to the endless blah, blah, blah about the book they're working on. You know the misery created by looming deadlines. You are patient as the entire world stops and revolves around the worn out, strung out, moody (bordering on schizophrenic) writer who believes that everything he has written so far is total crap that no one will ever read. Carrie, my beautiful wife and partner, thank you for being there for me every step of the way. Thank you for your patience as this project progressed over the past year, helping with the endless edits, and keeping everything going while our world stopped for this book. There would be no *Fanatical Prospecting* without YOU. I love you.

Every time I spoke to my friend and client Jack Mitchell over the past year he asked, "How's the book going?" Jack, you have no idea how big a kick in the pants your sincere interest in this project means to me. Thank you.

Jodi Bagwell, Jodi Bagwell, thank you for pushing me to finally write this book.

Luke DeCesare, Jeff Werner, Lori Sylvester—you were the catalysts for this book and it is because of you that I got off my rear end and made the commitment to write it. I've had so much fun working with you the past three years and I'm grateful for our friendship. Thank you.

Dan O'Boyle, Art Vallely, Don Mikes, Rick Slusser—thank you for the trust you have placed in me. There are no words for the gratitude I feel for the opportunity you've given me to work with you and your team at Penske. Art, your story about chasing trucks on your wedding anniversary trip at the Ritz is priceless—that's fanatical!

Andy Feldman, thank you for your enthusiasm for *Fanatical Prospecting*. We're building something very special together.

Chris Gredig and the entire AccuSystems team, thank you for giving this book the final push it needed to get off of the launch pad.

Anthony Iannarino, Mark Hunter, Miles Austin, John Spence, and Mike Weinberg: I am humbled that you guys allow me to be a part of your Mastermind group. Because of you I am better, more agile, and more focused than ever before. Mike, thank you for your inspiring foreword. You rock!

Greg Derry, thank you for "letting" me tell your story. Keep that lunch box handy.

Brian Stanton and David Pannell—I love you guys. There would be no *Fanatical Prospecting* without you. We started the movement together in OneaWeekville.

Brooke Coxwell, April Huff, Brad Adams, Kayleigh Wilcher—you get it done, making it possible for me to get it done. Thank you for everything you do.

I dedicated this book to Bob Blackwell, a man I consider to be one of the finest sales minds in the world. Bob was my sales manager when I was in my mid-twenties. He was tough to work for. No bullshit, just the fundamentals.

Bob shaped and honed the raw talent I had for sales. He turned me into a sales professional. Under Bob's tutelage I learned how to prospect, manage the sales process, and close deals. He instilled in me the work ethic required for success in sales.

Working for Bob was the best thing that ever happened to me and my family. It is a debt that we will never be able to repay.

About the Author

Jeb Blount is a Sales Acceleration expert who helps sales organizations reach peak performance *fast* by optimizing talent, leveraging training to cultivate a high-performance sales culture, developing leadership and coaching skills, and applying more effective organizational design.

Through his companies—Sales Gravy, Channel EQ, and Innovate Knowledge—Jeb advises many of the world's leading organizations and their executives on the impact of emotional intelligence and interpersonal skills on sales, leadership, customer experience, channel development, and strategic account management.

Under Jeb's leadership, Sales Gravy has become a global leader in sales acceleration solutions, including sales recruitment and staffing, sales on-boarding automation, custom sales training curriculum development and delivery, sales coaching, and online learning.

Jeb spends more than 200 days each year delivering keynote speeches and training programs to high-performing sales teams and leaders across the globe.

As a business leader, Jeb has more than 25 years of experience with Fortune 500 companies, SMBs, and start-ups. He has been named one of the top 50 most influential sales and marketing leaders (*Top Sales Magazine*), a Top 30 social selling influencer (*Forbes*), a top 10 sales expert to follow on Twitter (Evan Carmichael), a top 100 most innovative sales blogger (iSEEit), a top 20 must-read author—*People Buy You*—for entrepreneurs (YFS Magazine and *Huffington Post*), and the most downloaded sales podcaster in iTunes history, among many other accolades.

His flagship website, SalesGravy.com, is the most visited sales-specific website on the planet.

He is the author of seven books, including:

- *People Love You: The Real Secret to Delivering a Legendary Customer Experience* (John Wiley & Sons, 2013)
- *People Follow You: The Real Secret to What Matters Most in Leadership* (John Wiley & Sons, 2011)
- *People Buy You: The Real Secret to What Matters Most in Business* (John Wiley & Sons, 2010)
- *Sales Guy's 7 Rules for Outselling the Recession* (Macmillan 2009)
- *Business Expert Guide to Small Business Success* (Business Expert Publishing, 2009)
- *Power Principles* (Palm Tree Press, 2007).

To schedule or learn more about **Fanatical Prospecting Boot Camps**, call **1–888–360–2249**, e-mail andy@salesgravy.com, or visit FanaticalProspecting.com.

To schedule Jeb to speak at your next event, call **1–888–360–2249**, e-mail jeb@salesgravy.com, or visit JEB123.com.

Index

Note: Page references in *italics* refer to figures.

Three Cardinal Rules of, *216,* 216–224
timing of e-mail, 233–234
emotion, bridging with, 144–145
engagement
social selling and, 130
text messaging and, 242–243
enthusiasm
conveying, 135–137, 148–151
enthusiastic mindset, 10
exercise, 257–258

F
failure, attracting, 26–27
familiarity. *See* Law of Familiarity
Fanatical Prospecting
Fanatical Prospecting Boot Camp, 51, 155
Gold Level access to, 48
Web site resources of, 51, 60, 113, 129
fanatical prospecting techniques
avoiding sales slumps, 28, 31–35
balanced approach for, 20–24
cold calling and, 13–19
as contact sport, 73–74
defined, 3
Law of Replacement and, 29–31
mindsets of fanatical prospectors, 9–12
motivation for, 266–270
need for, 1–8
objectives of, 71–83
as persistent and consistent, 98
Power Hours for, 58–59
social prospecting tools, 107, 128–130
telephone as most powerful tool for, 157–158
30-Day Rule for, 27–29
time spent on, 25–26
tracking sales calls, 36–40
Universal Law of Need and, 26–27
"when it is time to go home, make one more call" (mantra), 264–265
See also CRM; e-mail prospecting; gatekeepers; in-person prospecting (IPP); Law of

Familiarity; mental toughness; message; objectives; prospecting pyramid; reflex responses, brush-offs, objections (RBOs); social selling; telephone prospecting; text messaging; time management
fear, of "no," 18–19, 150–151, 158–160
first impression, importance of, 115, 194
Five Cs of social selling, 107, 123–128
Fiverr.com, 117
flexible mindset, 11–12
focus, 59–62
four pillars of mental toughness
desire, 250–252
learning, 254–257
mental resilience, 252–254
overview, 250
physical resilience, 257–260
"14 Signs Your Perfectionism Has Gotten Out of Control" (Gregoire), 44
Fuller, Ryan, 56

G
Gandhi, Mohandas, 254
Gao, Kevin, 217
gatekeepers, 193–200
avoiding, 195, 196–197, 202
dealing with, 194–196
defined, 193–194
Gitomer, Jeffrey, 148
go-around-back hack, 199–200
Golden Hours, 50, 52–55, 69
Gregoire, Carolyn, 44
"Grit: Perseverance and Passion for Long-Term Goals" (Duckworth), 247
Guide to Social Selling Tools, 129

H
handwritten notes
for avoiding gatekeepers, 196
networking with, 239
Harvard Business Review, 56, 218–219
Harvard University, 136, 140–141
headshots, for social selling, 116
honesty, 195